Richard Holt Hutton

Essays on some of the modern guides of English thought in matters of faith

Richard Holt Hutton

Essays on some of the modern guides of English thought in matters of faith

ISBN/EAN: 9783337858490

Printed in Europe, USA, Canada, Australia, Japan

Cover: Foto ©ninafisch / pixelio.de

More available books at **www.hansebooks.com**

ESSAYS

ESSAYS

ON SOME OF THE

MODERN GUIDES TO ENGLISH THOUGHT

IN MATTERS OF FAITH

BY

RICHARD HOLT HUTTON

London
MACMILLAN AND CO.
AND NEW YORK
1891

All rights reserved

First Edition printed by R. & R. CLARK, 1887
New Edition 1888. *Reprinted* 1891

ADVERTISEMENT

I HAVE to thank the proprietors and editor of *Good Words* for permitting me to republish from its pages a considerable portion of the first and last essay in this volume; the proprietors and editor of the *Contemporary Review* for permitting me to republish the essays on Cardinal Newman, Matthew Arnold, and George Eliot's Life and Letters; and the proprietors and editors of the *British Quarterly Review* for permitting me to republish that portion of the essay on George Eliot as Author, which contains the estimate of *Middlemarch*. A considerable portion of the latter paper first appeared in the first edition of my literary essays, but was withdrawn in the second edition because I perceived that George Eliot at that time had still to publish some of the most striking and characteristic of her works.

R. H. H.

ENGLEFIELD GREEN, SURREY,
September 1887.

CONTENTS

	PAGE
I. Thomas Carlyle	1
II. AND III. The two great Oxford Thinkers, Cardinal Newman and Matthew Arnold	
II. Cardinal Newman	47
III. Matthew Arnold	103
IV. George Eliot as Author	151
V. George Eliot's Life and Letters	269
VI. Frederick Denison Maurice	311

THOMAS CARLYLE

THOMAS CARLYLE

For many years before his death Carlyle was to England what his great hero, Goethe, long was to Germany,—the aged seer whose personal judgments on men and things were everywhere sought after, and eagerly chronicled and retailed. Yet it was hardly for the same reason. In Goethe's old age, the ripeness of his critical judgment, and the catholicity, not to say even the facility, of his literary taste, induced a sort of confidence that he would judge calmly and judge genially anything, whether in life or literature, that was not extravagant. Carlyle was resorted to for a very different reason. The Chelsea shrine, as was well known, gave out only one sort of oracle, and that sort was graphic and humorous denunciation of all conventional falsehood and pretentiousness, or what was presumed to be conventional falsehood and pretentiousness;—and consequently recourse was had to that shrine only when some trenchant saying was wanted that might help in the sweeping away of some new formula of the sentimentalists or of the panegyrists of worn-out symbols. His almost extravagant admiration for Goethe notwithstanding, Carlyle, after his genius had matured, was ever more disposed to sympathise with the great organs of destructive than with those of constructive force. He sympathised with Cromwell for what he destroyed, with Frederick in great measure for what he destroyed, with Mirabeau and Danton for what they destroyed, and even with Goethe in large degree for the negative tendencies of his thought. With the constructive tendencies of the past he could often deeply sympathise,—as he showed in *Past and Present*,—but with those of the present, hardly ever. If I were asked what his genius did for English thought and literature, I should say that it did chiefly the work of a sort of spiritual volcano,—showed us the perennial fire subversive of worn-out creeds which lies concealed in vast stores beneath the surface of society, and the thinness of the crust which alone separates us from that pit of Tophet, as he would himself have called it. And yet, in spite of himself, he always strove to sympathise with positive work. His teaching was incessant that the reconstruction of society was a far greater work than the destruction of the worn-out shell which usually preceded it,— only, unfortunately, in his own time, there was hardly any species of reconstructive effort which could gain his acquiescence, much less his approval. He despised all the more positive political and philanthropic tendencies of his time ; felt little interest in scientific discoveries; concerned himself not at all about its art; scorned its economical teaching; and rejected the modern religious instructors with even more emphatic contumely than the "dreary professors of a dismal science." To Carlyle the world was out of joint, and his only receipt for setting it right—the restoration of "the beneficent whip" for its idlers, rogues, and vagabonds—was never seriously listened to by thinking men. Consequently, all that he achieved was achieved in the world of thought and imagination.

He has often been called a prophet, and though I have too little sympathy with his personal conception of good and evil so to class him,—though religious seer as he was, he was in no sense Christlike,—he certainly had to the full the prophet's insight into the power of parable and type, and the prophet's eye for the forces which move society, and inspire multitudes with contagious enthusiasm, whether for good or ill. He fell short of a prophet in this, that his main interest, after all, was rather in the graphic and picturesque interpretation of social phenomena than in any overwhelming desire to change them for the better, warmly as that desire was often expressed, and sincerely, no doubt, as it was entertained. Carlyle's main literary motive-power was not, indeed, a moral passion, but a humorous wonder. He was always taking to pieces, in his own mind's eye, the marvellous structure of human society, and bewildering himself with the problem of how it could be put together again. Even in studying personal character, what he cared for principally was this. For men who could not sway the great spiritual tides of human loyalty and trust, he had—with the curious exception of Goethe—no very real reverence. His true heroes were all men who could make multitudes follow them as the moon makes the sea follow her,—either by spiritual magnetism, or by dominance of will, or by genuine practical capacity. To him imagination was the true organ of divinity, because, as he saw at a glance, it was by the imagination that men are most easily governed and beguiled. His story of the French Revolution is a series of studies in the way men are beguiled and governed by their imagination, and no more wonderful book of its kind has ever been written in this world, though I should be sorry to have to estimate accurately how much of his picture is true vision, and how much the misleading guesswork of a highly imaginative dreamer.

It is singular that one who manifested his genius chiefly through history—or should I rather say, by his insight into and delineation of some of the most critical characters in history, and some of the most vivid popular scenes in history?—should have been so totally devoid of one most essential element in the true historical sense,—the appreciation, I mean, of the inherited conditions and ineradicable habits of ordinary national life. There was something of the historical Don Quixote about Carlyle; he tilted at windmills, and did not know that he was tilting at windmills, but the windmills were the habits, the routine, of nations. He had so deep an appreciation of the vivid flashes of consciousness which mark all great popular crises, because they mark all great personal crises, that he wanted to raise all human life and all common popular life to the level of the high self-conscious stage. He never thoroughly appreciated the meaning of habit. He never adequately entered into the power of tradition. He judged of human life as if will and emotion were all in all. He judged of political life as if great men and great occasions ought to be all in all, and was furious at the waste of force involved in doing things as men had been accustomed to do them, wherever that appeared to be a partially ineffectual way. And his error in judging of peoples is equally traceable in his judgments on individuals. If a man had a strong interest in the routine and detail of life, he called him "sawdustish." If he had a profound belief in any popular ideas beyond those acknowledged by himself, Carlyle probably called him moonshiny. Such men as John Mill came under the one condemnation, such men as Mazzini under the other. And yet both John Mill and Mazzini may be said to have applied a more effectual knowledge of men to the historical conditions of their own time than Thomas Carlyle. Indeed, once go beyond the world of the vivid personal element in popular emotion and passion, and Carlyle's insight seems to have been very limited, and his genius to have disappeared.

It is in some respects curious that Carlyle has connected his name so effectually as he has done with the denunciation of Shams. For the passionate love of truth in its simplicity was not at all his chief characteristic. In the first place, his style is too self-conscious for that of sheer, self-forgetting love of truth. No man of first-rate simplicity—and first-rate simplicity is, I imagine, one of the conditions of a first-rate love of truth—would express commonplace ideas in so roundabout a fashion as he; would say, for instance, in recommending Emerson to the reading public: "The words of such a man—what words he thinks fit to speak—are worth attending to;" or would describe a kind and gracious woman as "a gentle, excellent, female soul," as he does in his *Life of Sterling*. There is a straining for effect in the details of Carlyle's style which is not the characteristic of an overpowering and perfectly simple love of truth. Nor was that the ruling intellectual principle of Carlyle's mind. What he meant by hatred of shams, exposure of unveracities, defiance to the "Everlasting No," affirmation of the "Everlasting Yea," and the like, was not so much the love of truth as the love of divine force,—the love of that which had genuine strength and effective character in it, the denunciation of imbecilities, the scorn for the dwindled life of mere conventionality or precedent, the contempt for extinct figments, not so much because they were figments, as because they were extinct and would no longer bear the strain put upon them by human passion. You can see this in the scorn which Carlyle pours upon "thin" men,—his meagre reverence for "thin-lipped, constitutional Hampden," for instance, and his contempt for such men as the Edgeworth described in John Sterling's life, whom he more than despises, not for the least grain of insincerity, but for deficiency in *quantity* of nature, and especially such nature as moves society.

Carlyle, in short, was the interpreter to his country, not so much of the "veracities" and "verities" of life, as of the moral and social spells and symbols which, for evil or for good, have exercised a great imaginative influence over the social organism of large bodies of men, and either awed them into sober and earnest work, or stimulated them into delirious and anarchic excitement. He was the greatest painter who ever lived, of a portion of the interior life of man, of such life as spreads to the multitude,—painting it not perhaps exactly as it really is, but rather as it represented itself to one who looked upon it as the symbol of some infinite mind, of which it embodied a temporary phase. I doubt if Carlyle ever really interpreted any human being's career—Cromwell's, or Frederick's, or Coleridge's—as justly and fully as many men of less genius might have interpreted it. For this was not, after all, his chief interest. His interest seems to me always to have been in figuring the human mind as representing some flying colour or type of the Infinite Mind at work behind the Universe, and so presenting this idea as to make it palpable to his fellow-men. Perhaps the central thought of his life was in this passage from *Sartor Resartus:* "What is man himself but a symbol of God? Is not all that he does symbolical,—a revelation to sense of the mystic God-given power that is in him, a gospel of freedom, which he, the 'Messias of Nature,' preaches, as he can, by act and word? Not a hut he builds but is the visible embodiment of a thought, but leaves visible record of invisible things, but is, in the transcendental sense, symbolical as well as real." Carlyle was far the greatest interpreter our literature has ever had of the infinite forces working through society, of that vast, dim background of social beliefs, unbeliefs, enthusiasms, sentimentalities, superstitions, hopes, fears, and trusts, which go to make up either the strong cement or the destructive lava-stream of national life, and to image forth some of the genuine features of the retributive providence of history.

Over practical politics it is needless to say that he wielded no direct power,—indeed, would have despised himself if he had wielded power. The deep scorn which he poured upon the whole machinery of modern politics, the loathing with which he looked upon the great national Palaver, the contempt which he felt for the modern conception of liberty as a barricade against most needful and necessary government,—all prevented him from offering any but the wildest and most impracticable suggestions to practical statesmen. Indeed, Carlyle's *Latter-Day Pamphlets*, *Chartism*, and even the modern chapters in *Past and Present*, to say nothing of *Shooting Niagara, and After*, were not adapted, even if they were intended, to produce any immediate effect on the political measures or methods of the day. Nevertheless, I doubt whether any writer of his time has produced a more powerful effect, both good and bad, on the political tone and creed of thinking men, or done more to destroy that blind belief in mere institutions, whether aristocratic, or plutocratic, or democratic, which was at one time the equivalent for a political creed.

In at least five different catastrophes of the great political decade between 1861 and 1871, Carlyle's powerful influence over the ground ideas of politics showed itself in very potent currents of English thought. In relation to the great civil war between North and South in the United States, there can be no doubt at all that Carlyle's fierce invectives against leaving " black Quashee " to the liberty of idleness, had worked very powerfully in the direction of persuading many intellectual men of great ability to side with the South, to apologise for " the peculiar institution " and the coarse aristocracy which fought so bravely to perpetuate it. And again, when Mr. Eyre put down with so much breathless and cruel violence the revolt of our negroes in Jamaica, the effect of Carlyle's teaching was more than ever discernible in the eager outbreak of partisanship for " the beneficent whip " that divided into two hostile camps the whole of British society. In these two instances I hold that Carlyle's teaching had produced little but evil fruit. Men had taken home his creed that idleness and ignorance need drilling by main force, if needful; and had failed to take home the conditions by which he strove, not very effectually, it must be owned, to limit it,—namely, that the disciplinarians who enforce that drill must themselves be foremost in disinterested and devoted work, and must discipline their inferiors solely in the interest of the ragged regiments which need discipline, not in the interests of their own pockets or fears. In enforcing the lesson that such disciplinarians do but embody the beneficent severity of Nature's own laws, Carlyle always forgot that liberty limited by austere laws is a very different thing indeed from liberty overridden by the iron heel of selfish power; and that selfish power is subject to fits of anger, indignation, and vindictive passion, which rob it of half, or more than half, the moral value of austerely enforced conditions. Again, in relation to the attack of Prussia and Austria on Denmark, there can be little doubt that Carlyle's eager admiration of Prussia, and the Prussian drill-system, did very much to reconcile those Englishmen who had fallen under his influence to one of the earliest and most cynical of the acts of international violence for which the last twenty-five years in the history of Europe have been remarkable.

On the other hand, in relation to the unification of Germany, the assumption by Prussia of the leading place in the German State, and the Seven Weeks'

War with the Bund, the outbreak of war between Germany and France, and finally, the episode of the Commune, Carlyle's general teaching tended to keep the opinion of Europe, on the whole, on the right side, though decidedly deflected towards the German side of the centre of justice. In all these cases, Carlyle's profound respect for discipline, reticence, earnestness, and loyalty to honest leadership, inclined him towards the true solution of the European difficulty, though in his detestation of the hysteria of France, and his scorn for the blindness of blundering democracy, he fell into the mistake of flattering the Germans up to the top of their bent, and encouraging them in that military insolence which bids fair to bring them one day again to serious grief.

But it was on questions more remote from practical politics than these that Carlyle's political influence was, I think, most salutary. His diatribes against idle aristocracies,—aristocracies bent upon protecting themselves, both from their worst enemies and their best friends,—aristocracies at least as anxious to escape all real duties as to repel all dangerous attacks, —have sunk deeper into the public mind, and done more directly or indirectly to make the members of these aristocracies feel that they have their social position to earn and to justify, than all the writings in the English tongue put together, outside Carlyle's, have accomplished in the same time. Has not his language in *Past and Present* concerning the idle nobleman passed into the very substance of English political thought, though it may not as yet have produced all the effect it might on our House of Lords? "His fathers worked for him, he says, or successfully gambled for him; here *he* sits, professes, not in sorrow, but in pride, that he and his have done no work, time out of mind. It is the law of the land, and is thought to be the law of the Universe, that he alone, of recorded men, shall have no task laid on him, except that of eating his cooked victuals, and not flinging himself out of window. Once more, I will say, there was no stranger spectacle ever shown under this sun. A veritable fact in this England of the Nineteenth Century. His victuals he does eat, but as for keeping on the inside of the window,—have not his friends, like me, enough to do? Truly, looking at his Corn-laws, Game-laws, Chandos-clauses, Bribery-elections, and much else, you do shudder over the plunging and tumbling he makes, held back by the lapels and coat-skirts; only a thin fence of window-glass before him, and in the street mere horrid iron spikes." To a very considerable extent, I think, the idle aristocracy have taken that to heart, and have made, recently at least, no such mad efforts to plunge out of window on to the horrid iron spikes beneath. So, again, nothing has done so much as Carlyle's diatribes against plutocracy to ennoble the modern gospel of industry, and lift it out of the ruts of gross competition to produce illusory cheapness and dishonest saleability. Nor have any man's lessons produced so great an effect as his in raising our modern standard as to the dignity of labour, and making us see that our object must be to produce true labouring men, rather than wholesale men-labourers, even though a good deal of labouring force be sacrificed for the purpose of saving the manhood.

But most of all Carlyle influenced politics by raising a kind of salutary, even if often extravagant, fear of the destructive capacities of democracies when not nobly led, and not in satisfactory moral relations with the classes of more leisure, more knowledge, and more opportunity for disinterested work. His wonderful book on the French Revolution burnt this fear deep into the minds of all capable of understanding it, and from them the salutary dread has spread to many quite incapable of understanding it. For my own part I believe that Carlyle, judging too much by an exceptional people awaking to their misery at a time when that misery was exceptionally great, exaggerated the wildness of the anarchy of which any Teutonic democracy, for instance, is capable, and underrated the conventionalism of feeling, as well as the sound moral convictions, which such a democracy shares with the middle-class. But none the less his picture produced a profound effect, and made men feel afresh how helpless so-called "upper-classes" are, if they are not in close and friendly relations with those great masses of men in trust for whose benefit alone the State really holds its right to control and guide them. It is here that Carlyle's greatest influence over modern politics was exerted, an influence equally mingled of dread, sympathy, and the sense of obligation due from the educated to the ignorant, and one which, on the whole, did wonders, like the ancient tragedy, to purify men "by pity and by fear." Carlyle, indeed, produced on our own age, by widely different means, more of the characteristic effects of the Greek drama than any other English writer. He was not at any time a Christian politician. He felt that profound sense of the pressure of destiny, and of the narrow sphere of individual liberty within the grasp of "the eternities and immensities," which makes men stern and awe-struck,—severe masters, and in some sense dutiful servants, but not, in the highest sense, spiritual brethren. And, like the tragic dramatists of the Greek time, he always conceived the State itself as a real thing involved in the network of evil and good, sin and retribution, weakness and strength, and involved quite as deeply and directly as the temporary rulers who stood at the helm, and who by their shortcomings or their great achievements represented the cowering or the strong hearts of their fellow-citizens.

Indeed, it will be apparent from what I have said that Carlyle was neither moralist, prophet, statesman, nor politician, so much as prophetic artist. He had the temperament and the powers of a great artist, with what was in effect a single inspiration for his art, and that, one which required so great a revolution in the use of the appropriate artistic materials, that the first impression he produced on ordinary minds was that of bewilderment and even confusion. This subject,—almost his only subject,—whether he wrote history or biography, or the sort of musings which contained his conceptions of life, was always the dim struggle of man's nature with the passions, doubts, and confusions by which it is surrounded, with special regard to the grip of the infinite spiritual cravings, whether good or evil, upon it. He was always trying to paint the light shining in darkness and the darkness comprehending it not, and therefore it was that he strove so hard to invent a new sort of style which should express not simply the amount of human knowledge, but also, so far as possible, the much vaster amount of human ignorance against which that knowledge sparkled in mere radiant points breaking the gloom. Every one knows what *Carlylese* means, and every expert literary man can manufacture a little tolerably good Carlylese at will. But very few of us reflect what it was in Carlyle which generated the style, and what the style, in spite of its artificiality, has done for us. Indeed, I doubt if Carlyle himself knew. In his *Reminiscences* he admits its flavour of affectation with a comment which seems to me to show less self-knowledge than usual. Of his friend Irving's early style, as an imitation of the Miltonic or old English Puritan style, he says: "At this time, and for years afterwards, there was something of preconceived intention visible in it—in fact, of real affectation, as there could not well help being. To his example also I suppose I owe something of my own poor affectations in that matter which are now more or less visible to me, much repented of or not." I suspect of the two alternatives suggested in this amusing little bit of characteristic mystification, the "not" should be taken as the truth. Carlyle could not repent of his affectation, for it was in some sense of the very essence of his art. Some critics have attempted to account for the difference in style between his early reviews in the *Edinburgh* and his later productions by the corrections of Jeffrey. But Jeffrey did not correct Carlyle's *Life of Schiller*, and if any one who possesses the volume containing both the life of Schiller and the life of Sterling will compare the one with the other, he will see at once that, between the two, Carlyle had deliberately developed a new organon for his own characteristic genius, and that so far from losing, his genius gained enormously by the process. And I say this not without fully recognising that simplicity is the highest of all qualities of style, and that no one can pretend to find simplicity in Carlyle's mature style. But as, after all, the purpose of style is to express thought, if the central and pervading thought which you wish to express, and must express if you are to attain the real object of your life, is inconsistent with simplicity, let simplicity go to the wall, and let us have the real drift. And this seems to me to be exactly Carlyle's case. It would have been impossible to express adequately in such English as the English of his *Life of Schiller* the class of convictions which had most deeply engraved themselves on his own mind. That class of convictions was, to state it shortly, the result of his belief—a one-sided belief, no doubt, but full of significance—that human language, and especially our glib cultivated use of it, had done as much or more to conceal from men how little they do know, and how ill they grasp even that which they partly know, as to define and preserve for them the little that they have actually puzzled out of the riddle of life. In the very opening of the *Heroes and Hero Worship* Carlyle says :—

"Hardened round us, encasing wholly every notion we form, is a wrappage of traditions, hearsays, mere *words*. We call that fire of the black thunder-cloud 'electricity,' and lecture learnedly about it, and grind the like of it out of glass and silk. But what is it? What made it? Whence comes it? Whither goes it? Science has done much for us, but it is a poor science that would hide from us that great deep sacred infinitude of Nescience whither we can never penetrate, on which all science swims as a mere superficial film. This world, after all our science and sciences, is still a miracle; wonderful, inscrutable, *magical*, and more, to whosoever will think of it."

That passage reminds one of the best of the many amusing travesties of Carlyle's style, a travesty which may be found in Marmaduke Savage's *Falcon Family*, where one of the "Young Ireland" party praises another for having "a deep no-meaning in the great fiery heart of him." But in Carlyle's mind this conviction of the immeasurable ignorance (or "nescience," as he preferred to call it in antithesis to science), which underlies all our knowledge, was not in the least a "deep no-meaning," but a constant conviction, which it took a great genius like his to interpret to all who were capable of learning from him. I can speak for myself at least, that to me it has been the great use of Carlyle's peculiar chiaroscuro style, so to turn language inside out, as it were, for us, that we realise its inadequacy, and its tendency to blind and mislead us, as we could never have realised it by any limpid style at all. To expose the pretensions of human speech, to show us that it seems much clearer than it is, to warn us habitually that "it swims as a mere superficial film" on a wide unplumbed sea of undiscovered reality, is a function hardly to be discharged at all by plain and limpid speech. Genuine Carlylese —which, of course, in its turn is in great danger of becoming a deceptive mask, and often does become so in Carlyle's own writings, so that you begin to think that all careful observation, sound reasoning, and precise thinking is useless, and that a true man should keep his intellect foaming and gasping, as it were, in one eternal epileptic fit of wonder—is intended to keep constantly before us the relative proportions between the immensity on every subject which we fail to apprehend, and the few well-defined focal spots of light that we can clearly discern and take in. Nothing is so well adapted as Carlyle's style to teach one that the truest language on the deepest subjects is thrown out, as it were, with more or less happy effect, at great realities far above our analysis or grasp, and is not a triumphant formula which contains the whole secret of our existence.

Let me contrast a passage concerning Schiller in the *Life of Schiller*, and one concerning Coleridge in the *Life of Sterling*, relating to very nearly the same subject, the one in ordinary English, the other in developed Carlylese, and no one, I think, will doubt which of the two expresses the central thought with the more power. "Schiller," says Carlyle,

"Does not distort his character or genius into shapes which he thinks more becoming than their natural one; he does not bring out principles which are not his, or harbour beloved persuasions which he half or wholly knows to be false. He did not often speak of wholesome prejudices; he did not 'embrace the Roman Catholic religion because it was the grandest and most comfortable.' Truth with Schiller, or what seemed such, was an indispensable requisite; if he but suspected an opinion to be false, however dear it may have been, he seems to have examined it with rigid scrutiny, and, if he found it guilty, to have plucked it out and resolutely cast it forth. The sacrifice might cause him pain, permanent pain; but danger, he imagined, it could hardly cause him. It is irksome and dangerous to tread in the dark; but better so than with an *ignis fatuus* to guide us. Considering the warmth of his sensibilities, Schiller's merit on this point is greater than it at first might appear."

And now let me take the opposite judgment passed upon Coleridge in the *Life of Sterling* :—

"The truth is, I now see, Coleridge's talk and speculation was the emblem of himself: in it, as in him, a ray of heavenly inspiration struggled, in a tragically ineffectual degree, with the weakness of flesh and blood. He says once 'he had skirted the howling deserts of Infidelity'; this was evident enough; but he had not had the courage, in defiance of pain and terror, to press resolutely across said deserts to the new firm lands of faith beyond; he preferred to create logical fata-morganas for himself on the hither side, and laboriously solace himself with these. To the man himself Nature had given, in high measure, the seeds of a noble endowment; and to unfold it had been forbidden him. A subtle lynx-eyed intellect, tremulous, pious sensibility to all good and all beautiful; truly a ray of empyrean light, but embedded in such weak laxity of character, in such indolences and esuriences, as had made strange work with it. Once more the tragic story of a high endowment with an insufficient will. An eye to discern the divineness of the heaven's splendours and lightnings, the insatiable wish to revel in their godlike radiancies and brilliancies, but no heart to front the seething terrors of them, which is the first condition of your conquering an abiding place there. The courage necessary for him above all things had been denied this man. His life with such ray of the empyrean in it had been great and terrible to him, and he had not valiantly grappled with it; he had fled from it; sought refuge in vague day-dreams, hollow compromises, in opium, in theosophic metaphysics. Harsh pain, danger, necessity, slavish harnessed toil, were of all things abhorrent to him. And so the empyrean element lying smothered under the terrene, and yet inextinguishable there, made sad writhings. . . . For the old Eternal Powers do live for ever, nor do their laws see any change, however we, in our poor wigs and Church tippets, may attempt to read their laws. To *steal* into Heaven—by the modern method of sticking, ostrich-like, your head into fallacies on earth, equally as by the ancient and by all conceivable methods—is for ever forbidden. High treason is the name of that attempt, and it continues to be punished as such. Strange enough! here once more was a kind of heaven-scaling Ixion; and to him, as to the old one, the just gods were very stern; the ever-revolving, never-advancing wheel (of a kind) was his through life; and from his cloud-Juno did not he too procreate strange Centaurs, spectral Puseyisms, monstrous illusory hybrids, and ecclesiastical chimæras,—which now roam the earth in a very lamentable manner?"

I think Carlyle was driving by implication at something which seems to me quite false in the latter passage, and possibly even in the former also. But no one can doubt, I think, which of these two styles conveys the more vividly the idea common to both—that it is very easy and very fatal to deceive ourselves into thinking or believing what we only wish to believe, and that a mind which cannot distinguish firmly between the two, loses all sense of the distinction between words and things. And how much more powerfully is the thought expressed in the strange idiom of the later style. The fundamental difference between the two styles is that while the former aims, like most good styles, at what Carlyle wants to say expressly, the later is, in addition, lavish of suggestions which come in aid of his express meaning, by bringing out in the background the general chaos of vague indeterminate agencies which bewilder the believing nature, and render a definite creed difficult. Take the very characteristic Carlylese phrase "in a tragically ineffectual degree," and note the result of grafting the stronger thought of tragedy on the weaker one of ineffectuality,—how it dashes in a dark background to the spectacle of human helplessness, and suggests, what Carlyle wanted to suggest, how the powers above are dooming to disappointment the man who fortifies himself in any self-willed pet theory of his own. So, too, the expressions "logical fata-morganas," "tremulous, pious sensibility," "a ray of empyrean embedded in such weak laxity of character," "spectral Puseyisms," "monstrous illusory hybrids," "ecclesiastical chimæras," all produce their intended *daunting* effect on the imagination, suggesting how much vagueness, darkness, and ignorance Carlyle apprehended behind these attempted philosophical "views" of the great *à priori* thinker. Observe, too, the constant use of the plurals "indolences and esuriences," "godlike radiancies and brilliancies," which just suggest to the mind in how very many different forms the same qualities may be manifested. And finally, observe the discouraging effect of the touch which contrasts the conventionality of caste-costume, "our poor Wigs and Church tippets," with the "Eternal Powers that live for ever"—a touch that says to us in effect, "Your conventions mystify you, take you in, make you believe in an authority which the Eternal Powers never gave." And all this is conveyed in such little space by the mere suggestion of contrasts. The secret of Carlyle's style is a great crowding-in of contrasted ideas and colours,—indeed, such a crowding in, that for any purpose but his it would be wholly false art. But his purpose being to impress upon us with all the force that was in him that the universe presents to us only a few focal points of light which may be clearly discerned against vast and almost illimitable tracts of mystery, that human language and custom mislead us miserably as to what these points of light are, and that much of the light—all, indeed, which he himself does not recognise—comes from putrefying and phosphorescent *ignes fatui*, which will only betray us to our doom, the later style is infinitely more effective than the first. He does contrive to paint the incapacity of the mind to grasp truth, its vast capacity to miss it, the enormous chances against hitting the mark precisely in the higher regions of belief, with a wonderful effect which his earlier style gave little promise of. It seems to me a style invented for the purpose of convincing those whom it charmed, that moral truth can only be discerned by a brilliant imaginative tact and audacity in discriminating the various stars sprinkled in a dark vault of mystery, and then walking boldly by the doubtful light they give; that there is much which cannot be believed except by self-deceivers or fools, but that wonder is of the essence of all right-mindedness; that the enigmatic character of life is good for us, so long as we are stern and almost hard in acting upon the little truth we can know; that any sort of clear solution of the enigma must be false, and that any attempt to mitigate the sternness of life must be ascribed to radical weakness and the smooth self-delusions to which the weak are liable.

In speaking of his style I have already suggested by implication a good deal of the drift of Carlyle's faith. What he loves to delineate is the man who can discern and grope his way honestly by a little light struggling through a world of darkness,—the man whose gloom is deep, but whose lucidity of vision, so far as it goes, is keen,—the man who is half hypochondriac, half devotee, but wholly indomitable, like Mahomet, Cromwell, Johnson. Thus he says of Cromwell:—

"And withal this hypochondria, what was it but the very greatness of the man, the depth and tenderness of his ideal affections; the quantity of *sympathy* he had with things? The quantity of insight he could yet get into the heart of things; the mastery he could get over things; this was his hypochondria. The man's misery, as men's misery always does, came of his greatness. Samuel Johnson is that kind of man. Sorrow-stricken, half-distracted, the wide element of mournful *black* enveloping him—wide as the world. It is the character of a prophetic man; a man with his whole soul *seeing* and struggling to see."

In his *Life of Frederick the Great*, writing on Voltaire, Carlyle describes the same sort of character as the ideal Teutonic character, a type which recommended itself to Voltaire because it was the reverse of his own.

"A rugged, surly kind of fellow, much-enduring, not intrinsically bad; splenetic without complaint; standing oddly inexpugnable in that natural stoicism of his; taciturn, yet with strange flashes of speech in him now and then,—something which goes beyond laughter and articulate logic, and is the taciturn elixir of these two,—what they call 'humour' in their dialect."

Every hero he had was great in proportion as he displayed at once this profound impression of the darkness and difficulty of life, and this vehement dictatorial mode of acting on the glimpses or visions he had by way of showing valour in defiance of the darkness. Carlyle's characteristic delight in Odin and the Scandinavian mythology is a mere reflection of this strong appreciation of the religion of the volcano, the thunder-cloud, and the lightning-flash, mingled with a certain grim enjoyment of the spectacle of the inadequacy of human struggle. If Carlyle loved also to describe keen, clear wits like Jeffrey and Voltaire—if he revelled, too, in the picture of thin, acrid natures like Robespierre's, it was as foils to his favourite portraits of grim, vehement, dictatorial earnestness. As his style is chiaroscuro, so his favourite figures and characters are chiaroscuro also. Carlyle did not love too much light,—did not believe in it even as the gift of God. Mankind to him were "mostly fools." To make the best of a bad business was to his mind the highest achievement of the best men. He had a great belief in the sternness of purpose behind creation, but little belief in the love there. In his *Reminiscences* he describes the attitude of Irving's schoolmaster, "old Adam Hope," towards his average scholars as being summed up thus: "Nothing good to be expected from you, or from those you come of, ye little

whelps, but we must get from you the best you
have, and not complain of anything." And so far as
I understand his religion, that is very much how
Carlyle represents to himself the attitude of the
Eternal mind towards us all. He tells us candidly
in his account of Irving that he had confessed to
Irving that he did not think as Irving did of the
Christian religion, and that it was vain for him to
expect he ever should or could. And, indeed, no
one who knows Carlyle's writings needed the avowal.
Carlyle had a real belief in the Everlasting mind
behind nature and history; but he had not only no
belief in anything like a true revelation, he had, I
think, almost a positive repulsion, if not scorn, for
the idea, as if an undue and "rose-water" attempt to
alleviate the burden of the universe by self-deception,
were involved in it. When, for instance, his coarse
favourite, Friedrich Wilhelm, dies—the king, I mean,
who assaulted his own daughter in his rage, struck
her violently, and would have kicked her—Carlyle
delights to tell you that he slept "with the primeval
sons of Thor," and to comment on his death thus:
"No Beresark of them, nor Odin's self, was a bit of
truer human stuff; I confess his value to me in these
sad times is rare and great. Considering the usual
Histrionic Papin's Digester, Truculent Charlatan, and
other species of kings, alone obtainable for the sunk
flunkey populations of an era given up to Mammon
and the worship of its own belly, what would not
such a population give for a Friedrich Wilhelm to

guide it on the road *back* from Orcus a little? 'Would give,' I have written, but alas, it ought to have been '*should* give.' What *they* 'would' give is too mournfully plain to me, in spite of ballot-boxes, a steady and tremendous truth, from the days of Barabbas downwards and upwards." If this be not meant as a hint that, for Carlyle, such a hero as Friedrich Wilhelm was rather the king to be desired than He for whom Barabbas was really substituted,—and this, perhaps, is an overstrained interpretation,—it certainly does suggest that Carlyle's mind habitually adhered by preference to the Scandinavian type of violent smoke-and-flame hero, even at those times when the lessons of his childhood carried him back to the divine figure of the crucified Christ.

I do not think that any portion of Carlyle's works contains clear traces of the sort of ground on which he came to reject the Christian revelation. His diaries and letters are full of perpetually reiterated vituperations of cant; but what cant is, except that it is either absolutely insincere, or—a deeper stage still—sincere insincerity, Carlyle never plainly says. In one place he suggests that the mere echoing of other persons' beliefs is pure cant, for he bewails himself much on the misery of living amidst echoes. "Ach Gott!" he says, "it is frightful to live among echoes." Well, if the echoing of other persons' beliefs—that is, believing their belief on their authority—be cant, we must all of us cant on all subjects on which we have not been able to satisfy ourselves.

In that case, it is cant to echo the astronomer's prediction of an eclipse, or the wine merchant's opinion of a brand of wine, or the farmer's of the condition of the crops. It would be cant to accept Carlyle's assertion that Sterling's was a "beautiful soul" which "pulsed auroras,"—indeed, as we suspect that to have been a bit of Carlylese cant, the echoing of it might really be cant. Nay, it would even be cant to take it on trust from him that "sea-green incorruptible" is a trustworthy description of Robespierre, or "fiery-real from the great fire-bosom of Nature herself" of Danton. We cannot all of us follow the researches of the historians any more than those of the astronomers or the tradesmen. If we are to have impressions at all on the subjects on which Carlyle himself has given us our impressions, we must "live among echoes." It cannot be cant simply to take on trust the work of others, or to echo on reasonable evidence what we have not had time to investigate for ourselves. Nay, to invent original views for ourselves when we have not in reality the means of constructing them with anything like the justice and truthfulness with which others, whom we might follow and trust, can construct them, is itself a very serious sort of cant, of which Carlyle was not unfrequently guilty. I should describe cant not as the echoing of others' views or faiths—which we very often ought to echo, because they are far better than any which we could possibly construct of our own—but as the pretence of bearing *personal* evidence to truths which are not original in us at all, and which are borrowed by us from others, on whose authority alone we accept them. Now, it is not every one who can bear personal testimony to the ultimate foundations even of religious truth, though every one with a religion at all can bear personal testimony to the spiritual strength it gives. No one knew this better than Carlyle, for he bore the most eloquent testimony to the depth of his own father's and mother's faith; and yet, so far as we can judge, his profound scorn for traditional faiths struck in principle—though, of course, he did not think so—at the sincerity of theirs. He wrote with his usual wrath to Mr. Erskine of those who looked at the universe through the "helps and traditions of others." "Others," he said, "are but offering him their miserable spy-glasses, Puseyite, Presbyterian, Free Kirk, Old Greek, Middle-age, Italian, imperfect, not to say distorted, semi-opaque, wholly-opaque, and altogether melancholy and rejectable spy-glasses, one and all if one has *eyes* left. On me, too, the pressure of these things falls very heavy; indeed, I often feel the loneliest of all the sons of Adam; and, in the jargon of poor grimacing men, it is as if one listened to the jabbering of spectres,—not a cheerful situation at all while it lasts. . . . I confess, then, Exeter Hall, with its froth-oceans, benevolence, etc. etc., seems to me amongst the most degraded platitudes this world ever saw; a more brutal idolatry, perhaps,—for they are white men, and their century is the nineteenth,—than that of Mumbo Jumbo itself.

... It is every way very strange to consider what 'Christianity' so-called has grown to within these two centuries, on the Howard and Fry side as on every other,—a paltry, mealy-mouthed 'religion of cowards,' who can have no religion but a sham one, which also, as I believe, awaits its abolition from the avenging power. If men will turn away their faces from God, and set up idols, temporary phantasms, instead of the *Eternal One*,—alas! the consequences are from of old well known." For Carlyle, at least, even the self-sacrificing labours of Howard and Elizabeth Fry in trying to improve the diabolical treatment of criminals once common in English prisons were founded on pure cant, on a mealy-mouthed religion of cowards.

Yet his own religion was not free from cant. For it was, by his own admission in later life, a religion which he could not reconcile with the facts of life as he apprehended them. At first his religion, which was cast in the stern old Hebrew type, insisted a great deal on the everlasting foundations of truth, on the permanent duty of honest industry, on the severe grandeur of constancy and good faith, on the sublimity of God's eternity, and on the magnificence of the heavens; further, it poured the utmost contempt on miracle as exploded by science, treated the external story of the Gospel as childish legend, which based the faith in human immortality on a kind of intuition, and ridiculed all positive revelation as Hebrew old clothes. This is what Carlyle's faith was in his man-

hood. But apparently, if Mr. Froude may be trusted,
it was more hesitating towards the end. He admitted,
we are told, that his deep faith in Providence was
without evidence, if not against the evidence. When
Mr. Froude told him, not long before his death, that
he (Mr. Froude) "could only believe in a God which
[sic] did something,—with a cry of pain which I shall
never forget he said, 'He does nothing.' For himself," adds Mr. Froude, "however, his faith stood firm.
He did not believe in historical Christianity. He
did not believe that the facts alleged in the Apostles'
Creed had ever really happened. The resurrection
of Christ was to him only the symbol of a spiritual
truth. As Christ rose from the dead, so were we to
rise from the death of sin to the life of righteousness.
Not that Christ had actually died and had risen again.
He was only *believed* to have died and *believed* to have
risen, in an age when legend was history, when stories
were accepted as true from their beauty or their significance." In a word, Christianity was not true, and
all who "were pretending to believe, or believing
that they believed, becoming hypocrites conscious or
unconscious, the last the worst of the two, not daring
to look the facts in the face, so that the very sense of
truth was withered in them," were on the side of
cant. "For such souls," says Mr. Froude, describing
Carlyle's belief in words, let us hope, a little stronger
than he himself would have used, "there was no hope
at all." Such was Carlyle's own "Exodus from
Houndsditch," as he termed it. After that exodus he

was compelled to admit that his faith in Providence was without evidence, or against the evidence, and that the Everlasting Will on whose absolute government of the world he rested, " does nothing." If anybody had then turned round on him and told him that *he* was not facing the facts truly but deceiving himself with phantasms, that he had no right to denounce the Materialism of those who simply put away their faith in Providence because they found it, as he found it, " without evidence," if not against the evidence, and who had given up trust in an Everlasting Will which, so far as they could see, he had rightly described when he said, " He does nothing," what could he have replied which any Christian might not equally reply to his taunts? He would probably have been wisely indifferent to the assertion that for his soul there was " no hope at all." He would perfectly well have recognised that, after all, he was not in the least insincere in holding by that passionate faith in Providence for which, when challenged, he could give no reason—nay, against which he could suggest many reasons. He would have felt perfectly sure that, in spite of the pain with which he declared to Mr. Froude that God "does nothing," it was his own dulness and deadness which made the admission, and not his own life and insight. But would he ever have seen that it was as truly cant in himself to deny the possibility of true faith in Christianity to men of education and knowledge, as it would have been cant in the Materialists, if, on the strength of such evidence as Mr. Froude gives us, they had denied sincerity to Carlyle?

The truth is, that no cant is worse than the cant of originality, and that no cant ought to have been more clearly recognised as cant by Carlyle. He himself was original only in what he *omitted* from the faith of his parents, for no man could have retained more vividly the impress of the religious type which they had handed down to him. That he retained his faith in Providence and immortality at all was the consequence of the faith long and carefully preserved by his ancestors, and by them transmitted to him. On the mere basis of his own imaginative vision he would have had no faith worth the name,—at most, indeed, a perception of the possibility of faith. Nay, is it not the lesson of Revelation itself that what we inherit in this way from our parents is *not* a prejudice but a growing faculty of insight; and that we ought to value nothing more highly than the type of character through which genuine belief in the spiritual world becomes possible? Did not the Jews accumulate the results of their prophetic teaching for long generations of prosperity, calamity, exile, and dependent political life, before the time came at which a Christian Revelation became possible? And is it to be supposed for a moment that that long education was not expressly given in order that a new spiritual power might be developed in that people? If valour is a great inheritance, if scientific habits of thought are a great inheritance, if the capacity for industry is a great inheritance, then the capacity for spiritual belief is the greatest inheritance of all. Carlyle's proposal that every religious man should set up anew on his own narrow basis of religious feeling, is one of the most revolutionary and anarchic ever made. I entirely believe that it is the duty of Christians to face boldly all the real facts which science or history or criticism may bring before them, and to resign every element in their former faith which is really and truly inconsistent with those facts. But then they should carefully sift facts, and sift also the meaning of inconsistency. The true use of historical religion should be to give each generation a different and much higher standpoint in belief than was enjoyed by the previous generation. The Church is not infallible; but the Church is not what Carlyle's theory seems to make it, an institution which accumulates formulas, paralyses effort, and imposes error. Originality in religion is only useful just as originality in ethics is useful, *i.e.* not as encouraging any man to throw off all the great heritage of conviction and habit which his fathers have transmitted to him, but as enabling him to give new vitality to the highest elements of that heritage, and to aid in the gradual elimination of the lower and less noble elements,—a work of discrimination for which, as for all works of discrimination, a fine and reverent judgment is absolutely essential. Carlyle's judgment was in these matters not reverent,—was far too much penetrated by the impulses of an excitable imagination and an angry self-will. His Rembrandt-like imagination lighted up special points and scenes in the world's history with marvellous force; but then for him all the rest of the world was non-existent. He judged of the whole by a very small tract round the focal part of his vision. For the rest all was darkness; and yet he thought and spoke and lived and taught as if all the rest was just like the little tract he had brought into the field of his magic-lantern. Hence his religious criticism, like so much of his historical work, was very like the unrolling of a diorama, which reveals to view what is showy and sensational, and leaves all that is solid and silent out of account.

I conceive, too, that at the root of Carlyle's transcendental scepticism was a certain contempt for the raw material of human nature, as inconsistent with the Christian view, and an especial contempt for the particular effect produced upon that raw material by what he understood to be the most common result of conversion.

I think his view of Christianity—reverently as he always or almost always spoke of the person of Christ —was as of a religion that had something too much of love in it, something slightly mawkish; and I believe that if he could but have accepted the old Calvinism, its inexorable decrees would in many respects have seemed to him more like the ground-system of creation than the gospel either of Chalmers or of Irving. His love of despots who had any ray of honesty or insight in them, his profound belief that mankind should try and get such despots to order their doings for them, his strange hankerings after the institution of slavery as the only reasonable way in which the lower races of men might serve their apprenticeship to the higher races—all seems to me a sort of reflection of the Calvinistic doctrine that life is a subordination to a hard taskmaster, directly or by deputy, and that so far from grumbling over its severities, we must just grimly set to work and be thankful it is not worse than it is. "Fancy thou deservest to be hanged (as is most likely)," he says in *Sartor Resartus*, "thou wilt feel it happiness to be only shot; fancy thou deservest to be hanged in a hair halter, it will be a luxury to die in hemp." That seems to me to represent Carlyle's real conviction. He could not believe that God does, as a matter of fact, care very much for "the likes of us," or even is bound to care. His imagination failed to realise the need or reality of divine love. "Upwards of five hundred thousand two-legged animals without feathers lie around us, in horizontal position, their heads all in nightcaps, and full of the foolishest dreams," he wrote, in describing a city at midnight. And you could easily see that his whole view of life was accommodated to that conception. And the Creator, in Carlyle's view, takes, I think, very much the same account of these "two-legged animals with heads full of the foolishest dreams," as Adam Hope did of his stupid scholars; not much is to be expected of us or got out of us, but God will get out of us the best He can, and "not complain of anything." Even the best of our race show that they are the best by estimating their own deserts at the very lowest, by saying "we are unprofitable servants." As for the common sort, they deserve not so much divine love and salvation as to be driven out of "the dog-hutch" of their own self-love into the pitiless storm. Such seems to me to be the general drift of Carlyle's religion. He indulged readily enough his incredulity as to the Christian miracles, historical evidence, and the rest; but his chief doubt was as to the stuff of which mankind is made, on which his verdict seems to me to be this: Not of the kind worth saving or to be saved, after Christ's fashion, at all, but to be bettered, if at all, after some other and much ruder fashion, the "beneficent whip," physical or moral, being, perhaps, the chief instrument.

To turn from the great writer to the man, the root of Carlyle's weakness was, I think, very near to the root of his strength. Luther said that he never did anything well till his wrath was excited, and that then he could do everything well. And so too Carlyle's wrath often roused his great imagination, but it quite as often paralysed or extinguished his never very strong judgment, especially when that wrath took the place of scorn, as it very often did. This is to my mind the ruling tone in his correspondence, and is the general effect of his private life as revealed to us in Mr. Froude's biography. Indeed you may say of the whole tone of his diary and letters that his chief desire and resolve, as expressed in it, is to keep the "rabble rout" beneath his feet, rather than to attain to the height of any intellectual or moral virtue which he had discerned in living contemporaries. For example, with all his love for Irving, you never find a thought passing through Carlyle's mind that he, Carlyle, might with advantage emulate Irving's large and generous nature, and his eager spiritual faith. Nor do you find a character anywhere, unless it be within his own family, that Carlyle for a single moment set above him as an ideal nobler than himself, to the elevation of which he would gladly aspire. His one ideal of life seems to be to tread down the "rabble rout" instead of to strain after any excellence above his own. What has struck me with most wonder in reading his letters is that a man could *remain* so high-minded, as Carlyle on the whole certainly did, and yet live so constantly in the atmosphere of scorn—scorn certainly more or less for himself as well as every one else, but especially for every one else, his own clan excepted. He spends all his energies in a sort of vivid passion of scorn. He tramples furiously sometimes on himself and sometimes on the miserable generation of his fellow-men, and then he is lost in wonder and vexation that such trampling results in no great good. The grim fire in him seems to have been in search of something to consume, and the following, taken from his early life when he was even less of a pessimist than in his later years, was the kind of fuel which, for the most part, it found. He is writing from Kinnaird, in Perthshire, where he was staying with

Mr. and Mrs. Charles Buller, as tutor to that Charles Buller whose premature death some years later deprived England of a young statesman of the highest promise :—

"I see something of fashionable people here (he wrote to Miss Welsh), and truly to my plebeian conception there is not a more futile class of persons on the face of the earth. If I were doomed to exist as a man of fashion I do honestly believe I should swallow ratsbane, or apply to hemp or steel before three months were over. From day to day and year to year the problem is, not how to use time but how to waste it least painfully. They have their dinners and their routs. They move heaven and earth to get everything arranged and enacted properly; and when the whole is done, what is it? Had the parties all wrapped themselves in warm blankets and kept their beds, much peace had been among several hundreds of his Majesty's subjects, and the same result, the uneasy destruction of half a dozen hours, had been quite as well attained. No wonder poor women take to opium and scandal. The wonder is rather that these queens of the land do not some morning, struck by the hopelessness of their condition, make a general finish by simultaneous consent, and exhibit to coroners and juries the spectacle of the whole world of *ton* suspended by their garters, and freed at last from *ennui* in the most cheap and complete of all possible modes. There is something in the life of a sturdy peasant toiling from sun to sun for a plump wife and six eating children, but as for the Lady Jerseys and the Lord Petershams, peace be with them."

No man not a man of genius could have written this, and much that is of the same type; but then, mere rage at the superficialities of the world was not enough for one whom it never could have contented to be a satirist. Hardly anywhere in all these letters and journals do we find Carlyle fastening with delight on traces of the nobler and truer standard of thought (at least outside his own clan), while we constantly find him fastening with a sort of fever of excitement on traces of the ignoble and false standard. Where in the world could Carlyle have found nobler evidence of this higher standard of worth than in the works of the great genius of his age, Sir Walter Scott? Yet what does he say of these works?—

"It is a damnable heresy in criticism to maintain either expressly or implicitly that the ultimate object of poetry is sensation. That of cookery is such, but not that of poetry. Sir Walter Scott is the great intellectual *restaurateur* of Europe. He might have been numbered among the Conscript Fathers. He has chosen the worser part, and is only a huge Publicanus. What are his novels —any one of them? A bout of champagne, claret, port, or even ale drinking. Are we wiser, better, holier, stronger? No. We have been amused." (Vol. i. p. 371.) . . . "Walter Scott left town yesterday on his way to Naples. He is to proceed from Plymouth in a frigate, which the Government have given him a place in. Much run after here, it seems; but he is old and sick, and cannot enjoy it; has had two shocks of palsy, and seems altogether in a precarious way. To me he is and has been an object of very minor interest for many, many years. The novel-wright of his time, its favourite child, and *therefore* an almost worthless one. Yet is there something in his deep recognition of the worth of the past, perhaps better than anything he has *expressed* about it, into which I do not yet fully see. Have never spoken with him (though I might sometimes without great effort), and now probably never shall." (Vol. ii. p. 208.)

It is curious, by the way, that Carlyle, an immense reader, appears to have been wholly ignorant of the meaning of the word "publicanus," and to have confounded it with the English word "publican." But it is much more curious that he should have passed so grossly false a judgment on Sir Walter Scott. For if ever there were a man whose writings showed a profound appreciation of moral worth as distinct from conventional worth, it was Sir Walter Scott. Again, take the case of Wordsworth. If ever a man held and preached Carlyle's own transcendental doctrine both as a creed and as a practical rule of life, it was Wordsworth. Wordsworth genuinely held and embodied in his own life the spiritual view of things, and he genuinely abhorred the life of luxury, and loved the life of "plain living and high thinking." In a word, Wordsworth was a poetical Carlyle, without Carlyle's full insight into the superficialities and conventionalities of bodies politic, but otherwise a genuine and powerful spiritual ally. But what does Carlyle think of Wordsworth? Instead of delighting to detect in him a kindred spirit, he writes of him in this way:—

"Sir Wm. Hamilton's supper (three nights ago) has done me mischief; will hardly go to another. Wordsworth talked of there (by Captain T. Hamilton, his neighbour). Represented verisimilarly enough as a man full of English prejudices, idle, alternately gossiping to enormous lengths, and talking, at rare intervals, high wisdom; on the whole, endeavouring to make out a plausible life of *halfness* in the Tory way, as so many on all sides do. Am to see him if I please to go thither; would go but a shortish way for that end." (Vol. ii. pp. 338-339.)

And it is the same throughout. What Carlyle feels to be false he denounces with all the eloquence of a great imagination. But the evidence that what he is driving at is not the dissemination of a gospel of new truth to his fellow-men, but rather the intellectual annihilation of an error for which he feels the utmost scorn lies in the fact that he never seems to have felt the slightest admiration for those contemporaries who really held with him, but only a profound scorn for those contemporaries who lived in the mists of the illusions which he contemned.

Perhaps Carlyle's artistic fastidiousness even exaggerated the effects of his scornful temper. It is rather remarkable in a man of his peasant birth that there seems to have been an intolerant fastidiousness about him, not only in relation to people, but to sounds and sights. This must, I suppose, be ascribed to the fine artistic vein in his temperament. He says quite frankly in his *Reminiscences:* "In short, as has been enough indicated elsewhere, I was advancing towards huge instalments of bodily and spiritual wretchedness in this my Edinburgh purgatory; and had to clean and purify myself in penal fire of various kinds for several years coming; the first, and much the worst, two or three of which were to be enacted in this once-loved city. Horrible to think of in part even yet! The bodily part of them was a kind of base agony (arising mainly in the want of any extant or discoverable *fence* between my coarser fellow-creatures and my more sensitive self), and might and could easily (had the age been pious or thoughtful) have been spared a poor creature like me. Those hideous disturbances to sleep, etc., a very little real care and goodness might prevent all that; and I look back upon it still with a kind of angry protest, and would have my successors saved from it." And in a later page he adds his confession that he liked, on the whole, social converse with the aristocracy best. "Certain of the aristocracy, however, did seem to me still very noble; and, with due limitation of the grossly worthless (none of whom had we to do with), I should vote at present that, of classes known to me in England, the aristocracy (with its perfection of human politeness, its continual grace of bearing and of acting, steadfast 'honour,' light address and cheery stoicism), if you see well into it, is actually yet the best of English classes." That is a very curious testimony to the effect of Carlyle's artistic feeling in modifying his own teaching as to "the gospel of work." It was not the gospel of work which had made even the noblest of the aristocracy what they were.

Unfortunately, as it seems to me, in his wife, whose mind Carlyle had a very great share in forming, he found a pupil only too apt in assimilating the contemptuous side of his own doctrine; and so, as Mr. Froude puts it, the sharp facets of the two diamonds, as they wore against each other, "never wore into surfaces which harmoniously corresponded." Mrs. Carlyle said, in the late evening of her laborious life, "I married for ambition. Carlyle has exceeded all my wildest hopes and expectations, and I am miserable." No wonder, when no love for something above themselves, but rather scorn for everything mean, was the only deep ground of their mutual sympathy. The wonder rather is that that scorn for what was mean should have remained, on the whole, so sound as it did, and should never have degenerated into a misanthropy at once selfish and malignant. Yet this certainly never happened. It is in the highest sense creditable both to Carlyle and his wife, that with all the hardness of their natures, and all the severe trials, which partly from health and partly from the deficiency in that tenderness which does so much to smooth the path of ordinary life, they had to undergo, they kept their unquestionable cynicism free to the last from all the more ignoble elements, and perfectly consistent with that stoical magnanimity in which it began.

To sum up my view of Carlyle, it is, I think, as the author of *The French Revolution*—the most unique book of the century—that he will be chiefly remembered. For that book represents not only the author but the man.

In origin a peasant, who originated a new sort of

culture and created a most artificial style full at once of affectation and of genuine power ; in faith a Calvinistic sceptic, who rejected Christianity while clinging ardently to the symbolic style of the Hebrew teaching; in politics a pioneer of democracy, who wanted to persuade the people to trust themselves to the almost despotic guidance of Lord-protectors whom he could not tell them how to find ; in literature a rugged sort of poet, who could not endure the chains of rhythm, and even jeered at rhyme,—Carlyle certainly stands out a paradoxical figure, solitary, proud, defiant, vivid. No literary man in the nineteenth century is likely to stand out more distinctly than Thomas Carlyle, both for faults and genius, to the centuries which will follow.

II AND III

THE TWO GREAT OXFORD THINKERS
CARDINAL NEWMAN AND MATTHEW ARNOLD

II

CARDINAL NEWMAN

CARDINAL NEWMAN

It may be thought that there is something incongruous between the two great Oxford thinkers whom I am associating together—Cardinal Newman and Matthew Arnold—the one a prince of the Church which holds as articles of faith the immaculate conception of the Virgin, the invocation of saints, and the efficacy of indulgences; the other a rationaliser who dissolves away the very substance, nay, the very possibility, of Revelation, recognises no God but "a stream of tendency not ourselves which makes for righteousness," no saviour except "sweet reasonableness" in a human life, and no resurrection except the resurrection from a selfish to an unselfish heart. But the more impressive is the contrast between Cardinal Newman and Matthew Arnold, the more remarkable is the relation between them. Newman was far and away the most characteristic and influential Oxonian of the second quarter of this century; Matthew Arnold the most characteristic and influential Oxonian of its third quarter. Both drank deep of the genius of the great University to which they belong. The Cardinal is perhaps most widely known by his invocation to that "kindly light" which amidst the "encircling gloom" of this troubled existence he implored to lead him on. Matthew Arnold is perhaps most widely known by his description—borrowed from Swift—of the spirit for which we ought to yearn, as one of "sweetness and light." Both are great masters of the style in which sweetness and light predominate. But are poets—the one a theologian first and a poet afterwards; the other a poet first, and a theologian I will not say,—for a theologian without theism is almost a contradiction in terms—but a rationaliser of theology, an anxious inventor of supposed equivalents for theology—afterwards. In both there is a singular combination of gentleness and irony. Both give us the amplest sympathy in our desire to believe, and both are merciless when they find us practically dispensing with the logic which they have come to regard as final. Both are witnesses to the great power of religion—the one by the imaginative power he shows in getting over religious objections to his faith; the other by the imaginative power he shows in clothing a vacuum with impressive and majestic shadows till it looks something like a faith. Again, both, with all their richness of insight, have had that strong desire to rest on something beyond that insight, something which they can regard as independent of themselves, which led Newman first to preach against the principle of private judgment, and to yearn after an infallible Church, while it led Matthew Arnold to preach what he calls his doctrine of verification—namely, that no religious or moral instinct is to be trusted unless it can obtain the endorsement on a large scale of the common consent of the best human experience. Surely there is no greater marvel in our age than that it has felt profoundly the influence of both, and appreciated the greater qualities of both—the leader who with bowed head and passionate self-distrust, nay, with "many a pause of prayer and fear," has led hundreds back to surrender their judgment to a Pope whose rashness Dr. Newman's own ripe culture ultimately condemned, and the poet who in some of the most pathetic verses of modern times has bewailed the loss of the very belief which, in some of the most flippant and frigid of the diatribes of modern times, he has done all that was in his power to destroy. Cardinal Newman has taught men to take refuge in the greatness of the past from the pettiness of the present. Mr. Arnold has endeavoured to restore the idolatry of the *Zeitgeist*, the "time-spirit," which measures truth by the dwindled faith of the existing generation, and which never so much as dreams that one day the dwindled faith of the existing generation may in its turn be judged, and condemned, by that truth which it has denied. Surely, that the great University of Oxford should have produced first the one and then the other—first the great Romaniser, and then the great rationaliser—is such a sign of the times as one ought not lightly to pass by. When I consider carefully how the great theologian has vanished from his pulpit at St. Mary's, and how, finally transformed into a Cardinal, he has pleaded from his Birmingham Oratory with the same touching simplicity as in his old tutorial days for the truth that to the single heart "there are but two things in the whole universe—our own soul and God who made it"—and then how the man who succeeded him in exercising more of the peculiar influence of Oxford over the world than any other of the following generation—and where is there a promise of any younger Oxford leader who is likely to stand even in the place of Mr. Arnold?—tells us with that mild intellectual arrogance which is the leading characteristic of his didactic prose, "I do not think it can be said that there is even a low degree of probability for the assertion that God is a person who thinks and loves,"—when I consider this contrast, I realise more distinctly than in looking at any of the physical changes of the universe what Shakespeare meant when he wrote, "We are such stuff as dreams are made of." What are messages flashed under the ocean, what is our more rapid flight through space, what is the virtual contraction of the distances on this little molehill of a planet till the most distant points upon it are accessible to almost all, compared with the startling mental revolution effected within thirty or forty years at most? When the highest intellect of a great place of learning in one generation says in effect, "Because I believe so utterly in God and His revelation, I have no choice but to believe also in the Pope," while the highest intellect of the same great school in the next generation says, "As there is not even a low degree of probability that God in the old sense exists, let us do all that we can with streams of tendency, and morality touched with emotion, to supply his place," we must at least admit that the moral instability of the most serious convictions of earth is alarming enough to make the whole head sick and the whole heart faint. Perhaps, however, I may be able in some degree to attenuate, before I have dealt with both these great men, the more painful aspects of the paradox on which I am insisting.

Most of us know, by bust, photograph, or picture, the wonderful face of the great Cardinal;— that wide forehead, ploughed deep with parallel horizontal furrows which seem to express his careworn grasp of the double aspect of human nature, its aspect in the intellectual and its aspect in the spiritual world, —the pale cheek down which

"long lines of shadow slope
Which years, and curious thought, and suffering give,"

—the pathetic eye, which speaks compassion from afar, and yet gazes wonderingly into the impassable gulf which separates man from man, and the strange mixture of asceticism and tenderness in all the lines of that mobile and reticent mouth, where humour, playfulness, and sympathy are intricately blended with those severer moods that "refuse and restrain." On the whole, it is a face full in the first place of spiritual passion of the highest order, and in the next, of that subtle and intimate knowledge of the details of human limitation and weakness which makes all spiritual passion look utterly ambitious and hopeless, unless indeed it be guided amongst the stakes and dykes and pitfalls of the human battlefield by the direct providence of God.

And not a little of what I say of Cardinal Newman's countenance may be said also of his style. A great French critic has declared that "style *is* the man." But surely that cannot be asserted without much qualification. There are some styles which are much better than the man, through failing to reflect the least admirable parts of him; and many that are much worse—for example, styles affected by the artificial influence of conventional ideas, like those which prevailed in the last century. Again, there are styles which are thoroughly characteristic of the man in one sense, and yet are characteristic in part because they show his delight in viewing both himself and the universe through coloured media, which, while they brilliantly represent some aspects of it, greatly misrepresent or completely disguise all others. Such a style was Carlyle's, who may be said to have seen the universe with wonderful vividness as it was when in earthquake and hurricane, but not to have apprehended at all that solid crust of earth symbolising the conventional phlegmatic nature which most of us know only too well. Gibbon, again, sees everything —even himself—as if it were a striking moral pageant.

How characteristically he describes his father's disapprobation of his youthful passion for Mademoiselle Curchod (afterwards Madame Necker),—"I sighed as a lover, I obeyed as a son." It was evidently the moral pageant of that very mild ardour, and that not too reluctant submission, of which he was thinking; not of the emotion itself. And Macaulay, again, has a style like a coat of mail with the visor down. It is burnished, brilliant, imposing, but it presents the world and human life in pictorial antitheses far more vivid and brilliant than real. It is a style which effectually conceals all the more homely and domestic aspects of Macaulay's own nature, and represents mainly his hunger for incisive contrast. But if ever it were true that the style is the man, it is true, I think, of Newman—nay, of both Newman and Matthew Arnold. And therefore I may venture without impropriety to dwell somewhat longer on the style of both, and especially of the former, than would be ordinarily justifiable. Both styles are luminous, both are marked by that curious "distinction" which only genius, and in general only poetic genius, can command. Both show a great delight in irony, and use it with great effect. Both writers can, when they choose, indulge even in extravagance, and give the rein to ridicule without rousing that displeasure which any such excess in men of high intellectual power is apt to excite. Both styles are styles of white light rather than of the lurid, or glowing, or even rainbow order. Both, in poetry at least, and Newman's in both poetry and prose, are capable of expressing the truest kind of pathos. Both have something in them of the older Oxford suavity, though in very different forms. I have heard it said that the characteristic Oxford manner is "ostentatiously sweet," as the characteristic Cambridge manner is ostentatiously clumsy. But neither Cardinal Newman nor Matthew Arnold have the slightest trace of this excess of suavity, of the *eau sucrée* attributed to the University. Newman's sweetness is the sweetness of religious humility and ardour, Arnold's is the sweetness of easy condescension. Newman's sweetness is wistful, Arnold's is didactic; the one yearns to move your heart, the other kindly enlightens your intellect. Even Newman's prose style is spiritual in its basis, Arnold's intellectual. Even when treating spiritual topics, even when saying the best things Arnold has ever said as to "the secret of Jesus," his manner, though gracious, is gently dictatorial. Again, when Newman gives the rein to his irony, it is always with a certain earnestness, or even indignation against the self-deceptions he is ridiculing. When Arnold does so, it is in pleasurable scorn of the folly he is exposing. I may illustrate the very different irony of the two men by two passages of a somewhat analogous kind, in which each of them repels the imputation of having something new and wonderful of his own to communicate to the world. Here is the striking passage in which Arnold describes the embarrassment with which he should find himself addressing a select circle of his special admirers in the best room of the "Spotted Dog":—

"The old recipe," he says, "to think a little more and talk a little less, seems to me still the best recipe to follow. So I take comfort when I find the *Guardian* reproaching me with having no influence, for I know what influence means—a party, practical proposals, action; and I say to myself, 'Even supposing I could get some followers, and assemble them, brimming with affectionate enthusiasm, in a committee-room at some inn, what on earth should I say to them? What resolutions could I propose? I could only propose the old Socratic commonplace, *Know thyself*, and how black they would all look at that!' No; to inquire, perhaps too curiously, what the present state of English development and civilisation is, which, according to Mr. Lowe, is so perfect, that to give votes to the working class is stark madness; and, on the other hand, to be less sanguine about the divine and saving effect of a vote on its possessor than my friends in the committee-room at the 'Spotted Dog'; that is my inevitable portion. To bring things under the light of one's intelligence, to see how they look there, to accustom one's self simply to regard the Marylebone Vestry, or the Educational Home, or our Divorce Court, or our gin palaces open on Sunday and the Crystal Palace shut, as absurdities, is, I am sure, invaluable exercise for us just at present. Let all persist in it who can, and steadily set their desires on introducing, with time, a little more soul and spirit into the too too solid flesh of English society."

I turn to Father Newman's mode of making a somewhat similar protestation. He has been recalling the Tractarian horror of private judgment in theology, and is considering the position taken by some of the Anglicans, that it would be enough if they should only succeed in making a little party of their own, opposed to private judgment, within a Church that rests entirely upon private judgment:—

"For me, my dear brethren, did I know myself well, I should doubtless find I was open to the temptation as well as others to take a line of my own, or what is called, to set up for myself; but whatever might be my real infirmity in this matter, I should, from mere common sense and common delicacy, hide it from myself, and give it some good name in order to make it palatable. I never could get myself to say, 'Listen to me, for I have something great to tell you, which no one else knows, but of which there is no manner of doubt.' I should be kept from such extravagance from an intense sense of the intellectual absurdity, which, in my feelings, such a claim would involve; which would shame me as keenly, and humble me in my own sight as utterly, as some moral impropriety or degradation. I should feel I was simply making a fool of myself, and taking on myself, in figure, that penance, of which we read in the lives of saints, of playing antics and making faces in the market-place. Not religious principle but even worldly pride would keep me from so unworthy an exhibition. . . . Do not come to me at this time of day with views perfectly new, isolated, original, *sui generis*, warranted old neither by Christian nor unbeliever, and challenge me to answer what I really have not the patience to read. Life is not long enough for such trifles. Go elsewhere, not to me, if you wish to make a proselyte. Your inconsistency, my dear brethren, is on your very front. . . . I began myself with doubting and inquiring, you seem to say; I departed from the teaching I received; I was educated in some older type of Anglicanism—in the school of Newton, Cecil, or Scott, or in the Bartlett's Buildings school, or in the Liberal Whig school; I was a Dissenter or a Wesleyan, and by study and thought I became an Anglo-Catholic. And then I read the Fathers, and I have determined what books are genuine and what are not ; which of them apply to all times, which are occasional, which historical, and which doctrinal ; what opinions are private, what authoritative ; what they only seem to hold, what they ought to hold ; what are fundamental, what ornamental. Having thus measured and cut and put together my creed by my own proper intellect, by my own lucubrations, and differing from the whole world in my results, I distinctly bid you, I solemnly warn you, not to do as I have done, but to take what I have found, to revere it, to use it, to believe it, for it is the teaching of the old Fathers, and of your mother, the Church of England. Take my word for it that this is the very truth of Christ ; deny your own reason, for I know better than you ; and it is as clear as day that some moral fault in you is the cause of your differing from me. It is pride, or vanity, or self-reliance, or fulness of bread. You require some medicine for your soul. You must fast ; you must make a general confession ; and look very sharp to yourself, for you are already next door to a rationalist or an infidel."—*Lectures on Anglican Difficulties*, pp. 126-134.

Or as he put the same thing in another passage, in which he described how the authorities of the Anglican Church had ruled *ex cathedrâ*, that the Anglican divinity was all wrong :—

"There are those who, reversing the Roman maxim, are wont to shrink from the contumacious and to be valiant towards the submissive ; and the authorities in question gladly availed themselves of the power conferred on them by the movement against the movement itself. They fearlessly handselled their Apostolical weapons upon the Apostolical party. One after another in long succession they took up their song and their parable against it. It was a solemn war-dance which they executed round victims who, by their very principle, were bound hand and foot, and could only eye with disgust and perplexity this most unaccountable movement on the part of those 'Holy Fathers, the representatives of the Apostles, and the Angels of the Churches.' . . . When bishops spoke against them, and bishops' courts sentenced them, and the universities degraded them, and the people were against them, from that day their 'occupation was gone,' . . . henceforward they had nothing left for them but to shut up the school and retire into the country. Nothing else was left for them unless, indeed, they took up some other theory, unless they changed their ground, unless they ceased to be what they were, and became what they were not; unless they belied their own principles, and strangely forgot their own luminous and most keen convictions; unless they vindicated the right of private judgment, took up some fancy religion, retailed the Fathers, and jobbed Theology."

Both passages are admirable in their very different irony. But how wide apart is the character of that irony. Matthew Arnold's is the irony of true intellectual scorn, directed against all who appeal to vulgar prejudices and wish to rally party-feeling by *ad captandum* cries. He is delighted to boast that he has nothing to say to such people, and can hardly congratulate himself sufficiently on the thought that they would have nothing to say to him. If he can but make them feel how thorough is his contempt for that whole field of popular combinations in which political manœuvres are attempted, he is quite satisfied with himself. Newman's irony, on the other hand, is directed against what he regarded as the real self-deception which went on in the minds of some of his own most intimate associates and friends of former days. He is all on fire to make them feel that if they had really given up private judgment in theology, they could not consistently hold a position which is tenable only on the score that a vast number of most uncertain and arbitrary private judgments, approved by no Church as a whole, nor even by any influential section of any, have concurred to define and fortify it. Keen as his irony is, there is a certain passion in it too. He cannot endure to see what he thinks such unreality, such self-deception, in those whom he has trusted and loved. He seeks to cut them almost by main force out of a position which he thinks humiliating to them, and which for himself he would certainly regard as wanting in candour and sincerity. And the difference between the nature and bias of Arnold's irony and Newman's irony runs into the difference between their styles in general. Both are luminous, but Arnold's prose is luminous like a steel mirror, Newman's like a clear atmosphere or lake. Arnold's prose style is crystal, Newman's liquid.

And with this indication of the characteristic difference I will now turn to my immediate subject, Cardinal Newman's style only. It is a style, as I have said, that more nearly represents a clear atmosphere than any other which I know in English literature. It flows round you, it presses gently on every side of you, and yet like a steady current carries you in one direction too. On every facet of your mind and heart you feel the light touch of his purpose, and yet you cannot escape the general drift of his movement more than the ship can escape the drift of the tide. He never said anything more characteristic than when he expressed his conviction that, though there are a hundred difficulties in faith, into all of which he could enter, the hundred difficulties are not equivalent to a single doubt. That saying is most characteristic even of his style, which seems to be sensitive in the highest degree to a multitude of hostile influences which are at once appreciated and resisted, while one predominant and over-ruling power moves steadily on.

I will try and illustrate my meaning briefly. Take the following passage concerning the lower animals :—

"Can anything be more marvellous or startling, unless we were used to it, than that we should have a race of beings about us whom we do see, and as little know their state, or can describe their interests or their destiny, as we can tell of the inhabitants of the sun and moon? It is, indeed, a very overpowering thought, when we get to fix our minds on it, that we periodically use—I may say hold intercourse with—creatures who are as much strangers to us, as mysterious, as if they were the fabulous unearthly beings, more powerful than man, and yet his slaves, which Eastern superstitions have invented. We have more real knowledge about the angels than about the brutes; they have, apparently, passions, habits, and a certain accountableness; but all is mystery about them. We do not know whether they can sin or not, whether they are under punishment, whether they are to live after this life; we inflict very great sufferings on a portion of them, and they, in turn, every now and then, retaliate upon us, as if by a wonderful law. . . . Cast your thoughts abroad on the whole number of them, large and small, in vast forests, or in the water, or in the air, and then say whether the presence of such countless multitudes, so various in their natures, so strange and wild in their shapes, living on the earth without ascertainable object, is not as mysterious as anything Scripture says about the angels."

Now, does not the style of that passage perfectly represent the character of the mind which conceived it, as well as the special meaning it conveys? Inferior styles express the purpose but conceal the man; Newman's expresses the purpose by revealing the man. This passage—and I could find scores which would suit my purpose as well, and some, though not so short and detachable, that would suit it better—is as luminous as the day, but that is not its special characteristic, for luminousness belongs to the ether, which is the same whether the atmosphere be present or absent, and Newman's style touches you with a visible thrill, just as the atmosphere transmits every vibration of sound. You are conscious of the thrill of the writer's spirit as he contemplates this strange world of countless animated beings with whom our spiritual bond is so slight; the sufferings we inflict, and the retaliations permitted in return; the blindness to spiritual marvels with which custom strikes us; the close analogy between the genii of Eastern superstition and the domestic animals who serve us so industriously with physical powers so much greater than our own; the strangeness and wildness of the innumerable forms which hover round us in forest, field, and flood; and yet, with all those undercurrents of feeling, observe how large is the imaginative reach of the whole, how firmly the drift—to make it easier to believe in angelic hosts—is sustained; how steady is the subordination of the whole to the object of attenuating the difficulty of the spiritual mystery in which he desires men to believe. Once more, how tender is the style in the only sense in which we can properly attribute tenderness to style, its avoidance of every harsh or violent word, its shrinking aside from anything like overstatement. The lower animals have, he says, "apparently passions, habits, and a certain accountableness." Evidently Dr. Newman could not have suggested, as Des Cartes did, that they are machines, apeing feelings without having them; he never doubts their sufferings; he could not, even by a shade, exaggerate the mystery he is delineating. Every touch shows that he wishes to delineate it as it is, and not to overcolour it by a single tint. Then how piercing to our dulness is that phrase, "It is indeed a very overpowering thought *when we get to fix our minds on it.*" We are not overpowered, he would say, only because we cannot or do not fix our minds on this wonderful intercourse of ours with *intimates*, after a kind, of whose inner being we are yet entirely ignorant. And how reticent is the inference, how strictly it limits itself to its real object, to impress upon us how little we know even of the objects of sense, and how little reason there is in using our ignorance as the standard by which to measure the supersensual.

I have taken this passage as a fair illustration of Dr. Newman's style in relation to one of the class of subjects with which he most often deals. Let me take another illustration from his style when he is describing purely outward facts, though of course "style" means less, and ought to mean less, when it expresses only vivid physical vision, with perhaps a dash of wonder in it, than when it expresses a variety of moral emotions. Newman's external descriptions are not magnificent. A magnificent style in describing ordinary physical objects almost always means a style that suggests what the eye neither saw nor could see. And Dr. Newman's style is far from magnificent, for it is delicately vivid. The subject is one of the locust plagues devastating North Africa :—

"The swarm to which Juba pointed grew and grew till it became a compact body as much as a furlong square, yet it was but the vanguard of a series of similar hosts, formed one after another out of the hot mould or sand, rising into the air like clouds, enlarging into a dusky canopy, and then discharged against the fruitful plain. At length the large innumerous mass was put into motion, and began its career, darkening the face of day. As became an instrument of divine power, it seemed to have no volition of its own ; it was set off, it drifted with the wind, and thus made northward straight for Sicca. Thus they advanced, host after host, for a time wafted in the air, and gradually declining to the earth, while fresh hordes were carried over the first, and neared the earth after a longer flight in their turn. For twelve miles they extended from front to rear, and the whizzing and hissing could be heard for twelve miles on every side of them. The bright sun, though hidden by them, illumined their bodies, and was reflected from their quivering wings, and as they heavily fell earthward they seemed like the innumerable flakes of a yellow-coloured snow, and like snow did they descend, a living carpet, or rather pall, upon fields, crops, gardens, copses, groves, orchards, vineyards, olive-woods, orangeries, palm-plantations, and the deep forests, sparing nothing within their reach, and where there was nothing to devour, lying helpless in drifts, or crawling forward obstinately, as they best might, with the hope of prey. They could spare their hundred thousand soldiers twice or thrice over and not miss them; the masses filled the bottoms of the ravines and hollow ways, impeding the traveller as he rode forward on his journey, and trampled by thousands under his horse's hoofs. In vain was all this overthrow and waste by the roadside; in vain all their loss in river, pond, and watercourse. The poor peasants hastily dug pits and trenches as the enemy came on; in vain they filled them from the wells or with lighted stubble. Heavily and thickly did the locusts fall; they were lavish of their lives; they choked the flame and the water which destroyed them the while, and the vast living hostile armament still moved on. . . . They come up to the walls of Sicca and are flung against them into the ditch. Not a moment's hesitation or delay; they recover their footing, they climb up the wood or stucco, they surmount the parapet, or they have entered in at the windows, filling the apartments and the most private and luxurious chambers; not one or two, like stragglers at forage or rioters after a victory, but in order of battle and with the array of an army. Choice plants or flowers, about the impluvia and xysti, for amusement and refreshment, myrtles, oranges, pomegranates, the rose and the carnation have disappeared.

They dim the bright marbles of the walls and the gilding of the ceilings. They enter the triclinium in the midst of the banquet, they crawl over the viands and spoil what they do not devour. Unrelaxed by success and enjoyment, onward they go; a secret mysterious instinct keeps them together as if they had a king over them. They move along the floor in so strange an order that they seem to be a tessellated pavement themselves, and to be the artificial embellishment of the floor, so true are their lines and so perfect the patterns they describe. Onward they go, to the market, to the temple sacrifices, to the bakers' stores, to the cookshops, to the confectioners, to the druggists—nothing comes amiss to them; wherever man has aught to eat or drink there are they, reckless of death, strong of appetite, certain of conquest."

Now, that is a passage in which only a few of the greater qualities of style can be exhibited, but are not those few exhibited in perfection? Could there be a more luminous and orderly grasp of the strange phenomenon depicted, of its full physical significance and moral horror; could there be a more rich and delicate perception of the weirdness of that strange fall of "yellow snow"? Could there be a deeper feeling conveyed of the higher instrumentality under which plagues like these are launched upon the world?

And now to bring to a close what I have to say of Dr. Newman's style—though the subject grows upon one—let me quote one or two of the passages in which his style vibrates to the finest notes, and yet exhibits most powerfully the drift and undercurrent by which his mind is swayed. Perhaps he never expresses anything so powerfully as he expresses the deep pining for the rest of spiritual simplicity, for the peace which passes understanding, that underlies his nature. Take this from one of his Roman Catholic sermons: "Oh, long sought after, tardily found, the desire of the eyes, the joy of the heart, the truth after many shadows, the fulness after many foretastes, the home after many storms; come to her, poor children, for she it is, and she alone, who can unfold to you the secret of your being, and the meaning of your destiny." Again, in the exquisite tale of martyrdom from which I have already quoted the account of the locusts, the destined martyr, whose thirst for God has been awakened by her intercourse with Christians, thus repels the Greek rhetorician, who is trying to feed her on the husks of philosophic abstractions, as she expresses the yearnings of a heart weary of its desolation: "Oh that I could find Him!" Callista exclaimed passionately. "On the right hand and on the left I grope, but touch Him not. Why dost thou fight against me; why dost thou scare and perplex me, oh First and only fair?" Or take one of Dr. Newman's most characteristic poems—the few poems which have really been fused in the glow of his heart before they were uttered by his tongue. The lines I am going to quote were written on a fancy contained in the writings of Bede; the fancy that there is a certain "meadow as it were," in which the souls of holy men suffer nothing, but wait the time when they should be fit to bear the vision of God:—

"They are at rest :
    We may not stir the heaven of their repose
With loud-voiced grief, or passionate request,
    Or selfish plaint for those
Who in the mountain grots of Eden lie,
And hear the fourfold river as it hurries by.

"They hear it sweep
    In distance down the dark and savage vale,
But they at eddying pool or current deep
    Shall never more grow pale ;
They hear, and meekly muse as fain to know,
How long untired, unspent, that giant stream shall flow.

"And soothing sounds
    Blend with the neighbouring waters as they glide;
Posted along the haunted garden's bounds
    Angelic forms abide,
Echoing as words of watch, o'er lawn and grove,
The verses of that hymn which seraphs chant above."

In another of these poems Dr. Newman has referred to the sea described in the book of Revelation :—

"A sea before
The throne is spread ; its pure still glass
Pictures all earth scenes as they pass.
    We on its shore
Share in the bosom of our rest,
God's knowledge, and are blest."

It has always seemed to me that Newman's style succeeds, so far as a human form of expression can, in picturing the feelings of earth in a medium as clear, as liquid, and as tranquil, as sensitive alike to the minutest ripples and the most potent tidal waves of providential impulse, as the sea spread before the throne itself.

I have dwelt so much on Dr. Newman's style because in his case at least, I take the style to be the reflection of the man. But when I say this, it must not be supposed that in describing his style as a clear atmosphere or liquid medium, which makes itself felt everywhere, and yet urges him whom it envelops steadily in one direction, I mean to suggest that Cardinal Newman is wanting in the most marked personal character. A very brief reference to his career will show how very false an impression that would convey. Newman's early life at Oxford was, as we know, a very tranquil, and rather a solitary one. "Never less alone than when alone," were the words in which Dr. Copleston, the Provost of Oriel, addressed him on an accidental meeting in one of his Oxford walks. And he tells us, "It was not I who sought friends, but friends who sought me. Never man had kinder or more indulgent friends than I have had, but I have expressed my own feelings as to the mode in which I gained them," in the year 1829, "in the course of a copy of verses. Speaking of my blessings, I said—'blessings of friends which to my door, *unasked, unhoped*, have come'" (*Apologia*, p. 73). That is, others were more attracted towards the mind which had its own highest attraction in the invisible world, than he towards them. Keble was from the first Newman's chief object of hero-worship, for Newman at least never lost sight of quality in sheer force, never made the mistake which is usually attributed to Carlyle. When, after his election as a fellow of Oriel, he went to receive the congratulations of the other fellows, "I bore it," he wrote, "till Keble took my hand, and then felt so abashed and unworthy of the honour that I seemed desirous of quite sinking into the ground." This was years before the publication of *The Christian Year*. But even Keble's influence was less personal than theological. *The Christian Year* appeared in 1827, and immediately took the strongest hold of Newman. Indeed, the whole history of his life shows how absurd is the view which has sometimes been taken by able men, that Newman's life has been a continuous struggle against scepticism. No one can read his long series of sermons, and his remarkable though much shorter series of poems, and still less re-read them by the light of his lectures "On Anglican Difficulties," his *Apologia* and his *Grammar of Assent*, without being profoundly convinced that the Roman Catholic in Newman is as deep as his *thought*, the High Churchman as deep as his *temperament*, and the Christian as deep as his *character*, being intertwined with it inextricably—nay, not only intertwined, but identified. I can understand what Dr. Newman was as an Anglican, because the first part of the most characteristic work of his life was done as an Anglican, and I believe that it was Reason, and Reason almost alone, working on the assumptions which were so deeply rooted in him in 1843, which made him a Roman

Catholic. I cannot understand what he was as an Evangelical Protestant, because even so far as he ever *was* an Evangelical Protestant, it was only during his earliest youth, and the whole drift of his nature seems to have carried him away from the moorings of his early creed. But what would be left of Dr. Newman if you could wipe the Christian heart out of his life and creed I could as little guess as I could what would have been left of Sir Walter Scott if you could have emptied out of him the light of old romance and legend; or of Carlyle, if you could have managed somehow to graft upon him a conventional "gigmanic" creed. Keble's conception of the poetry in the Christian faith, and the nature-symbolism it contained, took a hold upon Newman which made his career what it became. In many respects, of course, his own mind vastly enlarged and deepened the intellectual view of Keble, turned it into something more masculine, more logical, more constructive; but it would be almost as unreasonable to speak of Keble himself as fighting all his life against a mordant scepticism as of Newman's doing so. It is true, of course, that Newman has seen, as Keble probably never saw, how profoundly the moral assumptions with which the conscious intellectual life begins, influence our faith or want of faith. He has done as much justice to the logical strength of certain types of sceptical thought as he has to the logic of Christian thought itself. But that, since his first "conversion," as he calls it, he ever felt even the smallest temptation to reject Christianity, whether before he became a Roman Catholic or since, is simply incredible. We have his own explicit assertion for the latter denial, and the evidence of his singularly self-consistent life for the former.

I have pointed out that Newman early rested on the conviction of the existence of "two, and two only, supreme and luminously self-evident beings, myself and my Creator" (*Apologia*, p. 59). Of all points of faith, he tells us elsewhere, "the being of a God is to my mind encompassed with the most difficulty and borne in on our minds with most power" (*Ibid.* p. 374). And to the aid of this central conviction came Keble's teaching, that the sacramental system has its roots deep in the natural creation itself, or, as Dr. Newman, expressing his obligations to Keble, puts it, "that material phenomena are both the types and the instruments of real things unseen, a doctrine which embraces not only what Anglicans no less than Catholics believe about sacraments properly so called, but also the article of the communion of Saints in its fulness, and likewise the mysteries of the faith."

Now the more earnestly Newman embraced the doctrine that the natural universe is full of the types and the instrumentality of spiritual beings unseen—and no one can read Newman's poems without feeling how deeply this conviction had struck its roots into him—the more perplexing the external realities of human history and human conduct, barbarous or civilised, mediæval or modern, seemed to him. His faith in the sacramental principle taught him to look for a created universe from which the Creator should be reflected back at every point; but he actually found one from which disorder, confusion, enmity to God, was reflected back at every point. Here are his own words:—

"Starting then with the being of a God (which, as I have said, is as certain to me as the certainty of my own existence, though when I try to put the grounds of that certainty into logical shape I find a difficulty in doing so in mood and figure to my satisfaction), I look out of myself into the world of men, and there I see a sight which fills me with unspeakable distress. The world seems simply to give the lie to that great truth of which my whole being is so full, and the effect upon me is in consequence, as a matter of necessity, as confusing as if it denied that I am in existence myself. If I looked into a mirror and did not see my face I should have that sort of feeling which actually comes upon me when I look into this living busy world and see no reflection of the Creator. This is to me one of the great difficulties of this absolute primary truth to which I referred just now. Were it not for this voice speaking so clearly in my conscience and my heart I should be an atheist, or a pantheist, or a polytheist when I looked into the world. I am speaking for myself only, and I am far from denying the real force of the arguments in proof of a God drawn from the general facts of human society; but these do not warm me or enlighten me; they do not take away the winter of my desolation or make the buds unfold and the leaves grow within me and my moral being rejoice. The sight of the world is nothing else than the prophet's vision, full of 'lamentations and mourning and woe.' To consider the world in its length and breadth, its various history, the many races of men, their starts, their fortune, their mutual alienation, their conflicts, and then their ways, habits, governments, forms of worship, their enterprises, their aimless courses, their random achievements and acquirements, and then the impotent conclusion of long-standing facts, the tokens so faint and broken of a superintending design, the blind evolution of what turn out to be great powers or truths, the progress of things as if from unreasoning elements, not towards final causes, the greatness and littleness of man, his far-reaching aims, his short duration, the curtain hung over his future, the disappointments of life, the defeat of good, the success of evil, physical pain, mental anguish, the prevalence and intensity of sin, the prevailing idolatries, the corruptions, the dreary hopeless irreligion, that condition of the whole race, so fearfully yet exactly described in the Apostle's words, 'Having no hope, and without God in the world,' all this is a vision to dizzy and appal, and inflicts on the mind the sense of a profound mystery which is absolutely beyond human solution."—*Apologia*, pp. 376-378.

This is a passage taken from the *Apologia*, but long before Dr. Newman became a Roman Catholic, even at a time when he held confidently that the Roman Catholic Church was anti-Christian, he had pressed home the same deep conviction that the spectacle of the moral universe and of human history is so utterly abhorrent to the heart taught from within, that it can only be explained at all on the principle that the human race has been implicated in some "great aboriginal calamity" which can only be obviated by some equally great supernatural interference in human affairs, specially adapted to remedy that calamity. Even before he threw himself into the Tractarian movement, even before he went abroad with Mr. Hurrell Froude in 1832 on that memorable journey in which, whether quarantined in lazarettos, or conversing with Roman ecclesiastics, or lying sick almost to death in Sicily, or tossing in an orange boat on the Mediterranean, he was so haunted by the belief that he had a "work to do in England," that he shrank from every kind of contact with influences which seemed to him incongruous with that work,— he had urged on Oxford students and Oxford audiences of every kind, with passionate earnestness, his warnings against trusting what Matthew Arnold delights to call the *Zeitgeist*, the "modern spirit," the spirit of the age.

"Our manners are courteous [he says], we avoid giving pain or offence ; our words become correct ; our relative duties are carefully performed ; our sense of propriety shows itself even in our domestic arrangements, in the embellishment of our houses, in our amusements, and so also in our religious profession. Vice now becomes unseemly and hideous to the imagination, or, as it is sometimes familiarly said, 'out of taste.' Thus elegance is gradually made the test and standard of virtue, which is no longer thought to possess an intrinsic claim on our hearts, or to exist *further* than it leads to the quiet and comfort of others. Conscience is no longer recognised as an independent arbiter of actions, its authority is explained away ; partly it is superseded in the minds of men by the so-called moral sense which is regarded merely as the love of the beautiful ; partly by the rule of expediency which is forthwith substituted for it in the details of conduct. Now, conscience is a stern, gloomy principle; it tells us of guilt and of prospective punishment. Accordingly, when its terrors disappear, then disappear also in the creed of the day those fearful images of divine wrath with which the Scripture abounds."—*Parochial Sermons*, vol. i. p. 311.

And then he utters that celebrated sentence—

"I will not shrink from uttering my firm conviction that it would be a gain to this country were it vastly more superstitious, more bigoted, more gloomy, more fierce in its religion than at present it shows itself to be. Not, of course, that I think the tempers of mind herein implied desirable, which would be an evident absurdity, but I think them infinitely more desirable and more promising than a heathen obduracy, and a cold, self-sufficient, self-wise tranquillity."—*Parochial Sermons*, p. 320.

In short, when Newman went abroad in 1832, with his consumptive friend Hurrell Froude, his thought by day and his dream by night seems to have been of the quickening of a Church which would fight against this *Zeitgeist*—against the religion of the day, against the theophilanthropic ideas of the Society for the Diffusion of Useful Knowledge, and fix the minds of its children upon those eternal realities, which the "modern spirit" of our own time is as anxious to soften, blanch, and water down, as the mediæval spirit was to travesty by isolating and exaggerating their austere and terrible warnings. There was a passion at this time in all Newman said and did. He told himself to learn to hate evil as the only adequate preparation for loving good. He was conscious of a driving force which carried him on—

> "Wave reared on wave its godless head
> While my keen bark, by breezes sped,
> Dash'd fiercely through the ocean bed,
> And chafed towards its goal."

He passed through Roman Catholic countries, carefully avoiding their worship; he fell sick of malaria when in Sicily, and told his servant that he should not die, adding to himself, "because I have not sinned against the light," a phrase which he says he has never understood, but which no doubt meant that he had not forfeited the right to be, what he felt himself destined to be, God's instrument for quickening the Church of England. When tossing at sea in the straits of Bonifazio, this austerer mood relented, and he felt for once that more gentle spirit which has marked all the later portions of his career. Almost every one now knows the poem to which I allude; I recall one verse only to show how different is its keynote to that of the eager flame of zeal with which during this journey he seems in general to have been burnt up:—

> "So long Thy power hath blest me, sure it still
> Will lead me on,
> O'er moor and fen, o'er crag and torrent, till
> The night is gone,
> And in the morn those angel faces smile,
> Which I have loved long since and lost awhile."

But mostly during this journey he harps on the lukewarmness of the age, and the indifference to eternal truth which it displays. Becalmed at sea, he implores patience, and confesses that he feels very sorely "the languor of delay." He muses much, too, on certain tendencies which he finds in his own character, tendencies which he believes to be pure, but which he knows are likely to be confounded by the world with craft and pride:—

"How didst thou start, thou Holy Baptist, bid
To pour repentance on the sinless brow !
Then all thy meekness from thy hearers hid
Beneath the ascetic's port and preacher's fire,
Flowed forth, and with a pang thou didst desire
He might be chief, not thou.

"And so on us at whiles it falls to claim
Powers that we dread, or dare some forward part ;
Nor must we shrink as cravens from the blame
Of pride, in common eyes, or purpose deep,
But with pure thoughts look up to God, and keep
Our secret in our heart."

Nay, he has a dream of St. Paul, which tells him that St. Paul too was exposed to the same unjust charges to which he himself was liable:—

"I dreamed that with a passionate complaint
I wish'd me born amid God's deeds of might,
And envied those who had the presence bright
Of gifted prophet and strong-hearted saint,
Whom my heart loves and fancy strives to paint.
I turned, when straight a stranger met my sight,
Come as my guest, and did awhile unite
His lot with mine ; and lived without restraint.

> Courteous he was and grave, so meek in mien
> It seem'd untrue, or told a purpose weak,
> Yet in the mood he could with aptness speak,
> Or with stern force, or show of feelings keen,
> Marking deep craft, methought, or hidden pride ;—
> Then came a voice, 'St. Paul is at thy side.' "

In this spirit Newman went back to commence the Tractarian movement. "There was," he has since confessed, "at that time a double aspect in my bearing towards others. My behaviour had in it a mixture both of fierceness and of sport, and on this account, I daresay, it gave offence to many, nor can I here defend it." The truth was that he really did feel to the bottom of his heart that he was doing a work of which he himself knew neither the scope nor the goal, and that, so far as he was acquitted by his own conscience, he did not much care what men said of him. He believed that it was given to him to open to the Church of England a new career, to raise it up as a new power to witness against the sins and whims and false ideals of the day, and the various idolatries of the *Zeitgeist*.

Where did he go wrong? Of course one does not like to say of a man of the highest genius, and of a kind of genius specially adapted to the subject on which he writes, that he is wrong, and that a man of no genius, who criticises him, is right ; but still, as I believe that he did go seriously wrong, and should be a Roman Catholic myself if I did not, I must give my explanation of the error I think I see. It seems to me, then, that he went wrong in his primary assumption that what he calls "the dogmatic principle" involves the existence of an infallible human authority, which can say, without possibility of error, 'this is what God has revealed, and this again is radically inconsistent with what He has revealed.' I will quote his own account of his convictions on this subject from the *Apologia*. It is a very striking passage, and very instructive as to the course of this great thinker's personal history :—

"Supposing, then, it to be the will of the Creator to interfere in human affairs, and to make provisions for retaining in the world a knowledge of Himself, so definite and distinct as to be proof against the energy of human scepticism,—in such a case, I am far from saying that there was no other way, but there is nothing to surprise the mind, if He should think fit to introduce a power into the world invested with the prerogative of infallibility on religious matters. Such a provision would be a direct, immediate, certain, and prompt means of withstanding the difficulty ; it would be an instrument suited to the need ; and when I find that this is the very claim of the Catholic Church, not only do I feel no difficulty in admitting the idea, but there is a fitness in it which recommends it to my mind. And thus I am brought to speak of the Church's infallibility as a provision, adapted by the mercy of the Creator, to preserve religion in the world, and to restrain that freedom of thought, which of course in itself is one of the greatest of natural gifts, and to rescue it from its own suicidal excesses."—*Apologia*, p. 382.

That seems to me a definite contention that the reason of man is naturally so restless, so disposed to devour its own offspring, as to need the bit and bridle of an infallible *human* authority in addition to the guidance of God's spirit. But is not that in a sense really putting man above God, or at best putting God's providence as revealed in human institutions above God's spirit as revealed in conscience and reason? I should have supposed that to a thinker with so passionate a belief in God as the deepest of all realities, the true security for the ultimate stability of our reason, for the ultimate subjection of our reason to the power and fascination of revelation, would have been simply this, that God after all sways our spirits, and draws them to Himself. But Newman has so keen an insight into the morbid side of the cravings of Rationalism for devouring its own offspring that he can hardly believe that we shall ever rest on what God has revealed, unless that revelation receives a genuinely human embodiment in an infallible institution set upon a rock for all men to recognise as stamped by Providence with one of God's greatest attributes, inability to err. This is saying, in other words, that when Newman passes from the world within to the world without, he discerns far more keenly the evils, the miseries, the weaknesses, the diseases, the woes, the corruptions of our nature, than he does its affinity with the divine life. Like a great physician, when he looks out of himself, his sight is sharper for the signs of disorder and internal malady than for the signs of life and strength. It is, I think, profound pity for the restlessness and insatiability of human reason which has made him a Roman Catholic. He is always seeking for some caustic which may burn away the proud flesh from our hearts, for some antiseptic which shall destroy the germs of canker in our intellect. He has a wonderful insight into the natural history of all our morbid symptoms. His hand is ever on the feeble and rapid pulse of human impatience, his eye is keen to discern the hectic flush on the worn face. He sees in the Roman Catholic Church a great laboratory of spiritual drugs which will lower fever and arrest the growth of fungoid parasites, and he cannot help grasping at the medicaments she offers.

Newman never shows more unique genius than in mastering the morbid symptoms, both of human conscience and human reason, though he is spiritually greatest when, after showing us how deep is his knowledge of all the intricate maladies of human nature, he shakes the trouble from him, and passes quietly into the peaceful rest of perfect faith. But his attachment to the Roman Catholic Church is, I think, in great measure given to its functions as a mediciner of souls, to its various appliances of penance, its exhaustive study of casuistry, and its elaborate pharmacopœia of spiritual tonics and febrifuges.

But to go back to the evil for which he maintains that an infallible Church is the only remedy, namely, the tendency of reason to undermine every faith for which we have not the daily evidence of universal experience :—he holds, truly I think, that no church, no witness to God, can stand without a steady dogmatic basis, and that, without submission to some visible vicegerent of God, no dogmatic basis of religious truth can ever be established. Well, I should be the last to assail dogma, as Matthew Arnold, for instance, has assailed it. It seems to me that even the fact of writing as I do implies a dogma—the dogma that my readers and I really exist. If God announces His holiness and love to man, He announces implicitly His own existence. If He announces the redemption of man, He announces the existence of the Redeemer. If we are convinced that a divine light has illumined our consciences, that fact alone implies a good many intellectual truths, which will more and more impress themselves on us as we recognise the fact and conform our lives to it. Theological dogma is nothing in the world but a *rationale* of the relations in which God places Himself towards us in the act of revealing Himself. But why does revelation imply the human possession of any *infallible* rationale of these relations? The Jews had a revelation continued during many centuries, a revelation which made them undoubtedly the specific medium through which divine truth was revealed to the world. But they had no infallible authority to which they could appeal on points in dispute. And it cannot be said that there never were any points in dispute. As a matter of fact, one of the greater prophets has assured us that, at one time during the history of that people, "the prophets" themselves "prophesy falsely, and the priests bear rule by their means, and my people love to have it so." How were the Jewish people to know, except by trusting their impressions of character,—a character educated by God Himself,—that Jeremiah was divinely taught in revealing to them that other prophets, who also claimed to be the organs of divine revelation, in this case at least made that claim falsely? Again, not only had the Jewish Church no infallible exponent of the drift of the divine teaching, but where is the evidence that even the primitive Christian Church made any such claim? What was the apostolate of Judas Iscariot except a divine warning against attributing too final an authority even to those earthen vessels chosen by the Redeemer Himself? Moreover, how should an infallible authority—even if one existed—on the dogmatic truths involved in revelation imply the right understanding of these truths, unless the believer be guided by the spirit of God in receiving them? The same words mean totally different things to the humble mind and the arrogant mind, to the selfish mind and to the self-denying. Even the infallible human authority could inculcate only a lesson of error and illusion when addressing itself to a fallible and sinful believer. I cannot for the life of me see how the infallible human authority for dogma could, even if it existed, be of any service to rebellious, misguided, passionate men, unless it could infuse the grace to understand spiritually, as well as authorise the right form of words to be understood. Surely revelation, once communicated, must live and exert itself, and deepen for itself the spiritual channels in which it is to run, just as the original moral teaching, engraved both on tables of stone and on the heart, has lived and exerted itself, and deepened for itself the moral channels in which it is to run. Both revelations have been misunderstood; both have been perverted; both have been defied; both have been ridiculed; both have been scorned; yet both have exerted an ever deepening and widening influence, and have found out the true hearts for which they were intended.

I cannot help thinking, then, that Dr. Newman's belief, that the most fitting power to subdue the anarchy of human passions and intellectual pride is an infallible Church, is an error, and an error of that most serious kind which, by throwing the Church which boasts infallibility off its guard, produces an abundant crop of special dangers and mistakes. So far from the assumption of infallibility having actually "preserved religion in the world," and "restrained the freedom of thought" which is so apt to run into "suicidal excesses," I cannot help thinking that that assumption has done more not only to foster "suicidal excesses" in the Church which makes it, but to drive the churches which deny it into "suicidal excesses" of another kind, than any other equally important factor in the history of revelation. I do not deny, on the contrary, I heartily join Dr. Newman in believing, that the only attitude of mind in which we can hope to profit by revelation is that of profound humility towards an infallible authority above us; but by whom is it wielded, by man or by God? Where is the evidence, or the vestige of evidence, that since Christ's ascension it has ever been put in commission in human hands at all? Was not one apostle rebuked as Satan the moment after his confession had been treated as putting him in possession of the keys of the new kingdom? Was not another avowedly doubtful whether in certain instances he spoke by inspiration or only out of his own fallible judgment? That an infallible authority should impart wisdom to fallible men I can understand; that it should make over its own infallibility on any terms to fallible men I cannot understand. And it seems to me that the result of the assumption in all countries which have accepted the infallible Church has been to secure indeed the intellectual ascendency of dogma, but often at the cost of destroying the moral ascendency of the truths of which dogma is but the skeleton. Roman Catholics who, like Dr. Newman, nourish themselves on a genuinely spiritual view of their own theology, seem to me to be among the salt of the earth. But what seems to be far commoner amongst Roman Catholic nations than even amongst Protestant nations is the habit of assenting with the mind to what the heart ignores; and is not this the direct consequence of attaching so much importance to the infallibility of a Church of which the earthly corner-stone may be such a Judas as Alexander Borgia? In the remarkable lecture — which as a youth I had the privilege of hearing — on "The Political State of Catholic Countries no Prejudice to the Sanctity of the Church," I remember the full sympathy and even enthusiasm with which I heard Dr. Newman say what I trust a great many Protestants would say with him, that the Church

"Aims not at making a show, but at doing a work. She regards this world and all that is in it as a mere shade, as dust and ashes, compared with the value of one single soul. She holds that unless she can in her own way do good to souls, it is no use her doing anything; she holds that it were better for sun and moon to drop from heaven, for the earth to fail, and for the many millions upon it to die of starvation in extremest agony, as far as temporal affliction goes, than that one soul, I will not say should be lost, but should commit one single venial sin, should tell one wilful untruth, though it harmed no one, or steal one poor farthing without excuse. She considers the action of this world and the action of the soul simply incommensurate, viewed in their respective spheres; she would rather save the soul of one single wild bandit of Calabria, or whining beggar of Palermo, than draw a hundred lines of railroad through the length of Italy, or carry out a sanitary reform in its fullest details in every city of Sicily, except so far as these great national works tended to some spiritual good beyond them."

But, then, does the Church habitually mean by saving the soul what I am sure Dr. Newman means? Does it mean putting an abiding purity into the bandit or the beggar—making him holy with the holiness of Christ? And if the Church does mean this, does her presumed infallibility help to accomplish it ? In the same remarkable lecture Dr. Newman drew a picture which I remember to have supposed at the time that he took from Ireland.

"Take a mere beggar-woman, lazy, ragged, filthy, and not over scrupulous of truth (I do not say she has arrived at perfection)"—[here he was so overcome by his own deep sense of humour that he laughed behind his MS., then crossed himself, and I think said a Pater Noster to himself before resuming]—"but if she is chaste and sober and cheerful, and goes to her religious duties, and I am supposing not at all an impossible case, she will, in the eyes of the Church, have a prospect of heaven, quite closed and refused to the State's pattern man, the just, the upright, the generous, the honourable, the conscientious, if he be all this not from a supernatural power—(I no not determine whether this is likely to be the fact, but I am contrasting views and principles) —not from a supernatural power, but from mere natural virtue."

I should have supposed it impossible to be at heart and in motive *really* just and upright, and absolutely a contradiction in terms to be *really* "conscientious," from any mere natural quality. Indeed, "virtue" does not seem to me, in its highest meaning, a natural quality at all, but distinctly a supernatural one, though I would not for a moment deny it even to an atheist who should follow, after a severe struggle, the guidance of divine light, while supposing himself to be following only his own best instincts. But my main criticism on that passage is that even in the country of which I suppose Dr. Newman to have been thinking when he depicted the chaste, sober and religious, though lazy, ragged, and untruthful beggar-woman, the Catholic Church has failed to bring home to the great mass of the population the supernatural character of those elementary duties on which Dr. Newman himself insists so justly. Ireland was for a long time the favourite Catholic example of a spiritual nation, not well trained in those secular virtues which are at the roots of prosperity. Is Ireland that favourite example still? Does not that utter want of moral and spiritual courage, in consequence of which the peasantry, far and wide, have submitted to the decrees of cruel and unscrupulous Ribbonmen, and have sheltered murderers from their well-earned punishment, attest that the infallible Church has *not* succeeded in bringing home even the most elementary of spiritual duties to the hearts and consciences of the people? I cannot help believing that the assumption of infallibility as to *dogma* has tended to divert the attention of the Church of Rome most seriously and unduly from the great danger of all churches—namely, the willingness to accept true *words* about God in the place of real spiritual acts founded on the love of His righteousness.

I cannot conclude this study of Dr. Newman without a few words on one of the most momentous of his books, the great book on *Development of Christian Doctrine*, which was destined to anticipate so curiously, in the ecclesiastical field, much that Mr. Darwin had to tell us in the field of biology. It is a great book, and one from which Protestants might learn much—much that they might use against Dr. Newman, much also that they might accept from him and apply for their own benefit. Now, it does not, as it seems to me, admit of doubt that we ought to examine most carefully, as evidence of what a divine revelation was, if we once believed that such a revelation has been given, what impression it actually produced on the generation which received it and on its immediate successors. We cannot and ought not to treat what we believe to come from above as we should what comes from our own mixed nature. We must admit fully the possibility that Revelation may contain elements which we cannot easily apprehend, elements which it takes even the faithful observance of many generations to apprehend and justify, elements which assert their full influence over believers very gradually, but then turn out to be of unspeakable importance. It has therefore always seemed to me that Protestants are far too anxious to depreciate the immense importance of the appeal to the actual Christianity of the Apostolic fathers and the Church of the second century. To know fully what Christianity was, we must know not only what the apostles have left to us in a documentary form as the drift of their teaching, but what was the immediate effect of what they taught, what the early Church believed that it had really received from them, what the type of Christianity was after it had been impressed on a generation born in communion with the Church. No book has done more to show the importance of this historic treatment than Dr. Newman's *Essay on Development;* none, I think, to lay down truer rules for genuine development; none, perhaps, to illustrate those rules less fortunately or with more preconceived bias. But who can fail to be grateful to the man who has insisted that a genuine "development" of revealed truth must preserve intact the original type, must keep continuously to the principles of the primitive doctrinal teaching, must show the power adequately to assimilate nutriment foreign yet subservient to it and to throw off alien material, must be able to show early indications that such a development would be likely, must be logically consistent with all that was originally taught, must be able to protect itself by "preservative additions" which secure the type instead of altering it, and, finally, must show tenacity of life? How far Dr. Newman's instances of those tests of development make good his own position is a very different question indeed —is, indeed, a question like that whether the House of Commons can be considered a "preservative addition" to the monarchy, or rather an addition which, while it has preserved it for centuries, is likely some day to supersede it. But what I hold to be the enormous value of Dr. Newman's essay is that it puts us on the way to a *true* investigation of the claims of our various churches to represent the primitive revelation of Christ. Do we or do we not preserve the original type? Do we or do we not show a continuity of principle with that primitive

Christianity? Do we show any power of assimilating life from without, and imposing the structural law of Christian hearts upon that life from without? Can we show the power to reject as alien to us what is poisonous to Christian habits of life? Can we show early anticipations of our modern religious developments? Can we prove our logical continuity with the old teaching? Are our "preservative additions" monstrous innovations tending to the neglect of the deepest truths, or real provisions for the security of the Christian life? And is there true buoyancy and vital tenacity in our developments, or an ever-growing languor of life? All these are questions which are no less relevant, and far more important, in regard to developments of revelation, than they are in biology in determining whether certain changes of structure cause an improvement or a marked degeneration of the stock which exhibits them. One of the great evidences of Cardinal Newman's genius is the proof that his mind was running on the tests of genuine developments and corruptions in doctrine, long years before the mind of the day had been awakened by Darwin and his contemporaries to the true touchstone of development or degeneration in biological forms.

Before I conclude, I will make some attempt to answer the question what the drift of Cardinal Newman's best teaching really is.

In the first place, though a great idealist—one of the greatest of idealists in this sense, that for him all material things are symbols, and all spiritual things the most vivid of realities—no one has pressed home upon us more powerfully, I might almost say more painfully, the difference between an unreal state of mind and a real state of mind, between unreal words and real words. Such a sermon as that on "The Religious Use of Excited Feelings" (*Parochial Sermons*, vol. i. sermon ix.), has in it all that is sound in the practice of religious revivals, as well as the antidote for all that is unsound. It is a death-blow to that unreality of mind which revels in agonies of remorse and tumults of devotion, and which does not reflect that, as Dr. Newman teaches, "emotion and passion are in our power indeed to repress, but not to *excite;* that there is a limit to the tumults and swellings of the heart, foster them as we will, and when that time comes the poor misused soul is left exhausted and resourceless." No utilitarian teacher has pressed home so sternly as Newman the need of *deeds* to give any real significance to words, or even to our feelings; no one has made us recognise as he has done that right words and even right feelings are but the shadows of things, and that it is only by the help of actions that we can ever learn to fathom the depth of our own words, or to turn to good account our otherwise idle emotions. "Let not your words run on," he tells us; "force every one of them into action as it goes" (*Ibid.* vol. i. p. 70). "In dreams we sometimes move our arms to see if we are awake or not, and so we are awakened. This is the way to keep your heart awake also. Try yourself daily in little deeds, to prove that your faith is more than a deceit" (*Parochial Sermons*, vol. i. p. 71). How scathing is his language towards men who indulge in the inculcation of truths which they do not embody in their own lives. He tells us his opinion of mere men of literature in no ambiguous language : "A man of literature is considered to preserve his dignity by doing nothing, and when he proceeds forward into action he is thought to lose his position, as if he was degrading his calling by enthusiasm and becoming a politician or a partisan. Hence mere literary men are able to say strong things against the opinions of their age, whether religious or political, without offence, because no one thinks they mean anything by them. They are not expected to go forward to act upon them, and mere words hurt no one" (*Ibid.* vol. v. p. 42). And yet he says, "To make professions is to play with edged tools unless we attend to what we are saying. Words have a meaning whether we mean that meaning or not; and they are imputed to us in their real meaning when our not meaning it is our own fault" (*Ibid.* vol. v. p. 33). No one has done so much as Newman to teach us at once how little and how much words may mean, how to one man they are the mere tools by which to move others, for their own selfish advantage, while to another they are the buoys floating on the surface by which the sunken reefs and quicksands are mapped out, and the whole configuration of the invisible depths of human nature, as it has been ascertained by innumerable soundings, is brought to light.

Again, no one has laid to heart like Newman, and made us lay to heart also, the comparatively small influence of mere logic, and the vast influence of unconscious assumptions—intellectual, moral, and spiritual—over the whole history of our inward lives. It is not too much to say that Newman has been the first to illustrate the almost *automatic* influence exerted by prepossessions and assumptions, once fairly implanted in the heart and mind, in leavening the whole nature; that he may be said to have taught us that all minds, however deeply steeped in a world of false teaching, are given some chance of struggling and finding their way to something better, and that our spiritual life depends on our eagerly using that chance, and voluntarily submitting ourselves ever more and more, as time goes on, both consciously and unconsciously, to the higher influence which has thus touched our lives. Newman anticipated not only the modern doctrine of evolution in its relation to religion, but also the modern doctrine of the automatic and unconscious influence of ideal ferments over the character of our thought, and the effect produced by the latent heat which in critical moments they will give out on the formation of our convictions.

"There is good reason," he told the University of Oxford forty-two years ago, "for saying that the impression made upon the mind need not even be recognised by the parties possessing it. It is no proof that persons are not possessed, because they are not conscious, of an idea. Nothing is of more frequent occurrence, whether in things sensible or intellectual, than the existence of such unperceived impressions. What do we mean when we say that certain persons do not know themselves, but that they are ruled by views, feelings, prejudices, objects, which they do not recognise? How common is it to be exhilarated or depressed, we do not recollect why, though we are aware that something has been told us, or has happened, good or bad, which accounts for our feeling, could we but recall it! What is memory itself but a vast magazine of such dormant, but present and excitable ideas? Or consider when persons would trace the history of their own opinions in past years, how baffled they are in the attempt to fix the date of this or that conviction, their system of thought having been all the while in continual, gradual, tranquil expansion; so that it were as easy to follow the growth of the fruit of the earth, 'first the blade, then the ear, after that the full corn in the ear,' as to chronicle changes which involved no abrupt revolution, or reaction, or fickleness of mind, but have been the birth of an idea, the development in explicit form, of what was already latent within it. Moreover, it is a question whether that strange and painful feeling of unreality which religious men experience from time to time, when nothing seems true, or good, or right, or profitable, when faith seems a name, and duty a mockery, and all endeavours to do right absurd and hopeless, and all things forlorn and dreary, as if religion was wiped out of the world, may not be the direct effect of the temporary obscuration of some master-vision which unconsciously supplies the mind with spiritual life and peace."— *University Sermons*, pp. 321-322.

No one, then, can doubt that Cardinal Newman has in relation to religion forestalled the leading scientific ideas of his younger contemporaries—the conception of evolution, and the conception of latent, or as some people call it, unconscious thought—in moulding human life; that his unique position consists in this, that while most of those for whom these ideas have had a great fascination have used them rather for the purpose of superseding Revelation, and explaining or trying to explain how we might have attained all the advantages of faith without faith, Newman has steadily used these scientific ideas in subordination to that master-key of all our being which he has found in Revelation. And yet, instead of being diverted from the study of natural laws by his profound devotion to things spiritual, that devotion seems to have quickened tenfold his keenness of eye for the natural history of man's mind, which he always rightly regards as the very basis upon which all supernatural teaching is necessarily founded and superinduced.

How shall I gather up in one expression the great Cardinal's characteristics? Shelley, with that curious want of discrimination for spiritual things which he combined so strangely with a delight in what is unearthly, called Byron, in his *Adonais*, "the Pilgrim of Eternity." Of course it was *Childe Harold's Pilgrimage* which suggested to him this most inappropriate epithet, for never was there a fine thought and expression more cruelly misapplied than when this term was applied to Byron, who, as Matthew Arnold has so grandly said, bore

> "With haughty scorn that mocked the smart
> From Europe to the Ætolian shore
> The pageant of his bleeding heart."

All that was most delirious and most transient in what Shakespeare calls "life's fitful fever" Byron experienced and confided to the world, while of eternity in time he never seems to have had a dream. But for eighty-six years Newman has lived amongst us as though he had no continuing city here, and comparatively very early in life he became aware that this was his destiny. In one very beautiful sonnet he speaks of his youthful hopes of "Isaac's pure blessing and a verdant home," but tells us that he has been led on step by step till he was found "a pilgrim pale with Paul's sad girdle bound." And no one has made us feel as he has done the detachment of the pilgrim from all earth's closest ties, at the very time when he enters so vividly into every change that affects the moral and religious prospects not only of his own Church but of our whole nation. The vivid pulse of time is to him the faint symbol of eternal interests behind and beyond time. In his wonderful poem on death, which he calls "The Dream of Gerontius," he makes the angel say to the passing soul, "It is the very energy of thought that keeps thee from thy God." And while it was energy of thought, no doubt, which kept Newman—I wish it had kept him permanently—from the Church in which he found refuge—nay, which kept him for two years from that Church even after he had taken final leave of his Anglican friends, it is energy of thought, too, which has kept his life from being merged in the great Church he has joined, and which has indeed made him almost as much of a pilgrim since he joined it as he was for the ten previous years when "through words and things" he went "sounding on his dim and perilous way." He has ever been a pilgrim, and a "pilgrim of eternity," if a pilgrim of eternity means a pilgrim who is severed by his love for eternal things from that whirl and eddy of temporary interests in which so many of us turn giddy and lose our heads. May I not indeed sum up Newman in the noble words in which his friend Keble describes the seer and the watchman who gaze through a twilight "neither clear nor dark," in their vigil for the signs of God's coming?

> "That is the heart for thoughtful seer,
> Watching, in trance, nor dark nor clear,
> Th' appalling future as it nearer draws:
>   His spirit calm'd the storm to meet,
>   Feeling the rock beneath his feet,
> And tracing through the cloud th' eternal cause.

> "That is the heart for watchman true,
> Waiting to see what God will do,
> As o'er the Church the gath'ring twilight falls:
>   No more he strains his wistful eye
>   If chance the golden hours be nigh,
> By youthful hope seen beaming round her walls.

> "Forc'd from his shadowy paradise,
> His thoughts to Heaven the steadier rise:
> There seek his answer when the world reproves:

> Contented in his darkling round
> If only he be faithful found
> When from the East th' eternal morning moves."

And yet even this would give too strong an impression of the mere hermit and recluse. Newman is neither. The tenderness of his heart is at least as unique as the detachment of his soul from earthly interests. And I cannot express this better than by concluding with the exquisitely beautiful words in which, two years before he finally left it, Newman took his farewell of the Church of England:—

"O kind and affectionate hearts, O loving friends, should you know any one whose lot it has been, by writing or by word of mouth, in some degree to help you . . . if he has ever told you what you knew about yourselves or what you did not know, has read to you your wants or feelings and comforted you by the very reading; has made you feel that there was a higher life than this daily one and a brighter world than that you see; or encouraged you, or sobered you, or opened a way to the inquiring, or soothed the perplexed; if what he has said or done has ever made you take interest in him and feel well inclined towards him, remember such a one in time to come though you hear him not, and pray for him that in all things he may know God's will, and at all times he may be ready to fulfil it."

II AND III
THE TWO GREAT OXFORD THINKERS
CARDINAL NEWMAN AND MATTHEW ARNOLD

III
MATTHEW ARNOLD

MATTHEW ARNOLD

THE difference between the intellectual and moral atmospheres which seem to have been breathed by Newman and Arnold is so astonishing that one can hardly realise that, for sixty-four years at least, they have been, what they still are, contemporaries. Bunyan, whose *Pilgrim's Progress* was published in 1678, says of his dream: "I espied a little before me a cave, where two giants, Pope and Pagan, dwelt in old time, by whose power and tyranny the men whose bones, blood, ashes, etc., lay there, were cruelly put to death. But by this place Christian went without much danger, whereat I somewhat wondered; but I have learned since that Pagan has been dead many a day; and as for the other, though he be yet alive, he is, by reason of age, and also of the many shrewd brushes that he met with in his younger days, grown so crazy and stiff in his joints, that he can now do little more than sit in his cave's mouth, grinning at pilgrims as they go by, and biting his nails because he cannot come at them." That appeared 208 years ago; and yet I have just been

descanting on one great man who has given in his
hearty adhesion to one of those giants after years
of meditative hesitation, while the second has been
made captive—I will not say by the other giant risen
from the grave, for I heartily admit that much of Mr.
Arnold's spirit is distinctively Christian, but at least
by a successor who has in him more, I think, of
Pagan than of Bunyan's Christian lore. What a
curious light is this on Mr. Arnold's doctrine of
the *Zeitgeist*, the "Time-spirit," which he so much
admires. In lecturing in Edinburgh on Butler, he
said of the *Analogy:* "The great work on which
such immense praise has been lavished is, for all real
intents and purposes now, a failure; it does not
serve. It seemed once to have a spell and a power;
but the *Zeitgeist* breathes upon it, and we rub our
eyes, and it has the spell and the power no longer."
And in another place he has said: "The Spirit of
Time is a personage for whose operations I have the
greatest respect; whatever he does is in my opinion
of the greatest effect." Well, is it so very great
after all? The *Zeitgeist* breathed upon Bunyan and
made him believe that Paganism was dead for ever,
and that the Papacy was in its dotage. It breathes
upon us in the nineteenth century, and while some
of its children rub their eyes, and find that Giant
Pope is the true sponsor for revelation after all,
others rub their eyes, and find that Giant Pagan is
still in his youth; that there is indeed no revelation,
and that Christianity, so far as it is true at all, is a

truth of human nature, not of theology. To my mind the *Zeitgeist* is a will-o'-the-wisp, who misleads us at least as much as he enlightens. In the scene on the Brocken in Goethe's *Faust*, the will-o'-the-wisp, when ordered by Mephistopheles—who also, we may remember, has the greatest admiration for the *Zeitgeist*—to conduct them to the summit, replies—

> "So deep my awe, I trust I may succeed
> My fickle nature to repress indeed;
> But zigzag is my usual course, you know."

And that, I think, might very justly be said of Mr. Arnold's Time-spirit. Its usual course is zigzag. It breathes on us, and we can no longer see a truth which was clear yesterday. It breathes again, and like invisible ink held to the fire, the truth comes out again in all its brightness. However, the drift of all this is, that Mr. Arnold, while he sees much which Cardinal Newman has neglected, has certainly neglected more which Cardinal Newman sees, so that they seem to live in worlds as different as their countenances. On the one countenance are scored the indelible signs of what a great Jewish prophet calls "the Lord's controversy"; on the other, whose high benignant brow rises smooth and exulting above a face of serene confidence, there sits the exhilaration which speaks of difficulties surmounted and a world that is either fast coming, or, in the thinker's opinion, must soon come, over to his side. Mr. Arnold is a master of the grand style. He has the port of a great teacher. He derives from his father, the reformer of Rugby, that energy of purpose which makes itself felt in a certain authority of tone. We should never dream of applying to him Wordsworth's fine lines—

"The intellectual power through words and things
 Goes sounding on its dim and perilous way."

Rather would his churches—for in some sense Mr. Arnold may be said to have churches of his own—quote the famous saying—

"Nil desperandum Teucro duce, et auspice Teucro."

He has succeeded in almost becoming himself what he has delineated in Goethe—

"For he pursued a lonely road,
 His eyes on Nature's plan;
 Neither made man too much a God,
 Nor God too much a man."

Certainly Mr. Arnold has not fallen into the latter error, whether into the former or not. He seems to have no doubts or difficulties in steering his course. He can eviscerate the Bible, and restore its meaning with the supernatural personality excluded. He has shown us how to "evolve" the Decalogue from the two primitive instincts of human nature. He has reconciled Isaiah with the "Time-spirit," and taught even sceptics to read him with exceptional delight. He has shown the Puritans what they might gain from the children of Athens, and the Athenian spirit, wherever it still exists, what it should learn from the Puritans. Take up the volume of his Prose Passages—and I know no book fuller of fascinating reading—and we shall find in it the rebukes which cultivated Germany administers to English Philistines, the rebukes which Conservative good taste addresses to rash Reformers, and the rebukes which brooding self-knowledge delivers to superficial politicians. We may learn there how Ireland would have been dealt with by statesmen who dive beneath the surface; and even how helpless and impotent is popular foreign policy in the hands of a minister guided by middle-class opinion. And when we have learned from his prose how keen and shrewd he is as an observer of the phenomena of his day, we may turn to his poetry, and lose ourselves in wonder at the truth and delicacy of his vision, the purity of his sympathies, the mellow melancholy of his regret, and the irrepressible elation which underlies even that regret itself. I think him so very great a poet that I will keep what I have to say on his poetry to the last; and will begin by referring to his more direct teaching, and especially to that teaching which implicitly accepts from science the exhortation to believe nothing which does not admit of complete verification, and which is intended to find for our age a truly scientific substitute for the theology of which the breath of the *Zeitgeist* has robbed us.

We must remember, then, that though Mr. Arnold proposes to demonstrate for us the truthfulness and power of the Bible, he commences by giving up

absolutely the assumption that there is any Divine
Being who thinks and loves, revealed in the Bible—a
proposition for which he does not consider that there
is even "a low degree of probability." One naturally
asks, "Well, then, what remains that can be of any
use?" Does not the Bible profess, from its opening
to its close, to be the revelation of a Being who thinks
about man and loves him, and who, because He thinks
about man and loves him, converses with him, mani-
fests to him His own nature as well as man's true
nature, and insists "thou shalt be holy because I am
holy." Mr. Arnold, however, is not at all staggered
by this. He holds that "we very properly and
naturally make" God a Being who thinks and loves
" in the language of feeling"; but this is an utterly
unverifiable assumption, without even a low degree of
probability. So that why we may "properly and
naturally" mislead ourselves by "language of feeling"
so very wide of any solid ground of fact, I cannot
imagine. We have always reproached the idolaters,
as Israel represented them, with worshipping a God
who is nothing in the world but the work of men's
hands, the cunning workmanship of a carver in wood
or stone. But why is it more proper or natural to
attribute, in the language of feeling, false attributes
to "the stream of tendency, not ourselves, which
makes for righteousness," than it is to attribute, in
the language of feeling, false attributes to the graven
images of an idol-founder? However, this is Mr.
Arnold's contention, though at other times he is

ready to admit that whenever emotion has been powerfully excited by supposed knowledge, and when that supposed knowledge turns out to be illusion, the emotion will disappear with the disappearance of our belief in the assumptions which we had formerly accepted. I should have thought that this would apply to the Bible, and that if ever we could be convinced that there is not even a low degree of probability for the conviction that God is a being who thinks and loves, all the emotions excited by the innumerable passages in which He is revealed as such a being would die away and be extinguished. But this is not Mr. Arnold's view. On the contrary, he holds that,

"Starting from what may be verified about God—that He is the Eternal which makes for righteousness—and reading the Bible with this idea to govern us, we have here the elements for a religion more solid, serious, awe-inspiring, and profound, than any which the world has yet seen. True, it will not be just the same religion which prevails now; but who supposes that the religion now current can go on always, or ought to go on? Nay, and even of that much-decried idea of God as the *stream of tendency in which all things seek to fulfil the law of their being*, it may be said with confidence that it has in it the elements of a religion, new indeed, but in the highest degree serious, hopeful, solemn, and profound."

It has always puzzled me very much to make out why Mr. Arnold should think, or say, that it is in any sense "verifiable," in his acceptation of that word, that the power which makes for righteousness is "eternal." But I believe, from a passage in *Literature and Dogma* (p. 61), that he really means by "eternal" nothing more than "enduring," and by "enduring," enduring in the history of man; so that the verifiable proposition which he takes as the foundation of a new religion is after all nothing more than this, that so far as history gives evidence at all, there has always been hitherto, since man appeared upon the earth, a stream of tendency which made for righteousness. Nevertheless, if the earth came to an end, and there be, as Mr. Arnold apparently inclines to believe, no life for man beyond his life on earth, then the enduring stream of tendency would endure no longer, and "the eternal" would, so far as it was verifiable, sink back into a transitory and extinct phenomenon of the terrestrial past. Well, then, so far as the Bible holds true at all in Mr. Arnold's mind, we must substitute uniformly for the God who there reveals and declares Himself and His love, a being who cannot either declare himself or feel, in our sense, the love which he is said to declare; one who must be discovered by man, instead of discovering himself to man, and who, when discovered, is nothing but a more or less enduring tendency to a certain deeper and truer mode of life, which we call righteous life. No wonder that "the religion in the highest degree serious, hopeful, solemn, and profound," to which Mr. Arnold hopes to convert the world, does not always appear, even to himself, either hopeful or solid. For example, in one of the most beautiful of his poems, "Stanzas from the

Grande Chartreuse," he explains, in a very different tone from that of the passage I have just quoted from *Literature and Dogma* (and I think a much more suitable and appropriate tone), how helpless and crippled his religious position really is, and how it came to pass that in visiting the home of one of the austere monastic orders he could feel a certain passion of regret without either much sympathy or much hope :—

> "For rigorous teachers seized my youth,
> And purged its faith, and trimmed its fire,
> Showed me the high, white star of Truth,
> There bade me gaze, and there aspire.
> Even now their whispers pierce the gloom:
> *What dost thou in this living tomb?*
>
> "Forgive me, masters of the mind!
> At whose behest I long ago
> So much unlearnt, so much resigned—
> I come not here to be your foe!
> I seek these anchorites, not in ruth,
> To curse and to deny your truth;
>
> "Not as their friend, or child, I speak!
> But as, on some far northern strand,
> Thinking of his own gods, a Greek,
> In pity and mournful awe, might stand
> Before some fallen Runic stone—
> For both were faiths, and both are gone.
>
> "Wandering between two worlds, one dead,
> The other powerless to be born,
> With nowhere yet to rest my head,
> Like these, on earth I wait forlorn.
> Their faith, my tears, the world deride—
> I come to shed them at their side."

In his poetry Mr. Arnold is often frank enough, as he certainly is here. In his prose he will not admit that the Church to which he looks as the Church of the future "is powerless to be born." But powerless to be born it is; a "stream of tendency," more or less enduring, which cannot even reveal itself, is not a power to excite emotion of any depth at all, unless it represents not only a tendency but a purpose. Religion, says Mr. Arnold, is "morality touched with emotion." But surely morality cannot be "touched with emotion" without reason, or at least excuse, for the emotion it is to excite. And yet this is what Mr. Arnold's language seems to point at. In one of his American lectures he appears to say that the emotions will remain even though the objects which properly excite them disappear; and in another passage of the same lecture he nevertheless intimates that even the very same thought may be so expressed as either to excite emotion or not to excite it, the difference between the two modes of expression being, except in its actual effect, quite undiscernible. But if Religion depends on an accident of that kind, Religion is an accident itself. An intention to make for Righteousness rightly excites emotion, but a tendency and an intention are different. Plague, pestilence, and famine, in God's hands, have often made for Righteousness. But without faith in God, plague, pestilence, and famine are more likely to touch immorality with emotion, than to touch morality with it.

How, then, is Mr. Arnold to conjure up the emotion which certainly does not seem to be naturally radiated from this more or less enduring "stream of tendency"? He strives to excite it by disclosing to us the promise of *life*, which is implicit in all conformity to this "stream of tendency"; for life is the word which, in Mr. Arnold's teaching, takes the place of faith. He values Christ's teaching because he says that it discloses the true secret of *life*—because it discloses a new life for the world, even after faith (as we understand it) is dead. This is the promise which he makes his favourite thinker, M. de Senancour, better known as the author of "Obermann," address to him:—

"Though more than half thy years be past,
And spent thy youthful prime;
Though, round thy firmer manhood cast,
Hang weeds of our sad time

"Whereof thy youth felt all the spell,
And traversed all the shade—
Though late, though dimm'd, though weak, yet tell
Hope to a world new-made!

"Help it to fill that deep desire,
The want which rack'd our brain,
Consumed our heart with thirst like fire,
Immedicable pain;

"Which to the wilderness drove out
Our life, to Alpine snow,
And palsied all our word with doubt,
And all our work with woe—

> "What still of strength is left, employ
> That end to help attain :
> *One common wave of thought and joy*
> *Lifting mankind again!*"

And that is the purpose to which Matthew Arnold has devoted what we may call his quasi-theological writings ; in other words, his writings produced to show that we may get all the advantages of theology without the theology—which we can and must do without. This new teaching is that which Tennyson has so tersely and finely expressed in "The Two Voices"—

> "'Tis life, whereof our nerves are scant ;
> Oh life, not death, for which we pant :
> More life, and fuller, that I want."

To the same effect Arnold quotes M. de Senancour: "The aim for men is to augment the feeling of joy, to make our expansive energy bear fruit, and to combat in all thinking beings the principle of degradation and misery." And Mr. Arnold's new version of Christianity promises us this life. "The all-ruling effort to live" is identical, he says, with "the desire for happiness," and this craving for life is, he asserts, sanctioned by Christ in the saying, "I am come that men might have *life*, and might have it more abundantly ; and ye will not come to me that ye may have life." I had always thought this a promise of life given by a being in whose hands is the power to bestow it. Not so Mr. Arnold. This power of attaining life, and attaining it in greater abundance, is, he declares, a mere natural secret which Christ had discovered, and which any man may rediscover for himself. It is a method of obtaining life, of obtaining "exhilaration." Indeed, exhilaration is, says Mr. Arnold, one of the greatest qualities of the Hebrew prophets. And this exhilaration is attainable by a merely natural process—namely, the renunciation by man of the superficial and temporary self, in favour of the deeper and permanent self. In *Literature and Dogma* Mr. Arnold has explained the "secret of Jesus," the true secret, as he holds, for riding buoyantly upon

> "That common wave of thought and joy,
> Lifting mankind again."

We are there told that the essence of Christianity is not the possession of supernatural life flowing from the love or gift of a supernatural being, but is simply the discovery and use of a certain secret of the wise heart. The secret is conveyed in Christ's promise: "He that loveth his life shall lose it, and he that hateth his life in this world shall keep it unto life eternal. Whosoever would come after me, let him renounce himself, and take up his cross daily and follow me." Christ's method, Mr. Arnold says,—

"Directed the disciple's eye inward, and set his consciousness to work; and the first thing his consciousness told him was that he had two selves pulling him different ways. Till we attend, till the method is set at work, it seems as if 'the wishes of the flesh and of the current thoughts' (Eph. ii. 3) were to be followed as a matter of course; as if an impulse to do a thing means that we should do it. But when we attend we find that an impulse to do a thing is really in itself no reason at all why we should do it, because impulses proceed from two sources quite different, and of quite different degrees of authority. St. Paul contrasts them as the inward man and the man in our members; the mind of the flesh and the spiritual mind. Jesus contrasts them as life properly so named and life in this world. And the moment we seriously attend to conscience, to the suggestions which concern practice and conduct, we can see plainly enough from which source a suggestion comes, and that the suggestions from one source are to overrule suggestions from the other."—*Literature and Dogma*, pp. 201-202. "The breaking the sway of what is commonly called one's self, ceasing our concern with it, and leaving it to perish, is not, he (*i.e.* Jesus Christ) said, being thwarted or crossed, but *living*. And the proof of this is that it has the character of life in the highest degree—the power of going right, hitting the mark, succeeding. That is, it has the character of happiness, and happiness is for Israel the same thing as having the Eternal with us—seeing the salvation of God."—*Literature and Dogma*, p. 203.

Now, surely it is hardly justifiable for Mr. Arnold, in describing the "secret of Jesus," to substitute for the words of Jesus words of his own so very different in tone and meaning from those in which that secret was first disclosed. Where does our Lord ever say that the evidence of spiritual life is in the consciousness it gives us of *hitting the mark*, of *succeeding?* If we are to take our Lord's secret, let us take it in His own language, not in Mr. Arnold's. Turn then

to His own language, and what do we find? We find,
"Blessed are the pure in heart, for they shall see
God." Does that mean the same thing as, "Blessed
are the pure in heart, for they shall hit the mark,
they shall succeed"? Again, "Blessed are the peace-
makers, for they shall be called the children of God."
Does that mean the same as, "Blessed are the peace-
makers, for they shall attain true success"? "Blessed
are ye when men shall revile you and persecute you,
and shall say all manner of evil against you falsely
for my sake. Rejoice and be exceeding glad, for
great is your reward in heaven." Does that promise
mean the same as "the more you are persecuted and
maligned, the greater is your reward on earth, no
matter whether there be any world beyond this or
not"? Yet that is what Mr. Arnold tries to make it
mean in order to reconcile his interpretation of the
"secret of Jesus" with the actual words of Jesus. I
believe that Mr. Arnold misreads even the language
of the conscience, when he makes it say that as we
advance in our development we become aware "of
two lives, one permanent and impersonal, the other
transient and bound to our contracted self; he
becomes aware of two selves, one higher and real, the
other inferior and apparent; and that the instinct in
him truly to live, the desire for happiness, is served
by following the first self and not the second" (*Last
Essays on Church and Religion*, pp. 116–117). What
we really become aware of is, that behind the loud-
voiced, strenuous, well-established self of our lower

nature, there is growing up a faint, embryo, struggling, nobler self, without strength, without permanence; but that on the side of that self there pleads another and higher power, offering us, if we listen to the nobler voice, infinite prospects of a new world of communion, a new buoyancy, a new career. It is not the nobler self which is, as Mr. Arnold says, strong and permanent. Nothing can be weaker or more fitful. But the promise is, that if we give ourselves to the weak and fitful but nobler voice, our doing so will bring us into direct communion with one who is really strong, who is really permanent, who is really eternal; not merely what Mr. Arnold means by eternal—namely, *more or less enduring*. I take it that the "secret of Jesus" is wholly misinterpreted if its promise of a communion between the weaker but nobler self and the eternal source of life and light be ignored. It falls in that case from the secret of Jesus to the secret of Matthew Arnold. Now the "secret of Jesus" is life indeed. The secret of Matthew Arnold is only better than death, because it gives its suffrage on the right side, though with the right suffrage it fails to connect the promise and the earnest of joy with which Jesus Christ connected it. I think every reasonable reader of the Bible must perceive that if this promise of permanent joy in an eternal love is not true, the whole chain of Hebrew prophecy is false and misleading, from the time of Abraham to the death of St. Paul.

But then Mr. Arnold will turn upon me with his

demand for verification : Can the promise be verified ? "Experience proves that whatever for men is true, men can verify." I should answer, certainly it is verifiable in a sense even truer and higher than that in which Mr. Arnold's own *rationale* of the moral secret, which he misnames the secret of Jesus, is verifiable. Even Mr. Arnold admits that his interpretation of the secret of Jesus has not always been verified.

"People may say," he tells us, "they have not got this sense that their instinct to live is served by loving their neighbours ; they may say that they have, in other words, a dull and uninformed conscience. But that does not make the experience less a true thing, the real experience of the race. Neither does it make the sense of this experience to be, any the less, genuine conscience. And it is genuine conscience, because it apprehends what does really serve our instinct to live, or desire for happiness. And when Shaftesbury supposes the case of a man thinking vice and selfishness to be truly as much for his advantage as virtue and benevolence, and concludes that such a case is without remedy, the answer is 'Not at all ; let such a man get conscience, get right experience.' And if the man does not, the result is not that he goes on just as well without it ; the result is that he is lost."—*Last Essays on Church and Religion*, pp. 115-116.

Well, if that is what Mr. Arnold means by verification, I think that it is easy to show that there is a much more perfect verification for the ordinary and natural interpretation of the "secret of Jesus" than for his mutilated interpretation of it. If it is verification to appeal to the best experience of the best, to the growing experience of those who have most intimately studied the various discipline of life, who can doubt what the reply must be to the question, Does experience testify to the self-sufficiency and adequacy to itself of what Mr. Arnold calls the permanent and higher self, or rather to its growing sense of inadequacy and dependence, and to its constant reference to that higher life in communion with which it lives? I do not hesitate to say that Mr. Arnold's mutilated interpretation of the "secret of Jesus," which omits indeed the very talisman of the whole, will receive no confirmation at all from the higher experience of the race, which testifies to nothing more persistently than this, that growing humility and the deepest possible sense of the dependence of the nobler self on communion with a righteous being external to it, is the unfailing experience of those in whom the nobler self is most adequately developed. Mr. Arnold's *rationale* of what he erroneously terms the "more permanent" and "stronger" self—but what experience proves to be indeed a very variable and very weak self, leaning on constant communion with another for its strength —is a mutilation of the true experience of man as delivered by the Bible, from Genesis to Revelation. Take the Psalmist: "Whom have I in heaven but thee, and there is none upon earth I desire in comparison with thee. My flesh and my heart faileth, but God is the strength of my heart, and my portion for ever." Take Isaiah: "Woe is me, for I am undone; because I am a man of unclean lips, and I dwell in the midst of a people of unclean lips; for mine eyes have seen the King, the Lord of Hosts." Take St. Paul: "I was with you in weakness, and in fear, and in much trembling. And my speech and my preaching was not with enticing words of man's wisdom, but in demonstration of the Spirit and of power: that your faith should not stand in the wisdom of men, but in the power of God." It is impossible to find in the Bible anything like a reference to the permanent and stronger self which asserts itself in us. The testimony is always to a nobler but weaker self, which leans on the sustaining grace of God. Well, but says Mr. Arnold in opposing Bishop Butler's view that the most we can hope for in this life is to escape from misery and not to obtain happiness,—in this contention Butler goes counter not only to the most intimate, "the most sure, the most irresistible instinct of human nature," but also "to the clear voice of our religion." "Rejoice and give thanks," exhorts the Old Testament. "Rejoice evermore," exhorts the New. That is most true, but what is the ground of these constant exhortations in both Old Testament and New? Surely not the strength and depth of the life, even the higher life, in man, but, on the contrary, the largeness and generosity of the succour granted to the righteous by God. On what, for instance, is grounded the injunction which Mr. Arnold quotes from the Old Testament? On this, that "the Lord hath done marvellous things: his right hand, and his holy arm, hath wrought salvation for him." And again on this, that "the Lord hath made known his salvation: his righteousness hath he openly showed in the sight of the nations." Can Mr. Arnold justify such a ground for rejoicing as that, on the lips of any one who disbelieves altogether in a God who "thinks and loves"? Again, what is the context of the injunction taken from the New Testament? "Rejoice evermore. Pray without ceasing. In everything give thanks: *for this is the will of God in Christ Jesus concerning you.*" The ground of rejoicing is a will—a will which is equally made the ground of prayer; without the ground for praying there could be no ground for rejoicing. Without a *known* will of God there could be neither the one nor the other. And it is the humility which recognises the strength, external to its own, which is the source at once of the joy and the prayer. The life which is so abundantly promised throughout the Bible is indeed not natural life, as Mr. Arnold explains it, but what we are more accustomed to call *grace*—the life poured in from outside.

Nor, indeed, can I understand how Mr. Arnold's explanation can hold at all, without this supernatural source of strength and joy. When Mr. Arnold says that it is the "permanent" and "stronger" self which conquers, and gives us life by the conquest, is it inappropriate to ask, *How* permanent, and *how* strong? Suppose, as has often happened, that the deeper and nobler self suggests a course which involves instant death, where is the permanence? Mr. Arnold will hear nothing of the promise of immortality. That is to him *Aberglaube*, over-belief, belief in excess of the evidence. In some of his most exquisite lines he speaks of death as the

> "Stern law of every mortal lot
> Which man, proud man, finds hard to bear,
> And builds himself, I know not what
> Of second life, I know not where."

So that he guarantees us assuredly no *permanence* for the nobler self. And then as to *strength:* Is the nobler self strong enough to endure the hard conditions which are often imposed on us by our best acts—the slander and persecution to which we expose ourselves, the misery which we bring on ourselves? The answer of the Bible is plain enough: No, it is not; but you may rely on the grace promised to the weakest, if you comply with the admonitions of that grace. Mr. Arnold can make no such reply. Unless the nobler self is intrinsically also the stronger self, in his opinion you are lost. It seems to me, then, that the injunction to "rejoice and give thanks," the injunction to "rejoice evermore," cannot be justified except in connection with a trust in One who can give us real succour from without, under the prospect of certain death and the still more certain collapse of human powers in the presence of great trials and temptations.

In a word, the faith taught by revelation is not, as Mr. Arnold himself admits, Mr. Arnold's faith. The former is intended to awaken and discipline a group

of genuine *affections,* using the word in the same sense
—though in the same sense raised to a higher plane
of life—as we use it of the human affections. Read
the Psalms, and you will find in them the germs of
all the affections generated in His disciples by Christ's
own teaching—the shame, the grief, the remorse, the
desolation, the hope, the awe, the love in its highest
sense, which human beings feel in the presence of a
human nature, holier, deeper, richer, stronger, nobler
than their own, when they have sinned against it and
are conscious of its displeasure, its retributive justice,
its joy in human repentance, and its forgiveness.
The whole drift of revelation is to excite these affections, to make us feel the divine passion which our
human passions elicit, to reach the deepest fountain
of our tears, and to fill us with that joy which, however deep, is all humility and all gratitude, because
its source is the love of another, and not the strength
or buoyancy of our own life. Well, this is not, and
could not be, Mr. Arnold's religion. In his expurgated
Bible, the affections in this sense have to be omitted.
He tells us quite plainly that the facts—or, as he calls
them, "the supposed facts"—by which the religious
affections have been fostered in us are illusions, that
our religion is nothing in the world but the culture
of that ideal life which man has happily a tendency
to develop. These are his words:

"The future of poetry is immense, because in poetry,
where it is worthy of its high destinies, our race, as time
goes on, will find an ever surer and surer stay. There is

not a creed which is not shaken, not an accredited dogma which is not shown to be questionable, not a received tradition which does not threaten to dissolve. Our religion has materialised itself in the fact—in the supposed fact; it has attached its emotion to the fact, and now the fact is failing it. But for poetry the idea is everything; the rest is a world of illusion—of divine illusion. Poetry attaches its emotion to the idea; the idea *is* the fact."

Well, if that be so, the emotion which Mr. Arnold insists on, in order to transform morality into religion, becomes a very mild and æsthetic kind of emotion indeed,—not one which can penetrate the sinner's heart with anguish, not one which can irradiate the penitent's heart with gratitude. Imagine the changes which you must make in the language of the Psalmist to empty it of what Mr. Arnold calls belief in "the supposed fact," and to conform the emotions to that which is attached to "the idea" alone :—

"Hide thy face from my sins, and blot out all mine iniquities. Create in me a clean heart, O God; and renew a right spirit within me. Cast me not away from thy presence; and take not thy Holy Spirit from me. Restore unto me the joy of thy salvation; and uphold me with thy free Spirit. . . . O Lord, open thou my lips; and my mouth shall show forth thy praise. For thou desirest not sacrifice, else would I give it; thou delightest not in burnt-offering. The sacrifices of God are a broken spirit: a broken and a contrite heart, O God, thou wilt not despise."

Take the divine illusion, as Mr. Arnold calls it, out of this, and how much of "the emotion" requisite for religion would remain? Has he not himself told us?—

"That gracious Child, that thorn-crown'd Man!
—He lived while we believed.

"While we believed, on earth he went,
And open stood his grave.
Men called from chamber, church, and tent;
And Christ was by to save.

"Now he is dead! Far hence he lies
In the lorn Syrian town;
And on his grave, with shining eyes
The Syrian stars look down.

"In vain men still, with hoping new,
Regard his death-place dumb,
And say the stone is not yet to,
And wait for words to come.

"Ah, o'er that silent sacred land,
Of sun, and arid stone,
And crumbling wall, and sultry sand,
Sounds now one word alone!

"From David's lips that word did roll,
'Tis true and living yet:
*No man can save his brother's soul,
Nor pay his brother's debt.*

"Alone, self-pois'd, henceforward man
Must labour!—must resign
His all too human creeds, and scan
Simply the way divine."

Well, then, where is the "emotion" with which "morality" must be touched, in order to transform it into religion, to come from? Mr. Arnold makes no answer,—except that it must be emotion excited by ideas alone, and not by supposed facts, which, as he says, will not stand the tests of scientific verification.

But with regard to that asserted demand of science for verification, let me just make one final observation: That in the sense in which Mr. Arnold uses it, to explode all belief in light coming to us from a mind higher than our own, it equally explodes belief in the authority of those suggestions of the deeper self to which what he calls the "secret of Jesus" teaches us to defer. For why are we to obey them? Mr. Arnold replies simply, human *experience* teaches us that it adds to our life, to our happiness, to the vitality of our true and permanent self, to do so. But how are we to get the verification without trying both the wrong way and the right? You cannot found on mere experience *without* the experience. And does, then, the way to virtue lead through sin alone? Mr. Arnold guards himself by saying that some "finely-touched" souls have "the *presentiment*" of how it will be—a presentiment, I suppose, derived by evolution from the experience of ancestors. But is it a duty, then, to found your actions on those obscure intimations which your ancestors' experience may have transmitted to you? Should you not test your ancestors' experience for yourself before adopting it? Should you not sin in order to be sure that sin saps your true life and diminishes your fund of happiness? I fear there is nothing for Mr. Arnold but to admit that this is not sin—that *trying* evil in order to be sure it *is* evil is not forbidden by any law, if there be no spiritual nature higher than man's, which lays its yoke upon us, and subdues us into the attitude of reverence and awe.

The principle which Mr. Arnold calls "verification" is in reality fatal to all purity. It makes experience of evil the ground of good. For myself, I believe that there is enough verification for the purposes of true morality in the recognition, without the test of experience, of the higher character of the nature confronted with our own; and that we may learn the reality of revelation, the reality of a divine influence which should be a law to us, and rebellion against which is, in the deepest sense, sin, without trying the effect of that rebellion, without making proof of both the alternatives before us. The life even of the truest *human* affections is one long protest against the principle that you can know nothing without what is termed experiment and verification in the scientific sense of the word. What creature which has learnt to love tries the effect of piercing the heart of another before it learns to reject that course as treachery? Revelation, as I understand it, is an appeal to the human affections—a divine discipline for them. It no more demands experiment and verification, in the scientific sense which men try to foist so inappropriately into our moral life, than a parent would think of demanding from his child that, in order to be sure that his wishes and commands are wise, the child should make experiments in disobedience, and only conform to his father's injunctions after he had learned by a painful experience that these experiments had ended in pain and discomfiture.

In insisting on the striking, I might almost say the

dismaying, contrast between the great Oxford leader, whose whole mind has been occupied with theological convictions from his earliest years of Oxford life to the present day, and the Oxford leader who has avowed himself unable to see even a slender probability that God is a being who thinks and loves, I have said that I hoped to do something to attenuate the paradox before I had done. This is probably the right place to say a few words on the subject, for undoubtedly it is the assumption running through Mr. Arnold's theoretical writings, that no belief is trustworthy which has not what he calls the verification of experience to sustain it, to which we owe his repudiation of all theology. Undoubtedly the twenty years or so by which he is Cardinal Newman's junior made an extraordinary difference in the intellectual atmosphere of Oxford, and of the English world of letters outside Oxford, during the time at which a thoughtful man's mind matures. Mr. Arnold was not too late at Oxford to feel the spell of Dr. Newman, but his mind was hardly one to feel the whole force of that spell, belonging as it does, I think, rather to the stoical than to the religious school—the school which magnifies self-dependence, and regards serene calm, not passionate worship, as the highest type of the moral life. And he was at Oxford too early, I think, for a full understanding of the limits within which alone the scientific conception of life can be said to be true. A little later, men came to see that scientific methods are really quite inapplicable to the sphere of moral truth, that the scientific assumption that whatever is true can be verified is, in the sense of the word "verification" which science applies, a very serious blunder, and that such verification as we can get of moral truth is of a very different, though I will not scruple to say a no less satisfactory, kind from that which we expect to get of scientific truth. Mr. Arnold seems to me to have imbibed the prejudices of the scientific season of blossom, when the uniformity of nature first became a kind of gospel, when the *Vestiges of Creation* was the book in vogue, when Emerson's and Carlyle's imaginative scepticism first took hold of cultivated Englishmen, and when Mr. Froude published the sceptical tales by which his name was first known amongst us. Mr. Arnold betrays the immovable prejudices by which his intellectual life is overridden in a hundred forms; for example, by the persistency with which he remarks that the objection to miracles is that they do not happen, the one criticism which I venture to say no one who had taken pains to study evidence in the best accredited individual cases, not only in ancient but in modern times, would choose to repeat. And again, he betrays it by the pertinacity with which he assumes that you can verify the secret of self-renunciation, the secret of Jesus, in the same sense in which you can verify the law of gravitation, one of the most astounding and, I think, false assumptions of our day. I make bold to say that no one ever verified the secret of self-renunciation yet, or ever even wished to verify it, who had not assumed the moral obligation it involves before even attempting a verification; while with the law of gravitation it is quite different: we believe it solely because it has been verified, or, in the case of the discoverer, because evidence was before him that it might very probably be verified.

But though Mr. Arnold's mind is of the stoical rather than the religious type, and though certain premature scientific assumptions, which were in vogue before the limits of the region in which the uniformity of nature has been verified, had been at all carefully defined, run through all his theoretical writings, it is nevertheless true that his whole intellectual strength has been devoted to sustaining, I cannot say the cause of religion—for I do not think his constant cry for more emotion in dealing with morality has been answered—but the cause of noble conduct, and to exalting the elation of duty, the rapture of righteousness. Allow for his prepossessions—his strangely obstinate prepossessions—and he remains still a figure on which we can look with admiration. We must remember that, with all the scorn which Matthew Arnold pours on the trust we place in God's love, he still holds to the conviction that the tendency to righteousness is a power on which we may rely even with *rapture*. Israel, he says, took "his religion in rapture, because he found for it an evidence irresistible. But his own words are the best: 'Thou, O Eternal, art the thing that I *long* for, thou art my hope, even from my youth; through thee have I been *holden up* ever since I was born; there is nothing *sweeter* than to take heed unto the commandments of the Eternal. The Eternal is my strength; my heart has trusted in Him, and I am *helped;* therefore my heart *danceth for joy,* and in my song I will *praise* him'" (*Literature and Dogma*, p. 319). And Mr. Arnold justifies that language, though it seems to me clear that with his views he could never have been the first to use it. Still, do not let us forget that he does justify it, that the great Oxonian of the third quarter of this century, though he is separated wide as the poles from Cardinal Newman in faith, yet uses even the most exalted language of the Hebrew seers with all the exultation which even Cardinal Newman could evince for it. I think it is hardly possible to think of such an attitude of mind as the attitude of a common agnostic. The truth is, that his deep poetical idealism saves Mr. Arnold from the depressing and flattening influences of his theoretical views. The poet of modern thought and modern tendencies cannot be, even though he strives to be, a mere agnostic. The insurrection of the agnosticism of the day against faith is no doubt one of its leading features; but the failure of that insurrection to overpower us, the potent resistance it encounters in all our hearts, is a still more remarkable feature. Matthew Arnold reflects both of these characteristics, though the former perhaps more powerfully than the latter.

In passing from the thinker to the poet, I am

passing from a writer whose curious earnestness and ability in attempting the impossible will soon, I believe, be a mere curiosity of literature, to one of the most considerable of English poets, whose place will probably be above any poet of the eighteenth century, excepting Burns, and not excepting Pope, or Cowper, or Goldsmith, or Gray; and who, even amongst the great poets of the nineteenth century, may very probably be accorded the sixth or fifth, or even by some the fourth place. He has a power of vision as great as Tennyson's, though its magic depends less on the rich tints of association, and more on the liquid colours of pure natural beauty; a power of criticism and selection as fastidious as Gray's, with infinitely more creative genius; and a power of meditative reflection which, though it never mounts to Wordsworth's higher levels of genuine rapture, never sinks to his wastes and flats of commonplace. Arnold is a great elegiac poet, but there is a buoyancy in his elegy which we rarely find in the best elegy, and which certainly adds greatly to its charm. And though I cannot call him a dramatic poet, his permanent attitude being too reflective for any kind of action, he shows in such poems as the "Memorial Verses" on Byron, Goethe, and Wordsworth, in the "Sick King in Bokhara," and "Tristram and Iseult," great precision in the delineation of character, and not a little power even of forcing character to delineate itself. What feeling for the Oriental type of character is there not in the Vizier

of the Sick King of Bokhara when he remonstrates
with the young king for taking too much to heart
the tragic end of the man who had insisted, under
the Mahometan law, on being stoned, because in a
hasty moment he had cursed his mother!—

"O King, in this I praise thee not!
  Now must I call thy grief not wise.
Is he thy friend, or of thy blood,
  To find such favour in thine eyes?

"Nay, were he thine own mother's son,
  Still, thou art king, and the law stands.
It were not meet the balance swerved,
  The sword were broken in thy hands.

"But being nothing, as he is,
  Why for no cause make sad thy face?—
Lo, I am old! three kings, ere thee,
  Have I seen reigning in this place.

"But who, through all this length of time,
  Could bear the burden of his years,
If he for strangers pain'd his heart
  Not less than those who merit tears?

"Fathers we *must* have, wife and child,
  And grievous is the grief for these;
This pain alone, which *must* be borne,
  Makes the head white, and bows the knees.

"But other loads than this his own
  One man is not well made to bear.
Besides, to each are his own friends,
  To mourn with him, and show him care.

"Look, this is but one single place,
  Though it be great; all the earth round,

If a man bear to have it so,
Things which might vex him shall be found.

"Upon the Russian frontier, where
The watchers of two armies stand
Near one another, many a man,
Seeking a prey unto his hand,

"Hath snatch'd a little fair-hair'd slave;
They snatch also, towards Mervè,
The Shiah dogs, who pasture sheep,
And up from thence to Orgunjè.

"And these all, labouring for a lord,
Eat not the fruit of their own hands;
Which is the heaviest of all plagues,
To that man's mind, who understands.

"The kaffirs also (whom God curse!)
Vex one another, night and day;
There are the lepers, and all sick;
There are the poor, who faint alway.

"All these have sorrow, and keep still,
Whilst other men make cheer, and sing.
Wilt thou have pity on all these?
No, nor on this dead dog, O King!"

And again, how deep is the insight into the Oriental character in the splendid contrast between Rome and the East after the Eastern conquests of Rome, in the second of the two poems on the Author of *Obermann*:—

"In his cool hall, with haggard eyes,
The Roman noble lay;
He drove abroad, in furious guise,
Along the Appian Way.

> "He made a feast, drank fierce and fast,
> And crown'd his hair with flowers—
> No easier nor no quicker pass'd
> The impracticable hours.
>
> "The brooding East with awe beheld
> Her impious younger world.
> The Roman tempest swell'd and swell'd,
> And on her head was hurl'd.
>
> "The East bow'd low before the blast
> In patient, deep disdain;
> She let the legions thunder past,
> And plunged in thought again.
>
> "So well she mused, a morning broke
> Across her spirit gray;
> A conquering, new-born joy awoke,
> And fill'd her life with day.
>
> "'Poor world,' she cried, 'so deep accurst,
> That runn'st from pole to pole
> To seek a draught to slake thy thirst—
> Go, seek it in thy soul!'"

Or take the famous description, in the lines at Heine's grave, of our own country taking up burden after burden, with "deaf ears and labour-dimm'd eyes," as she has just taken up the new burden of Burmah:—

> "I chide with thee not, that thy sharp
> Upbraidings often assail'd
> England, my country—for we,
> Heavy and sad, for her sons,
> Long since, deep in our hearts,
> Echo the blame of her foes.
> We, too, sigh that she flags;
> We, too, say that she now—

> Scarce comprehending the voice
> Of her greatest, golden-mouth'd sons
> Of a former age any more—
> Stupidly travels her round
> Of mechanic business, and lets
> Slow die out of her life
> Glory, and genius, and joy.
>
> "So thou arraign'st her, her foe;
> So we arraign her, her sons.
>
> "Yes, we arraign her! but she,
> The weary Titan, with deaf
> Ears, and labour-dimm'd eyes,
> Regarding neither to right
> Nor left, goes passively by,
> Staggering on to her goal;
> Bearing on shoulders immense,
> Atlantean, the load,
> Wellnigh not to be borne,
> Of the too vast orb of her fate."

Though not a dramatic poet, it is clear, then, that Matthew Arnold has a deep dramatic insight; but that is only one aspect of what I should call his main characteristic as a poet—the lucid penetration with which he discerns and portrays all that is most expressive in any situation that awakens regret, and the buoyancy with which he either throws off the pain, or else takes refuge in some soothing digression. For Arnold is never quite at his best except when he is delineating a mood of regret, and then his best consists not in yielding to it, but in the resistance he makes to it. He is not, like most elegiac poets, a mere sad muser; he is always one who finds a secret of joy in the midst of pain, who discovers a tonic for the suffering nerve, if only in realising the large power of sensibility which it retains. Take his description of the solitude in which we human beings live—heart yearning after heart, but recognising the eternal gulf between us—a solitude decreed by the power which

> "bade betwixt our shores to be
> The unplumb'd, salt, estranging sea!"

How noble the line, and how it sends a shiver through one! And yet not a shiver of mere regret or mere yearning; rather a shiver of awe at the infinitude of the ocean in which we are all enisled. It is the same with all Arnold's finest elegiac touches. In all of them regret seems to mingle with buoyancy, and buoyancy to have a sort of root in regret. What he calls (miscalls, I think) the "secret of Jesus"—"miscalls," because the secret of Jesus lay in the knowledge of His Father's love, not in the *natural* buoyancy of the renouncing heart—is in reality the secret of his own poetry. Like the East, he bows low before the blast, only to seek strength in his own mind, and to delight in the strength he finds there. He enjoys plumbing the depths of another's melancholy. Thus he says in relation to his favourite *Obermann*—

> "A fever in these pages burns
> Beneath the calm they feign;
> A wounded human spirit turns,
> Here, on its bed of pain.

> "Yes, though the virgin mountain-air
> Fresh through these pages blows;
> Though to these leaves the glaciers spare
> The soul of their white snows;
>
> "Though here a mountain-murmur swells
> Of many a dark-boughed pine,
> Though, as you read, you hear the bells
> Of the high-pasturing kine—
>
> "Yet, through the hum of torrent lone,
> And brooding mountain-bee,
> There sobs I know not what ground-tone
> Of human agony."

But even so, the effect of the verses is not the effect of Shelley's most exquisitely melancholy lyrics. It does not make us almost faint under the poet's own feeling of desolation. On the contrary, even in the very moment in which Arnold cries—

> "Farewell! Under the sky we part,
> In this stern Alpine dell.
> O unstrung will! O broken heart!
> A last, a last farewell!"

we have a conviction that the poet went off with a buoyant step from that unstrung will and broken heart, enjoying the strength he had derived from his communion with that strong spirit of passionate protest against the evil and frivolity of the world. It is just the same with his "Empedocles on Etna." He makes the philosopher review at great length the evils of human life, and decide that, as he can render no further aid to men, he must return to the elements.

But after he has made his fatal plunge into the crater of the burning mountain, there arises from his friend Callicles, the harp-player on the slopes of the mountain below, the following beautiful strain :—

"Through the black, rushing smoke-bursts,
Thick breaks the red flame ;
All Etna heaves fiercely
Her forest-clothed frame.

"Not here, O Apollo!
Are haunts meet for thee.
But, where Helicon breaks down
In cliff to the sea,

"Where the moon-silver'd inlets
Send far their light voice
Up the still vale of Thisbe,
O speed, and rejoice !

"On the sward at the cliff-top
Lie strewn the white flocks,
On the cliff-side the pigeons
Roost deep in the rocks.

"In the moonlight the shepherds,
Soft lull'd by the rills,
Lie wrapt in their blankets
Asleep on the hills.

"—What forms are these coming
So white through the gloom ?
What garments out-glistening
The gold-flower'd broom ?

"What sweet-breathing presence
Out-perfumes the thyme ?
What voices enrapture
The night's balmy prime ?—

"'Tis Apollo comes leading
His choir, the Nine.
—The leader is fairest,
But all are divine.

"They are lost in the hollows
They stream up again!
What seeks on this mountain
The glorified train?—

"They bathe on this mountain,
In the spring by their road;
Then on to Olympus,
Their endless abode.

"—Whose praise do they mention?
Of what is it told?—
What will be for ever;
What was from of old.

"First hymn they the Father
Of all things; and then,
The rest of immortals,
The action of men.

"The day in his hotness,
The strife with the palm;
The night in her silence,
The stars in their calm."

And we close the poem with a sense, not of trouble, but of refreshment. So in the tragic story of "Sohrab and Rustum"—in which the father, without knowing it, kills his own son, who dies in his arms—the poem ends not in gloom, but in a serene vision of the course of the Oxus as it passes, "brimming and bright and large," towards its mouth in the Sea of Aral, a course which is meant to be typical of the peaceful close of Rustum's stormy and potent and victorious, though tragic, career. It seems to be Matthew Arnold's secret in Art not to minimise the tragedy or sadness of the human lot, but to turn our attention from the sadness or the tragedy to the strength which it illustrates and elicits, and the calm in which even the tumultuous passions of the story eventually subside. Even the sad poem on the Grand Chartreuse closes with a wonderful picture of cloistered serenity, entreating the busy and eager world to leave it unmolested to its meditations—

"Pass, banners, pass, and bugles cease;
And leave our desert to its peace."

There is nothing which Matthew Arnold conceives or creates so well, nothing so characteristic of him, as the soothing digressions, as they seem—digressions, however, more germane to his purpose than any epilogue—in which he withdraws our attention from his main subject, to refresh and restore the minds which he has perplexed and bewildered by the painful problems he has placed before them. That most beautiful and graceful poem, for instance, on "The Scholar-Gipsy," the Oxford student who is said to have forsaken academic study in order to learn, if it might be, those potent secrets of Nature, the traditions of which the gipsies are supposed sedulously to guard, ends in a digression of the most vivid beauty, suggested by the exhortation to the supposed lover

of Nature to "fly our paths, our feverish contact fly,"
as fatal to all calm and healing life—

"Then fly our greetings, fly our speech and smiles!
 —As some grave Tyrian trader, from the sea,
  Descried at sunrise an emerging prow
 Lifting the cool-hair'd creepers stealthily,
  The fringes of a southward-facing brow
   Among the Ægæan isles;
 And saw the merry Grecian coaster come,
  Freighted with amber grapes, and Chian wine,
  Green, bursting figs, and tunnies steep'd in brine—
 And knew the intruders on his ancient home,

"The young light-hearted masters of the waves—
 And snatch'd his rudder, and shook out more sail;
 And day and night held on indignantly
 O'er the blue Midland waters with the gale,
  Betwixt the Syrtes and soft Sicily,
   To where the Atlantic raves
 Outside the western straits; and unbent sails
  There, where down cloudy cliffs, through sheets
      of foam,
  Shy traffickers, the dark Iberians come;
 And on the beach undid his corded bales."

Nothing could illustrate better than this passage Arnold's genius or his art. He wishes to give us a picture of the older type of audacity and freedom as it shakes itself impatiently rid of the paltry skill and timid cunning of the newer age, and plunges into the solitudes into which the finer craft of dexterous knowledge does not dare to follow. His whole drift having been that care and effort and gain and the pressure of the world are sapping human strength, he ends

with a picture of the old-world pride and daring
which exhibits human strength in its freshness and
vigour, and he paints it with all that command of
happy poetical detail in which Mr. Arnold so greatly
excels. No one knows as he knows how to use detail
without overlaying the leading idea which he intends
to impress on us. The Tyrian trader, launching out
into the deep, in his scorn for the Greek trafficker
hugging the shore with his timid talent for small
gains, brings home to us how much courage, freedom,
and originality we may lose by the aptness for social
intercourse which the craft of civilisation brings with
it. So he closes his poem on the new scrupulousness
and burdensomeness and self-consciousness of human
life by recalling vividly the pride and buoyancy of
old-world enterprise. I could quote poem after
poem which Arnold closes by some such buoyant
digression—a buoyant digression intended to shake
off the tone of melancholy, and to remind us that
the world of imaginative life is still wide open to us.
"This problem is insoluble," he seems to say; "but
insoluble or not, let us recall the pristine strength of
the human spirit, and not forget that we have access
to great resources still."

And this is where Arnold's buoyancy differs in
kind from Clough's buoyancy, though buoyancy is the
characteristic of both these essentially Oxford poets.
Clough is buoyant in hope, and sometimes, though
perhaps rarely, in faith; Arnold is buoyant in neither,
but yet he is buoyant—buoyant in rebound from

melancholy reflection, buoyant in throwing off the weight of melancholy reflection. "The outlook," he seems to say, "is as bad as possible. We have lost our old faith, and we cannot get a new one. Life is sapping the noblest energies of the mind. We are not as noble as we used to be. We have lost the commanding air of the great men of old. We cannot speak in the grand style. We can only boldly confront the truth and acknowledge the gloom ; and yet, and yet—

'Yet on he fares, by his own heart inspired.'"

Through hope or despair, through faith or doubt, the deep buoyancy of the imaginative life forbids Arnold to rest in any melancholy strain ; he only snatches his rudder, shakes out more sail, and day and night holds on indignantly to some new shore which as yet he discovers not. Clough's buoyancy is very different. It is not the buoyancy which shakes off depressing thoughts, but the buoyancy which overcomes them—

> "Sit, if you will, sit down upon the ground,
>   Yet not to weep and wail, but calmly look around.
>   Whate'er befell
>   Earth is not hell ;
> Now too, as when it first began,
> Life is yet life, and man is man.
> For all that breathe beneath the heaven's high cope,
> Joy with grief mixes, with despondence, hope.
>   Hope conquers cowardice, joy grief ;
>   Or, at least, faith unbelief.

> Though dead, not dead,
> Not gone, though fled,
> Not lost, though vanished,
> In the great gospel and true creed
> He is yet risen indeed,
> Christ is yet risen."

There is Clough's buoyancy of spirit, which goes to the heart of the matter. But Arnold, with equal buoyancy, seems to aim rather at evading than averting the blows of fate. He is somewhat unjust to Wordsworth, I think, in ascribing to Wordsworth, as his characteristic spell, the power to put aside the "cloud of mortal destiny" instead of confronting it—

> "Others will teach us how to dare,
> And against fear our breast to steel;
> Others will strengthen us to bear—
> But who, ah! who, will make us feel?
> The cloud of mortal destiny,
> Others will front it fearlessly—
> But who, like him, will put it by?"

That, I should have said, is not Wordsworth's position in poetry, but Matthew Arnold's. Wordsworth "strengthened us to bear" by every means by which a poet can convey such strength; but Arnold, exquisite as his poetry is, teaches us first to feel, and then to put by, the cloud of mortal destiny. But he does not teach us, as Wordsworth does, to bear it. We delight in his pictures; we enjoy more and more, the more we study it, the poetry of his exquisite detail; we feel the lyrical cry of his sceptical moods vibrating in our heart of hearts; we feel the reviving air of his buoyant digressions as he escapes from his own spell, and bids us escape too, into the world of imaginative freedom. But he gives us no new strength to bear. He gives us no new light of hope. He gives us no new nerve of faith. He is the greatest of our elegiac poets, for he not only makes his readers thrill with the vision of the faith or strength he has lost, but puts by "the cloud of mortal destiny" with an ease that makes us feel that after all the faith and strength may not be lost, but only hidden from his eyes. Though the poet and the thinker in Matthew Arnold are absolutely at one in their conscious teaching, the poet in him helps us to rebel against the thinker, and to encourage us to believe that the "stream of tendency" which bears him up with such elastic and patient strength is not blind, is not cold, and is not dumb. He tells us—

> "We, in some unknown Power's employ,
> Move on a rigorous line;
> Can neither, when we will, enjoy,
> Nor, when we will, resign."

But if the "unknown Power" be such that when we will to enjoy, we are taught to resign, and when we will to resign, we are bid, though it may be in some new and deeper sense, to enjoy, surely the "unknown Power" is not an unknowing Power, but is one that knows us better than we know ourselves.

IV

GEORGE ELIOT AS AUTHOR

GEORGE ELIOT AS AUTHOR

THE great authoress who called herself George Eliot is chiefly known, and no doubt deserved to be chiefly known, in England, as a novelist, but she was certainly much more than a novelist in the sense in which that word applies even to writers of great genius, to Miss Austen, or Mr. Trollope,—nay, much more than a novelist in the sense in which that word applies to Miss Brontë, or even to Thackeray, though it is of course true in relation to all these writers, that besides being much more, she is also, and necessarily, not so much. What is remarkable in George Eliot is the striking combination in her of very deep speculative power with a very great and realistic imagination. It is rare to find an intellect so skilled in the analysis of psychological problems so completely at home in the conception and delineation of real characters. George Eliot discusses the practical influences acting on men and women, I do not say with the *ease* of Fielding,—for there is a touch of carefulness, often of over-carefulness in all she does, —but with much of his breadth and spaciousness—

the breadth and spaciousness, one must remember, of a man who had seen London life in the capacity of a London police magistrate. Nay, her imagination has, I do not say of course the fertility, but something of the range and the delight in rich historic colouring, of Sir Walter Scott's, while it combines with it something too of the pleasure in ordered learning, and the laborious marshalling of the picturesque results of learning,—though her learning is usually in a very different field,—which gives the flavour of scholastic pride to the great genius of Milton. Not that I think George Eliot's verse entitles her to be described as a poet, though the poetic side of her mind has been deep enough and true enough to lend richness, depth, and harmony to her romances. I am only pointing out now how much she is besides a novelist,—how inevitable it was that in her novels she should range far beyond the region of the most successful novelists of recent times,—far beyond that little world of English society which has determined for novelists of the most different type of genius,—for Miss Austen, for Mrs. Gaskell, for Trollope, for Thackeray, and for many less successful, but still very successful contemporaries,—their peculiar field of work.

It is, indeed, a great help towards understanding her true genius to compare George Eliot with the school of society-novelists of whom I have spoken. What one remarks about the works of those who have studied any particular society as a whole far more deeply than they have studied the individual characters in it is, that their creations all stand on one level, are delineated, with great accuracy, down to the same not very considerable depth, and no further; that all, in short, are bas-reliefs cut out on the same surface. The novelists of this school are perfectly inexhaustible in resource on the special social ground they choose, and quite incapable of varying it. And all of them disappoint us in not giving more insight into those deeper roots of character which lie beneath the social surface. Probably the mobile sympathies which are so essential to artists of this class, and the faculty of readily realising, and of being easily satisfied with realising, the workings of other minds, are to some extent inconsistent with that imaginative intensity and tenacity which is needful for the deeper insight into human character. Certainly the accomplished artists I have named carve out their marvellously lifelike groups in a very shallow though sufficiently plastic material. How perfect and how infinitely various are the images left on the mind by the characters in Miss Austen's novels! Lord Macaulay has expressed just admiration of the skill which could paint four young clergymen, "all belonging to the upper part of the middle class, all liberally educated, all under the restraints of the same sacred profession, all young, all in love, all free from any disposition to ride a special hobby, and all without a ruling passion," without making them insipid likenesses of each other. And no doubt this does show great power; but it is equally remarkable that all of them are drawn just to the same depth, all delineated out of the same social elements. None of their minds are exhibited in any direct contact with the ultimate realities of life; none of them are seen grasping at the truth by which they seek to live, struggling with a single deadly temptation,—or, in short, dealing with any of the deeper elements of human life. The same may almost be said of Thackeray's, Mr. Trollope's, and Mrs. Gaskell's sketches. These authors, indeed, sometimes probe the motives of their leading characters, but they generally report that at a very small depth below the surface the analysis fails to detect any certain result. The whole graphic effect of their art is produced with scarcely any disturbance of the smooth surface of social usage. The artist's graver just scratches off the wax in a few given directions till the personal bias of taste and bearing is sufficiently revealed, while the pervading principle of the society in which the artist lives is strictly preserved.

It was very different with Miss Brontë. Her imagination was not, and under the circumstances of her life could not have been, at home with the light play of social influences. There is even an abruptness of outline, a total want of social cohesion among her characters. They are sternly drawn, with much strong shading, and kept in isolated spheres. They break, or rather burst, in upon each other, when they exert mutual influences at all, with a rude effort, that is significant enough of the shyness of a solitary creative imagination. Still, for this very reason, what characters Miss Brontë does conceive truly, she reveals much more deeply than the society-novelists of whom I have been speaking. She has no familiarity with the delicate touches and shades by which they succeed in conveying a distinct impression without laying bare the deeper secrets of character. She has not, like them, any power of giving in her delineations *traces* of thought and feeling which lie beyond her actual grasp. She has a full and conscious hold of all the moods she paints; and though her paintings are in nine cases out of ten far less lifelike, yet *when* lifelike they are far more profoundly imagined than those of Mr. Trollope, Miss Austen, Mrs. Gaskell, or even Thackeray himself. There is as little common life, diffused atmosphere of thought, and there are as few connecting social ideas, amongst the various figures in Miss Brontë's tales as is possible to conceive among fellow-men and fellow-countrymen. But what personal life there is, is of the deepest sort, though it is apt to be too exceptional and individual, and too little composed out of elements of universal experience.

The novelists of the society-school, who delineate not so much individual figures as a complete phase of society, have what one may call a *medium* ready to their hand in which to trace the characteristic features of the natures they delineate. They have a familiar world of manners to paint, in which a modulation, an omission, or an emphasis here and there, are quite sufficient to mark a character, or indicate a latent emotion. Not so an author who, like Miss Brontë, endeavoured to fit all her characters with a new and appropriate outward manner of their own as distinct and special as the inward nature it expressed. With her there was necessarily a directness of delineation, a strong downrightness in the drawing which is in very marked contrast with the method that charms us so much in the pictures of Miss Austen and her modern successors. Much of the art of the drawing-room novelists consists in the indirectness, the allusiveness, the educated reticence of the artists. They portray a society; they *indicate* an individuality. They delight in fine strokes; they will give a long conversation which scarcely advances the narrative at all, for the sake of a few delicate touches of shade or colour on an individual character. In the power to paint this play of common social life, in which there are comparatively but few keynotes of distinct personality, the charm of this school of art consists; while Miss Brontë's lay in the Rembrandt-like distinctness with which all that the mind conceived was brought into the full blaze of light, and the direct vigour with which all the prominent features were marked out.

George Eliot as a novelist has points of connection with both of these schools of art, besides some characteristics peculiarly her own. There is the same clearness of drawing, delicacy of finish, and absence of excitement, which characterise the modern semi-satirical school. But there is less of play in the surface-painting,—more of depth in the deeper characters imagined,—a broader touch, a stronger, directer fashion of delineation,—less of manner-painting, and more of the bare naturalism of human life. On the other hand, there is nothing of the Rembrandt-like style of Miss Brontë; the light flows more equally over George Eliot's pictures; one finds nothing of the irregular emphasis with which Currer Bell's characters are drawn, or of the strong subjective colouring which tinges all her scenes. George Eliot's imagination, like Miss Brontë's, loves to go to the roots of character, and portrays best by broad direct strokes; but there the likeness between them, so far as there is any, ends. The reasons for the deeper method and for the directer style are hardly likely to have been similar in the two cases. Miss Brontë can scarcely be said to have had any large instinctive knowledge of human nature;—her own life and thoughts were exceptional, cast in a strongly-marked but not very wide mould; her imagination was solitary; her experience was very limited; and her own personality tinged all she wrote. She "made out" the outward life and manner of her *dramatis personæ* by the sheer force of her own imagination; and as she always imagined the will and the affections as the substance and centre of her characters, those of her delineations which are successful at all are deep, and their manner broad.

George Eliot's genial, broad delineations of human life have, as I said just now, more perhaps of the breadth of Fielding than of any of the manner-painters of the present day. For these imagine life only as it appears in a certain dress and sphere, which are a kind of artificial medium for their art,—life as affected by drawing-rooms. George Eliot has little, if any, of their capacity for catching the under-tones and illusive complexity of this sort of society. She has, however, observed the phases of a more natural and straightforward class of life, and she draws her external world as much as possible from observation —though some of her Florentine pictures must have been suggested more by literary study than by personal experience—instead of imagining it, like Miss Brontë, out of the heart of the characters she wishes to paint. The English manners she delights in are chiefly of the simplest and most homely kind, —of the rural farmers and labourers, of the half-educated portion of the country middle-class, who have learnt no educated reticence, and of the resident country gentry and clergy in their relations with these rough-mannered neighbours. This is a world in which she could not but learn a direct style of treatment. The habit of concealing, or at most of suggesting rather than downright expressing, what is closest to our hearts, is, as we know, a result of education. It is quite foreign to the class of people whom George Eliot knows most thoroughly, and has drawn with the fullest power. All her deepest knowledge of human nature has probably been acquired among people who speak their thoughts with the directness, though not with the sharp metallic ring, of Miss Brontë's Yorkshire heroes. But instead of almost luxuriating, as Miss Brontë appears to do, in the startling emphasis of this mannerism, and making all her characters precipitate themselves in speech in the way best calculated to give a strongly-marked picture of the conception in her own brain, George Eliot has evidently delighted to note all the varieties of form which varying circumstances give to these direct and simple manners, and takes as much pleasure in painting their different shades as Miss Austen does in guiding her more elaborate conversations to and fro so as to elicit traits of personal character. Directness of delineation is, indeed, evidently natural to the author of *Adam Bede*, but it has no tendency whatever to take, with her, that form of concentrated intensity which it assumed in Miss Brontë; her style has all the general composure and range of tone of the life she paints, and shows her as more in sympathy with the dumb and stolid phases of rural society than with the more active forms of urbane converse. There was something of the poet in both. But George Eliot's poetry was rooted in the more intellectual emotions, Miss Brontë's was rooted in the most personal. George Eliot's poetic tendencies are rather of the kind to soften outlines and harmonise the effects of her pictures. Miss Brontë's, on the other hand, were adapted to express the passion of her own imagination; and while the effect was graphic and unique, it was monotonous, and not unfrequently unreal.

George Eliot's pictures are not only directer and simpler than those of the drawing-room novelists, but her deeper and frequently poetic imagination discriminates finely between the various degrees of depth which she gives to her characters, and throws more of universality and breadth into them. The manners of "good society" are a kind of social costume or disguise which is, in fact, much more effective in concealing how much of depth ordinary characters have, and in restraining the expression of universal human instincts and feelings, than in hiding the individualities, the distinguishing inclinations, talents, bias, and tastes of those who assume them. The slight restraints which are imposed by society upon the expression of individual bias are, in fact, only a new excitement to its more subtle and various, though less straightforward, development. Instead of speaking itself simply out, it gleams out in a hundred ways by the side-paths of a more elaborate medium. To avail yourself skilfully of all the opportunities which these social manners give you of being yourself, adds a fresh, though very egotistic, interest to life, and contributes much of the zest to the sort of study in which Thackeray and Trollope were the acknowledged masters. But this applies only to the lighter and more superficial part of human personality. Those stronger passions and emotions in which all men share more or less deeply; which are in the strictest sense personal, and yet in the strictest sense universal; which are private, because either the objects or the occasions which excite them most deeply are different for every different person, and universal, because towards some objects, or on some occasions, they are felt alike by all;—these most personal and most widely diffused of all the elements of human nature are sedulously suppressed in cultivated society; and even the most skilful of the drawing-room novelists find little room for delineating the comparative depth of their roots in different minds.

And yet these deepest portions of human character, which the simpler and less educated grades of society, in their comparative indifference to the sympathy they receive, do not care to hide, and which educated society half suppresses, or expresses only by received formulas quite without personal significance, are far truer measures of force and mass in human character than any other elements. They are, in fact, the only common measures which are applicable to all in nearly equal degree. After all, what we care chiefly to know of men and women is not so much their special tastes, bias, gifts, humours, or even the exact proportions in which these characteristics are combined, as the general depth and mass of the human nature that is in them,—the breadth and the power of their life, its comprehensiveness of grasp, its tenacity of instinct, its capacity for love, its need of trust. A thousand skilful outlines of character, based on mere individualities of taste and talent and temper, are not near as moving to us as one vivid picture of a massive nature stirred to the very depths of its commonplace instinct and commonplace faith. And the means of studying these broader aspects of human life are much fewer in the educated society which Miss Austen and Thackeray draw than in the country-towns, mills, and farmhouses which are dotted about George Eliot's *Scenes from Clerical Life, Silas Marner*, and her more elaborate English tales.

In the depth, force, and thorough naturalness of the human characteristics in the delineation of which she delights, George Eliot is not superior to Miss Brontë, who never fails to give us a distinct measure of the instinctive tenderness, depth of affection, and energy of will, of her creations. But in breadth of range George Eliot is far beyond Currer Bell. Intensity is the main characteristic of the authoress of *Jane Eyre*. She cannot paint quiet massive strength, still less easy, composed, and inert natures. George Eliot enters into these with even more insight than into the more concentrated. Eager prejudice, dumb pain, the passive famine of inarticulate desires, are painted by both authors with marvellous and almost equal power; but George Eliot has the wider and more tranquil sympathies, and sometimes almost seems to rival Sir Walter Scott in the art of delineating the repose of strong natures and the effortless strength they put forth.

Again, in one field—the field of religious faith—

the author of *Adam Bede* and *Romola* shows much broader insight than any of the writers I have named. The drawing-room school of novelists do not and cannot often go down to a stratum of life deep enough to come upon the springs of faith. Miss Austen never touches them. Thackeray turns dizzy with the very mobility of his own sympathies, and finding a distinct type of faith in every different man's mind, not only proclaims the inscrutability of all divine topics, but refuses altogether to assign any strong motive power to religious emotions in his delineations of human life. Miss Brontë, too, finds it needful to eliminate the supernatural, though she once or twice admits the preternatural, in her pictures. As an artist she is strictly a secularist, delineating religious enthusiasm only once, and then exhibiting it as the stimulus of a cold nature and as putting forth unlawful claims to overrule legitimate human affections. Even Sir Walter Scott, powerfully as he could paint fanaticism, and keen as was his pleasure in the marvellous, never attempted to paint the quieter and deeper forms of religious faith. He evidently did not admit any supernatural element into his conception of sensible men and women, and never paints its influence over a sober and tranquil will.

George Eliot holds that the stronger class of intellects meddle least with religious faith. But she sees far more clearly than any of them the actual space occupied by spiritual motives in human life,—

the depth, beauty, and significance which they, and they alone, give to human action. And, accordingly, in almost all her tales she introduces some character with conscious cravings for something beyond human happiness; while in the most popular of her works she delineates the most delicately beautiful and spiritual nature with which I have ever met in the whole range of fiction. Goethe's picture of the Fair Saint in *Wilhelm Meister* cannot properly be said to belong to fiction at all. Not only is it, in fact, a minute copy from real life, but it is not even woven by his imagination into the texture of his story. It is an episode of mere description, and the character is not delineated in action. Nay, in itself, the *Schöne Seele* which Goethe has so delicately mirrored for us cannot compare in simplicity and beauty with Dinah in *Adam Bede*.

Another element in which George Eliot shows the masculine breadth and strength of her genius adds less to the charm of her tales,—I mean the shrewdness and range of her miscellaneous observations on life. Nothing is rarer than to see in women's writings that kind of strong acute generalisation which Fielding introduced so freely. Yet the miscellaneous observations in which George Eliot so often indulges us, after the fashion of the day, are not always well suited to the particular bent of her genius—indeed, they often break the spell which that genius has laid upon her readers. She is not a satirist, and she half adopts the style of a satirist in these portions of her books. The influence of Thackeray had at first a distinctly bad effect on her genius, but in *Silas Marner* that influence began to wane, and quite disappeared in *Romola*, though I think it reappeared a little in *Felix Holt*. A powerful, somewhat slow, and direct style of portraiture is in ill-keeping with that flavour of sarcastic innuendo in which Thackeray delighted. It jars upon the ear in the midst of the simple and faithful delineations of human nature as it really is, with which George Eliot fills her books. It was all very well for Thackeray who made it his main aim and business to expose the hollowness and insincerities of human society, to add his own keen comment to his own one-sided picture. But then it was of the essence of his genius to lay bare unrealities, and leave the sound life almost untouched. It was rather a relief than otherwise to see him playing with his dissecting-knife after one of his keenest probing feats; you understand better how limited his purpose is,— that he has been in search of organic disease,—and you are not surprised, therefore, to find that he has found little that was healthy.

But George Eliot had a different power. She could delineate what is sound even more powerfully than what is unsound. She does not expose but paints human nature, its weakness and its strength; and the satirical tone in which Thackeray justified to his readers the severity of his criticisms, by trying to show that they were all of them open to criticisms at least as severe, was a setting not at all in harmony with George Eliot's style of art. This is, indeed, usually so deep, direct, and real, that the interruption needed to listen to the author's aside is a painful break. It would suit her books far better if, in this respect, she had followed Miss Brontë's eager and undeviating style of narration, and had never indulged in the pleasure of being her own critic. But if she felt bound to intersperse her narratives with comments and thoughts of her own, she could not have found a less suitable tone for them than that satirical contempt for his readers' unreal state of mind to which the author of *Vanity Fair* accustomed us. When in the midst of an admirable sketch of the farm-labourers on Mr. Poyser's farm, by no means ill-natured in itself, we come upon such a sentence as this, for instance :—" When Tityrus and Meliboeus happen to be on the same farm, they are not sentimentally polite to each other,"—we feel suddenly transported to the latitude of a clumsy *Vanity Fair*. Often it is only that observations, themselves not ungenial, are clothed in the half-scornful language which Thackeray's success induced so many light writers to adopt. For example, there is in the chapter which opens as follows nothing that is not genial and wise; but throughout the whole there runs a tone of bantering depreciation—a "what a vulgar world it is we live in" sort of air—which has no justification either in the tenor of what is said, or the particular incident on which it is a comment :—

" ' This Rector of Broxton is little better than a pagan !'

I hear one of my lady readers exclaim. 'How much more edifying it would have been if you had made him give Arthur some truly spiritual advice! You might have put into his mouth the most beautiful things—quite as good as reading a sermon.' Certainly I could, my fair critic, if I were a clever novelist, not obliged to creep servilely after nature and fact, but able to represent things as they never have been and never will be. Then, of course, my characters would be entirely of my own choosing, and I could select the most unexceptionable type of clergyman, and put my own admirable opinions into his mouth on all occasions."

This is, when read in its context, sarcasm quite out of its natural element, floundering like a fish out of water. Indeed, this foreign mannerism gives a certain air of laborious smartness to the chapters of comment in *Adam Bede*, which seems to me the only defect in that wonderful book. That which was only an external mannerism in the occasional commentary of *Adam Bede* grew into a rankling foreign substance in *The Mill on the Floss*, and it was a great relief to her admirers to find that in her later works George Eliot had in a great degree discontinued it.

For George Eliot was no satirist. Even where her banter is least heavy, hers was not the bent to bring out without effort, and yet in full relief, the weak points of men, as the genius of satire requires; and one feels painfully that, like most able people who do what it is not their bent to do, she overdoes it, and breaks a butterfly on the wheel. How lightly and tauntingly Thackeray would have given us the following! how broadly ludicrous Dickens might have made it! but in George Eliot's hands it is neither broad fun nor indirect satire, but laborious, painstaking, intellectual power, commenting with slow contempt on human foibles:—

"It is a pathetic sight and a striking example of the complexity introduced into the emotions by a high state of civilisation—the sight of a fashionably-drest female in grief. From the sorrow of a Hottentot to that of a woman in large buckram sleeves, with several bracelets on each arm, an architectural bonnet, and delicate ribbon-strings —what a long series of gradations! In the enlightened child of civilisation the abandonment characteristic of grief is checked and varied in the subtlest manner, so as to present an interesting problem to the analytic mind. If, with a crushed heart and eyes half-blinded by the mist of tears, she were to walk with a too devious step through a door-place, she might crush her buckram sleeves too, and the deep consciousness of this possibility produces a composition of forces by which she takes a line that just clears the doorpost. Perceiving that the tears are hurrying fast, she unpins her strings and throws them languidly backward—a touching gesture, indicative, even in the deepest gloom, of the hope in future dry moments when cap-strings will once more have a charm. As the tears subside a little, and with her head leaning backward at the angle that will not injure a bonnet, she endures that terrible moment when grief, which has made all things else a weariness, has itself become weary; she looks down pensively at her bracelets and adjusts their clasps with that pretty studied fortuity which would be gratifying to her mind if it were once more in a calm and healthy state."

George Eliot's humour, which is very great, is not

of the ironical kind. The covert meaning which aims at one thing while it appears to say another is not in her way. The humour in which she excels most has nothing in it of the self-command and reticence which give the edge to irony. The satirist just moves away sufficiently from the station at which for the moment his character is placed to show you how one-sided and shallow that character is; but he keeps on the mask of sympathy, though he allows you to see him smiling under it; and half the sting of his irony consists in his assuming that the weakness probed is too deeply rooted in human nature to mock at openly, though you need not shut your eyes to it.

There is nothing of this species of humour in George Eliot. She has a large share of that dramatic humour of which Shakespeare's is the model, which consists in a rapid and complete change of moral and intellectual latitude, in showing us the strangely different views of human things—vulgar, contemplative, and practical—which differently situated beings take. Of this kind of humour there is no more perfect and delightful specimen than the scene in which she paints the unflinching (or, as we might falsely call it, indelicate) feeling of the uneducated towards Death and the necessary accompaniments of Death, as illustrated by Lisbeth Bede's wishes about her husband's coffin and funeral.

"'What art goin' to do?' asked Lisbeth. 'Set about thy feyther's coffin?'

"'No, mother,' said Adam; 'we're going to take the wood to the village, and have it made there.'

"'Nay, my lad, nay,' Lisbeth burst out in an eager, wailing tone; 'thee wotna let nobody make thy feyther's coffin but thysen? Who'd make it so well? An' him as know'd what good work war, an 's got a son as is th' head o' the village, an' all Treddles'on too, for cleverness.'

"'Very well, mother, if that's thy wish, I'll make the coffin at home; but I thought thee wouldstna like to hear the work going on.'

"'An' why shouldna I like't? It's the right thing to be done. An' what's likin' got to do wi't? It's choice o' mislikins is all I'n got i' this world. One mossel's as good as another when your mouth's out o' taste. Thee mun set about it now this mornin' fust thing. I wunna ha' nobody to touch the coffin but thee.'

"Adam's eyes met Seth's, which looked from Dinah to him rather wistfully.

"'No, mother,' he said, 'I'll not consent; but Seth shall have a hand in it too, if it's to be done at home. I'll go to the village this forenoon, because Mr. Burge 'ull want to see me, and Seth shall stay at home and begin the coffin. I can come back at noon, and then he can go.'

"'Nay, nay,' persisted Lisbeth, beginning to cry, 'I'n set my heart on 't as thee shalt ma' thy feyther's coffin. Thee 't so stiff an' masterful, thee 't ne'er do as thy mother wants thee. Thee wast often angered wi' thy feyther when he war alive; thee must be the better to 'm now he's goen'. *He'd ha' thought nothin' on 't for Seth to ma' 's coffin.*'"

Some of George Eliot's most subtle and characteristic humour consists in giving to the conversation of her rural louts a distinct, though of course unconscious, bearing on the intellectual questions contemporaneously discussed by the most highly cultivated, without coming to any much more impressive results. Even when this is not the case, there is a humour in the mere sharpness of the contrast between the favourite subjects of her boors and those of refined society. Thus, in the inimitable conversation at the opening of *Silas Marner*,—the conversation in the Rainbow Inn,—the subject is simply and solely one to excite the professional interest of butchers and of all connoisseurs in grazing stock. But the pungency is given by the grotesqueness of the contrast between the professional interests of the lower and middle classes, and by that additional flavour of professionality which every descent in the scale of education certainly ensures.

"The conversation, which was at a high pitch of animation when Silas approached the door of the Rainbow, had, as usual, been slow and intermittent when the company first assembled. The pipes began to be puffed in a silence which had an air of severity ; the more important customers, who drank spirits and sat nearest the fire, staring at each other as if a bet were depending on the first man who winked ; while the beer-drinkers, chiefly men in fustian jackets and smock-frocks, kept their eyelids down and rubbed their hands across their mouths, as if their draughts of beer had been a funereal duty attended with embarrassing sadness. At last, Mr. Snell, the landlord, a man of neutral disposition, accustomed to stand aloof from human differences as those of beings who were all alike in need of liquor, broke silence, by saying in a doubtful tone to his cousin the butcher,—

"'Some folks 'ud say that was a fine beast you druv in yesterday, Bob?'

"The butcher, a jolly, smiling, red-haired man, was not disposed to answer rashly. He gave a few puffs before he spat and replied, 'And they wouldn't be fur wrong, John.'

"After this feeble delusive thaw, the silence set in as severely as before.

"'Was it a red Durham?' said the farrier, taking up the thread of discourse after the lapse of a few minutes.

"The farrier looked at the landlord, and the landlord looked at the butcher, as the person who must take the responsibility of answering.

"'Red it was,' said the butcher, in his good-humoured husky treble—'and a Durham it was.'

"'Then you needn't tell *me* who you bought it of,' said the farrier, looking round with some triumph; 'I know who it is has got the red Durhams o' this country-side. And she'd a white star on her brow, I'll bet a penny?' The farrier leaned forward with his hands on his knees as he put this question, and his eyes twinkled knowingly.

"'Well, yes—she might,' said the butcher slowly, considering that he was giving a decided affirmative. 'I don't say contrary.'

"'I knew that very well,' said the farrier, throwing himself backward again and speaking defiantly; 'if *I* don't know Mr. Lammeter's cows, I should like to know who does—that's all. And as for the cow you've bought, bargain or no bargain, I've been at the drenching of her—contradick me who will.'

"The farrier looked fierce, and the mild butcher's conversational spirit was roused a little.

"'I'm not for contradicking no man,' he said; 'I'm for peace and quietness. Some are for cutting long ribs —I'm for cutting 'em short, myself; but *I* don't quarrel with 'em. All I say is, it's a lovely carkiss—and anybody as was reasonable, it 'ud bring tears into their eyes to look at it.'

"'Well, it's the cow as I drenched, whatever it is,' pursued the farrier angrily; 'and it was Mr. Lammeter's cow, else you told a lie when you said it was a red Durham.'

"'I tell no lies,' said the butcher, with the same mild huskiness as before; 'and I contradick none—not if a man was to swear himself black: he's no meat o' mine, nor none of my bargains. All I say is, it's a lovely carkiss. And what I say I'll stick to; but I'll quarrel wi' no man.'

"'No,' said the farrier, with bitter sarcasm, looking at the company generally; 'and p'rhaps you aren't pigheaded; and p'rhaps you didn't say the cow was a red Durham; and p'rhaps you didn't say she'd got a star on her brow—stick to that, now you're at it.'

"'Come, come,' said the landlord; 'let the cow alone. The truth lies atween you: you're both right and both wrong, as I allays say. And as for the cow's being Mr. Lammeter's, I say nothing to that; but this I say, as the Rainbow's the Rainbow.'"

But as soon as Mr. Macey, the parish clerk and tailor, enters into the conversation, a faint shadow of the intellectual phases of "modern thought"—just sufficient to remind the reader of the form which they take in the present day, without in any way marring the truth of the picture—begins to fall on it. Mr. Macey has fallen upon some appropriate form of the difficulty of distinguishing between the "subjective" and the "objective." He it is who tells us that "there's allays two 'pinions; there's the 'pinion a man has of himsen, and there's the 'pinion other folks have on him. There'd be two 'pinions about a cracked bell if the bell could hear itself." And further, in discussing the error of a bride and bridegroom who had interchanged their respective responses in the marriage service, he throws up the difficult question as to the relation between "substance" and "form." "Is it the meaning or the words as makes folks fast in wedlock? For the parson meant right, and the bride and bridegroom meant right. But then, when I come to think on it, meanin' goes but a little way i' most things, for you may mean to stick things together, and your glue may be bad, and then where are you? And so I says to mysen, 'It isn't the meanin', it's the glue.' And I was worreted as if I'd got three bells to pull at once. . . . But where's the use o' talking? —you can't think what goes on in a 'cute man's inside."

There is also in George Eliot abundance of what always accompanies dramatic humour, — I mean a great fertility in illustrative analogies which go to the very heart of a one-sided view of any question. Of this Mrs. Poyser's justly admired wit is the most obvious example. When, for instance, she wishes to impress upon Dinah that her village convert's piety is an artificial result of her own personal influence, and cannot outlast her absence a day, what can be more felicitous than her simile? "There's that Bessy Cranage, she'll be flaunting in new finery three weeks after you're gone, I'll be bound: she'll no more go on in her new ways without you than a dog 'ull stand on its hind legs when nobody's looking."

But while George Eliot's imagination is opulent enough in its power of dramatic humour, in its capacity for easily migrating from one moral latitude to another, and fertile enough in illustration of any view, or any character it once grasps, one sees in the third volume of *The Mill on the Floss*, in the somewhat laborious gossip of the Florentine society in *Romola*, and constantly in *Middlemarch*, that there is no proportionate power of indirectly portraying character by the sidelights and shadows of easy general conversation,—a power which often distinguishes feminine novelists. In the picture of life as it passed in St. Ogg's or Middlemarch drawing-rooms, she falls so much below herself that this, it is quite clear, is not her natural field of art. With all her subtlety and intellectual power, which are obviously great, and her humour, which is greater, she falls far short of many who are greatly her inferiors in genius in her attempt to delineate character through this tranquil play of educated social intercourse. Take up almost any scene in Thackeray or Trollope, and you will find a conversation in which, without any formal discussion, every character seems to be answering by some slight modification in its own tone to the chords struck by the others. This sort of play of character is mainly a fruit of social elasticity. The type of mind in the uncultivated and the philosophising classes, whom George Eliot has made her chief study, is much stiffer and more monotonous. The latter change with the changes in their own mood, but do not suffer the same subtle modifications of tone and feeling from social influences which you perceive in society. George Eliot has but little skill in delineating this social phenomenon. Her imagination requires to have a distinct conception of the mood or thought to be seized before she can paint it There is nothing of that easy modulation (grasped by instinct rather than by imagination) in the conversation of her educated people, which constitutes half its charm, and which gives to the modern novelist so wide a field for indirect portraiture. Among Miss Austen's scenes, for instance, George Eliot might perhaps have written those between people of a totally different social level, as, for example, the humorous scenes between the Miss Steeles and the Miss Dashwoods in *Sense and Sensibility*. But *Middlemarch* and *Daniel Deronda* both show that the delicately-delineated play of feeling between Elizabeth Bennet and Mr. Darcy in *Pride and Prejudice*, or between Emma and Jane Fairfax in *Emma*, would have been quite out of her sphere. It is much more difficult for an Englishman to criticise her very elaborate picture of the gossip of Florentine market-places, but to me there seems a constant over-laboriousness even there.

Indeed, there are probably no two more different types of genius than that which excels in indirect and that which excels in direct delineation. And George Eliot, like Sir Walter Scott, is always most successful with the broadest and simplest modes in which human character expresses itself. In short, for masculine composure and range of sympathy, for strength of grasp in dealing with universal human feelings, for skill in habitually realising to us that individual differences of character are engrafted on a fundamental community of nature, she had no rival among the literary artists of her day. And though it was in part a logical consequence of these great gifts, yet, as I have shown, it is exceptional enough to deserve separate notice and adds indefinitely to the charm they exercise, that she had a keen sense of that infinite hunger of the spirit which nothing human could appease, though an inadequate appreciation of the inward conditions, by the true fulfilment of which that hunger is satisfied.

Adam Bede is always likely to remain George Eliot's most popular work. It is a story of which any English author, however great his name, could not fail to have been proud. Everything about it (if I except perhaps a touch of melodrama connected with the execution scene) is at once simple and great, and the plot is unfolded with singular simplicity, purity, and power. Her genius delighted in depicting the life of a little community; and even when she had got a really deep interest at work on her village stage, she was always anxious to remind herself and her readers how the general population were doing meanwhile in spite of it,—to picture them as they were, quite unconscious of the unfolding plot and living out their ordinary lives in the ordinary way, with but few half-curious glances at the slowly-maturing crisis.

This tendency gave a great charm to a tale in which the interest was really profound; for it turned the story from a mere narrative of individual perils, trials, joys, and sorrows, into a vivid illustration of the common human lot. There is a concentrated sort of egotism about common novels even of a high order of talent, which is one reason why the interest in them is apt to die away in riper years. Sir Walter Scott's novels are never iron-bound by this purely individual kind of interest: to children they seem far too discursive, too little limited to the particular story; but his tales retain among the mature the popularity which they have in youth, in great measure on this very account, that they range so pleasantly beyond the borders of the immediate narrative, and give us so wide a knowledge of the great common life in the heart of which the individual actors of the story are placed. But then, Sir Walter Scott had also an intense sympathy with action, an eager interest in the unwinding of his own tales, which generally at least prevented his discursiveness from passing the boundaries of legitimate art. He never failed to give us a general background, a vista of tradition concerning the times of which he writes; but he seldom failed to make it a background to some much more vivid interest which fills the foreground in his own mind.

George Eliot was to a great extent deficient

in this sympathy with action. She had obviously a strong dislike to all those artificial enhancements of interest which do not arise fairly out of the moral constitution of the characters; and this may have induced her sometimes to overlook the artistic value of a rapid current of action, of a certain shadow of suspense, as instruments in the exhibition of the deeper springs of human character. But if this indifference to the machinery of romance was a defect, it disappeared in *Adam Bede*, and was closely connected with its greatest beauties. In almost any other writer's hands the story of seduction which is at the basis of *Adam Bede* would have been heightened by innumerable factitious elements, and the various threads of interest would have been multiplied and interwoven at every point. George Eliot's natural aversion to these adventitious effects induced her to limit herself strictly to the simplest possible unfolding of the tragedy; and the consequence is, that the story gains in moral spaciousness far more than it could have lost in exciting elements.

Nor is this clearness of the moral space, this free movement of personal character, a common characteristic of modern novels. There are two common errors into which even the greatest authors manage to fall, and by which they produce a suffocating effect in their pictures, and give the impression that their characters are, as Thackeray calls them, "puppets," with the strings pulled from behind. One error, the commonest in the greater modern artists, is to smother character in society,—to limit the whole scope of the delineation to the little effects which can be produced on a crowded canvas, where there is no room for even one mind to be itself, or to be seen apart from the rippling of social influences upon it. The other error, the commonest in writers of the older school, is to smother character in incident, to accumulate motives and external excitements so thickly as to drown all spontaneous life in the artificial tension of passive emotion and involuntary impulse. One amongst several reasons why Scott's heroes and heroines are usually the poorest characters in his tales is, that they are made the centres of all these circumstantial interests—the puppets arbitrarily moved about by these hidden strings. In neither case is there proper space for the free play of personal life. Real men of any force have a free sphere of their own, influenced, but in no way determined, by the social or circumstantial influences which hem them round; and to encumber the principal characters with too great a pressure of subsidiary influences, whether of one kind or another, is almost inevitably to cramp the design and destroy the freedom of the life portrayed. Now there is nothing of all this in *Adam Bede*. There is no such concentration of distracting influences as to bewilder any of the characters out of their natural responsibility for themselves and their own actions. No doubt a rural society, a certain community of life, is depicted; but while this is kept constantly present to one's mind by the fidelity with which all the mutual relations of the village society are impressed on the language and bearing of the characters delineated, yet each character stands out distinct and clear, holding its own destiny in its own power. This gives dignity, freedom, and simplicity to the whole, and adds a kind of solemnity to the movement of the principal action in the story, which, had it been complicated by any extraneous or chance elements, must have produced a less profound and single effect on the imagination.

Even in *Adam Bede* there is an occasional looseness in the texture of the narrative which indicates the characteristic tendency of the author to sketch-in freely all her imagination has grasped, without reference to unity of design; but the intrinsic interest of the plot so far checks this tendency as to render it visible only when previously suggested by her other works. One sees it mainly in this, that some of the principal figures, quite essential to the whole effect of the tale, stand too much outside the thread of the story, and take no part in its evolution. In Goethe's novels this fault reaches its climax; for no one has any reason to suppose, merely because a figure appears there, and is very carefully painted in, that it is to be connected in any way with the unwinding of the tale. George Eliot is not chargeable with any fault so great as this; but, apart from any disposition to uphold mere technical or formal rules of art, there is a greater vividness of impression, a more concentrated effect produced on the mind, when the course of the narrative works *in conjunction* with the power of the artist to engrave the picture upon the memory, than when they work apart. Seth Bede, for instance, one of the best conceptions in the story, is almost entirely a spectator of its course; one might remember the whole essence of the plot, and almost forget his existence,—and yet he is not a mere side-sketch, like Bartle Massey or Mr. Craig, for his character is essential to bring out in full relief the characters of Adam and of Dinah. Even in this tale, then, the group of characters painted is a far more perfect work of art than the story, taken as a whole, which includes them; for only one or two are strongly impressed on the mind by virtue of their close connection with the action of the narrative; the images of the remainder, graphically as they are rendered, are conveyed to the reader mainly through dialogue and description.

But, this once admitted, there is no further qualification to make in one's admiration of the art of the story. The group of characters, conceived in themselves, and without reference to the narrative, seems to me perfect,—a rural cartoon of marvellous simplicity, and yet stately in its beauty. The strongheaded, manly, sharp-tempered, secular carpenter, with his energetic satisfaction in work, his impatience of dreamers, and his early passion for Hetty's earthly loveliness,—the tender-hearted, mystic-minded Seth, who so readily unlooses his hold of his one dream of happiness,—the pretty, vain, little, pleasure-loving dairymaid, with her inarticulate love of luxury and dread of shame, so shallow that she cannot even feel a passing anticipation of the fate before her, but flutters into it like a moth into the candle,—the spiritual, transparent-minded, meditative, yet clear-sighted Wesleyan factory-girl, whose delicate sensitiveness to the inward condition and wants of others never ruffles her own distinct apprehension of the personal duty before her,—the good-natured, self-deceiving, weak young squire, with his patronising generosity, and his disposition to comfort himself, in his self-reproach, with the good opinion of those who are totally ignorant of his grounds for self-reproach, —and the noble, easy-minded, tolerant rector who feels so little impulse to exert moral influence over others that the Wesleyan factory-girl is a problem to him, and who, even where he has natural authority, rather shrinks from the intrusion necessary to exert it,—with the many other vividly-painted figures more or less in the background,—the quick-witted, fretful Lisbeth, with her excessive fondness for the son she fears, and her half-contempt for the son whose religiousness she regards as an insurance to the family,— the more quick-witted and more audacious farmer's wife, whose reverence for the piety of her niece is so strongly mixed with dislike of eccentricity and dissent;—these, with the slighter but equally true outlines with which the picture is filled up, form one of the truest and most typical groups of English life I have ever seen delineated.

Moreover, the characters themselves are not more perfectly handled than the scene. It is impossible to forget where we are for a moment. The hum of village-life is heard throughout; the paramount influence of the manor-house, the substantial importance of the well-to-do farmer, the rector's authority in the parish,—are all conveyed without any effort through the force with which the author realises her scenes; and frequently we have a picture of idyllic beauty—as where Adam Bede finds Hetty picking currants in the garden—that reminds us of the soft poetic touch with which Goethe delineated a situation that had sunk deep into his mind.

The greatest effort and greatest success of the book consist, however, in the wonderful power of the contrast between Hetty and Dinah. From the first introduction of Dinah preaching to the crowd on the village green, and winning her little success over the vain heart of the blacksmith's daughter, and the first appearance of Hetty tossing her butter in the dairy, full of conscious delight at *her* little success in riveting Captain Donnithorne's admiration, the interest centres in these two figures. What common measure of human nature can apply to them both? Near as they are in position, and equal in attractions, and belonging alike to the same half-educated class, they represent evidently the highest and lowest grade in the scale of spiritual nature, and the thoughts that fill the mind of the one do not even rouse the faintest echo in the nature of the other. The art of the con-

trast is the greater that it is never forced on our
attention, and never exaggerated. Yet from the first
it is growing upon us. Dinah's gentle rejection of
the one brother whom she cannot love opens the tale,
while Hetty's conduct to the other whom she cannot
love forms its climax of interest. The interest is the
deeper and truer that it is not the commonplace
antithesis between right and wrong, but between the
finest and most delicate of spiritual consciences, and
that absolute inaccessibility to moral or spiritual
thought which marks a soft, shallow, pleasure-loving
nature preoccupied with self-love. The moral *material*
of which the two girls are made seems chargeable
with the difference rather than any conduct of their
own. Can any meeting-point be found between the
two? or, if not, any experience, however strange,
which shall bridge the apparently impassable gulf?
This is in great measure the theme of the story; and
the scene in which it is first fully realised—where
Dinah and Hetty are pictured in the adjoining bed-
rooms, each in their separate world—is one of the
most powerful pieces of imaginative writing which
the present generation has produced. I can but
extract the closing passage :—

"What a strange contrast the two figures made! Visible
enough in that mingled twilight and moonlight. Hetty,
her cheeks flushed and her eyes glistening from her imaginary drama, her beautiful neck and arms bare, her hair
hanging in a curly tangle down her back, and the baubles
in her ears. Dinah, covered with her long white dress,

her pale face full of subdued emotion, almost like a lovely corpse into which the soul has returned charged with sublimer secrets and a sublimer love. They were nearly of the same height; Dinah evidently a little the taller as she put her arm round Hetty's waist, and kissed her forehead.

"'I knew you were not in bed, my dear,' she said, in her sweet clear voice, which was irritating to Hetty, mingling with her own peevish vexation like music with jangling chains, 'for I heard you moving; and I longed to speak to you again to-night, for it is the last but one that I shall be here, and we don't know what may happen to-morrow to keep us apart. Shall I sit down with you while you do up your hair?'—'O yes,' said Hetty, hastily turning round and reaching the second chair in the room, glad that Dinah looked as if she did not notice her earrings.

"Dinah sat down, and Hetty began to brush together her hair before twisting it up, doing it with that air of excessive indifference which belongs to confused self-consciousness. But the expression of Dinah's eyes gradually relieved her; they seemed unobservant of all details. 'Dear Hetty,' she said, 'it has been borne in upon my mind to-night that you may some day be in trouble—trouble is appointed for us all here below, and there comes a time when we need more comfort and help than the things of this life can give. I want to tell you that if ever you are in trouble and need a friend that will always feel for you and love you, you have got that friend in Dinah Morris at Snowfield; and if you come to her, or send for her, she'll never forget this night, and the words she is speaking to you now. Will you remember it, Hetty?'—'Yes,' said Hetty, rather frightened. 'But why should you think I shall be in trouble? Do you know of anything?' Hetty had seated herself as she tied on her cap, and now Dinah leaned forwards and took her hands as she answered,

"'Because, dear, trouble comes to us all in this life: we set our hearts on things which it isn't God's will for us to have, and then we go sorrowing; the people we love are taken from us, and we can joy in nothing because they are not with us; sickness comes, and we faint under the burden of our feeble bodies; we go astray and do wrong, and bring ourselves into trouble with our fellow-men. There is no man or woman born into this world to whom some of these trials do not fall, and so I feel that some of them must happen to you; and I desire for you, that while you are young you should seek for strength from your Heavenly Father, that you may have a support which will not fail you in the evil day.'

"Dinah paused and released Hetty's hands, that she might not hinder her. Hetty sat quite still: she felt no response within herself to Dinah's anxious affection; but Dinah's words, uttered with solemn, pathetic distinctness, affected her with a chill fear. Her flush had died away almost to paleness; she had the timidity of a luxurious pleasure-seeking nature, which shrinks from the hint of pain. Dinah saw the effect, and her tender anxious pleading became the more earnest, till Hetty, full of a vague fear that something evil was sometime to befall her, began to cry. . . . Dinah had never seen Hetty affected in this way before, and with her usual benignant hopefulness, she trusted it was the stirring of a divine impulse. She kissed the sobbing thing, and began to cry with her for grateful joy. But Hetty was simply in that excitable state of mind in which there is no calculating what turn the feelings may take from one moment to another, and for the first time she became irritated under Dinah's caress. She pushed her away impatiently, and said with a childish sobbing voice, 'Don't talk to me so, Dinah. Why do you come to frighten me? I've never done anything to you. Why can't you let me be?'

"Poor Dinah felt a pang. She was too wise to persist, and only said mildly, 'Yes, my dear, you're tired; I won't hinder you any longer. Make haste and get into bed. Good-night.' She went out of the room almost as quietly and quickly as if she had been a ghost; but once by the side of her own bed she threw herself on her knees, and poured out in deep silence all the passionate pity that filled her heart. As for Hetty, she was soon in the wood again—her waking dreams being merged in a sleeping life scarcely more fragmentary and confused."

 This is powerful, and it seems scarcely possible that the conception of a problem so deep should be worked out with any adequate success; and yet the development is as powerful as the commencement, and the solution most powerful of all. To depict the sufferings of a sensitive but frail nature,—the remorse of guilt, the despair of shame,—this would be comparatively easy to an imagination so powerful as George Eliot's. But to deal with a nature too shallow for any real sense of guilt, too easily numbed by pain for clear thought at all, too cowardly for despair, and to show how, by the slow, dull pressure of mingled shame and hardship, momentarily broken by a new instinct, and then renewed after a more conscious act of guilt, a dim sense of spiritual things is literally *wrung* out of this sterile little pleasure-loving life, till under Dinah's kindly influence it becomes a distinct cry for help,—this is a task as great as any which an imaginative writer below the rank of a great poet ever attempted. Observe with what flexibility the author contracts her own powerful imagination within the limits of Hetty's nature, and delineates the growing wretchedness and numbness of her vacant mind during the futile journey in search of Captain Donnithorne, the helpless attempt to destroy herself, and the violent shrinking of her whole being from the brink of death.

"The horror of this cold, and darkness, and solitude—out of all human reach—became greater every long minute: it was almost as if she were dead already, and knew that she was dead and longed to get back to life again. But no: she was alive still; she had not taken the dreadful leap. She felt a strange contradictory wretchedness and exultation; wretchedness, that she did not dare to face death; exultation, that she was still in life—that she might yet know light and warmth again. She walked backwards and forwards to warm herself, beginning to discern something of the objects around her, as her eyes became accustomed to the night: the darker line of the hedge, the rapid motion of some living creature—perhaps a field-mouse—rushing across the grass. She no longer felt as if the darkness hedged her in: she thought she could walk back across the field, and get over the stile; and then, in the very next field, she thought she remembered there was a hovel of furze near a sheepfold. . . .

"She had found the shelter: she groped her way, touching the prickly gorse, to the door, and pushed it open. It was an ill-smelling close place, but warm, and there was straw on the ground: Hetty sank down on the straw with a sense of escape. Tears came—she had never shed tears before since she left Windsor—tears and sobs of hysterical joy that she had still hold of life, that she was still on the familiar earth, with the sheep near her. The very consciousness of her own limbs was a delight to her: she turned up her sleeves, and kissed her arms with the passionate love of life."

Seldom has any human experience been more powerfully painted, and yet the confession in prison which Dinah at last wins from her is still more powerful. In short, the whole thread of inward history which unites the first interview between them in Hetty's bedroom with the last in her cell is recounted with a power quite unsurpassed in fiction. With no more promising instrument to work upon than the most sterile and frivolous of characters, George Eliot has brought forth tones which are far more pathetic than could have been extorted from a nobler type of suffering and penitence, for they seem to attest more solemnly the capacities of all men—of man. The spiritual and the earthly natures find at last a single meeting-point in the infantine cry for divine mercy which poor little Hetty puts forth to Dinah rather than to God. How strange and painful it is to realise that the great author who painted this for us did not herself believe in the divine mercy which she makes Dinah proclaim!

The artistic conditions under which George Eliot works, are, when she chooses, singularly favourable to the exhibition of the only kind of "moral" which a genuine artist should admit. No one now ever thinks of assuming that a writer of fiction lies under any obligation to dispose of his characters exactly as he would perhaps feel inclined to do, if he could determine for them the circumstances of a real instead of an imaginary life. It was a quaint idea of the last generation to suppose that the moral tendency of a tale lay, not in discriminating evil and good, but in the zeal which induced the novelist to provide, before the end of the third volume, for plucking up and burning the tares. But though we have got over that notion, our modern satirists are leading us into the opposite extreme, and trying to convince us that even discrimination itself, in such deep matters, is nearly impossible. The author of *The Mill on the Floss* is hardly exempt from this tendency; but in *Adam Bede* it is not discernible.

The only moral in a fictitious story which can properly be demanded of writers of genius is, *not* to shape their tale this way or that, which they may justly decline to do on artistic grounds, but to discriminate clearly the relative nobility of the characters they do conceive; in other words, to give us light enough in their pictures to let it be clearly seen where the shadows are intended to lie. An artist who leaves it doubtful whether he recognises the distinction between good and evil at all, or who detects in all his characters so much evil that the readers' sympathies must either be entirely passive or side with what is evil, is blind to artistic as well as moral laws. To banish confusion from a picture is the first duty of the artist; and confusion must exist where those lines which are the most essential of all for determining the configuration of human character are invisible or indistinctly drawn. Moreover, I think it may be said, that in painting human nature an artist is bound to give due weight to the motives which would claim authority over him in other acts of his life; and as he would be bound at any time and in any place to do anything in his power to make clear the relation between good and evil, the same motive ought to induce him never to omit in his drawing to put in a light or a shadow which would add to the moral truthfulness of the picture.

But this conceded, an artist must still work according to the conditions of his own genius, and where that genius leads him only to give lively sketches, such as Miss Austen's for example, of the social externals of character, and barely to indicate the interior forces which determine its form and growth, it is unreasonable to expect more than a very superficial moral. Those stories alone can have deep morals which are concerned with the deepest moral phenomena; but where this is so they must show them in their true light. *Adam Bede* may be said to produce in this sense a deeper and nobler moral impression than any other English story of our day. It exhibits in close mutual relations characters of very various degrees of moral depth. It teaches us to discriminate truly between them. It has for its centre-piece one singularly beautiful and bright character which illuminates the whole narrative, and so aids us to realise the good and the evil in all the others; and hence every conscience as well as every imagination gains fresh force and distincter vision from its perusal.

The Mill on the Floss is in every way inferior, in some respects painfully inferior, to *Adam Bede*. It is a masterly fragment of fictitious biography in two volumes, followed by a second-rate one-volume novel, —the three connected into a single whole by very inadequate links. The deeper characters in the tale are not nearly so deep as those in *Adam Bede ;* and the shallower characters do not serve in the same way to bring into relief the nobler characteristics of the deeper. The moral foundations of the story are almost entirely laid on the same dreary level. Moral and spiritual *perspective* there is almost none. The one character which is intended to give depth to and light up the tale, at one time threatens to go out in smoke; and the shadows are anything but clear. There is occasional confusion, both artistic and moral, some exaggeration, and, I think, in the mere physiological attraction felt by the heroine for Stephen Guest, and all but yielded to, there is a serious artistic and moral blot. Yet *The Mill on the Floss* is a book of great genius. Its overflowing humour would alone class its author high among the humorists, and there are some sketches in it of English country life which have all the vivacity and not a little of the power of Sir Walter Scott's best works. The proud, warm-hearted, not very clear-headed miller, whose heart is broken by bankruptcy, and whose spirit is consumed with the thirst for revenge, is a character to live in the imagination. Yet *The Mill on the Floss* is so inferior in art to George Eliot's really greatest works that I may pass on to speak of the tale which, though not her greatest, certainly contains some of her subtlest intellectual studies—I mean *Romola*.

George Eliot's drawings, as I have before intimated, all require a certain space, like Raffael's cartoons, and are not of that kind which produce their effect by the reiteration of scenes each complete in itself. You have to unroll a large surface of the picture before even the smallest *unit* of its effect is attained. And this is far more true of *Romola* than of her English tales. In the latter, the constant and striking delineation of social features with which we are all familiar, satisfies the mind in the detail almost as much as in the complete whole. This cannot be so when even greater power is shown in mastering the life of a foreign nation in a past age. We do not care about the light Florentine buzz with which so great a part of the first volume is filled. Its allusions are half riddles, and its liveliness a blank to us. Small local colours depend for their charm on the familiarity of small local knowledge. Then, again, George Eliot is much greater as an imaginative painter of character than as an imaginative painter of action, and naturally much more inclined for the one than the other. What her characters do is always subordinate with her to what they are. This is the highest artistic power, but it carries its inconveniences with it. She does not carry her readers away, as it is called; it is generally easy to stop reading her; she satisfies you for the moment, and does not make you look forward to the end. She has a touch of Sir

Walter Scott's power to revivify the past, but not Scott's force in making you plunge into it with as headlong an interest as into the present. For this she compensates by a deeper and wider intellectual grasp; but still it is easy enough to understand why half-developed characters, sketched in with unfamiliar local colours on a background of history that has long melted away, should look strange and uninviting, especially when not carried off by any exciting current of events, to the ordinary reader's eye. It is marvellous that, in spite of these disadvantages, the wide and calm imaginative power of the writer should have produced a work which is likely to be permanently celebrated in English literature—in which Italy and England may feel a common pride.

The great artistic purpose of the story is to trace out the conflict between liberal culture and a most passionate form of Christian faith in that strange era (which has so many points of resemblance with the present), when the two in their most characteristic forms struggled for pre-eminence over Florentines who had been educated into the half-pedantic and half-idealistic scholarship of Lorenzo de Medici, who faintly shared the new scientific impulses of the age of Columbus and Copernicus, and whose hearts and consciences were stirred by the preaching, political as well as spiritual, of one of the very greatest as well as earliest of the reformers, the Dominican friar Savonarola. No period could be found when mingling faith and culture effervesced with more curious results. In some great and noble minds the new learning, clearing away the petty rubbish of mediæval superstition, and revealing the severe simplicities of the great age of Greece, grew into a feeling that supplied all the stimulus of fever, if not the rest of faith, and of these the author has drawn a very fine picture in the blind Florentine scholar, Romola's father, Bardo, who, with a restless fire in his heart, "hung over the books and lived with the shadows" all his life. Nothing is more striking and masterly in the story than the subtle skill with which the dominant influence of this scholarship over the imagination of the elder generation of that time—the generation which saw the first revival of learning—is delineated in the pictures of Bardo and Baldassarre. In the former you get something like a glimpse of the stately passion for learning, which, in a later age (though England was then a good deal behind Italy), took so vital a hold of the intellect of Milton, and overlaid his powerful imagination with all its rich fretwork of elaborate classical allusion. In the latter character, Baldassarre, the same impression is conveyed in a still more subtle and striking form, because by painting the intermittent flashes of intellectual power in a scholar's failing memory, and its alternations with an almost animal passion of revenge, we gain not only a more distinct knowledge of the relative value in which scholarship was there and then held as compared with other human attainments, but a novel sense of sympathy, which, in an age of diffused culture like this, it is not very easy to attain, with the extravagance, as we should now think it, of the value attached to the scholar's powers. There are few passages of subtler literary grandeur in English romance than that which paints the electrifying effect of a thrill of vindictive passion on Baldassarre's paralysed memory in recalling once more his full command of Greek learning, and the sense of power which thus returned to him :—

"He leaned to take up the fragments of the dagger; then he turned towards the book which lay open at his side. It was a fine large manuscript, an old volume of Pausanias. The moonlight was upon it, and he could see the large letters at the head of the page:

ΜΕΣΣΗΝΙΚΑ. ΚΒ'.

In old days he had known Pausanias familiarly; yet an hour or two ago he had been looking hopelessly at that page, and it had suggested no more meaning to him than if the letters had been black weather-marks on a wall; but at this moment they were once more the magic signs that conjure up a world. That moonbeam falling on the letters had raised Messenia before him, and its struggle against the Spartan oppression. He snatched up the book, but the light was too pale for him to read further by. No matter; he knew that chapter; he read inwardly. He saw the stoning of the traitor Aristocrates—stoned by a whole people, who cast him out from their borders to lie unburied, and set up a pillar with verses upon it, telling how Time had brought home justice to the unjust. The words arose within him, and stirred innumerable vibrations of memory. He forgot that he was old; he could almost have shouted. The light was come again, mother of knowledge and joy! In that exultation his limbs recovered their strength: he started up with his broken dagger and book, and went out under the broad moonlight. It was a nipping frosty air, but Baldassarre could feel no chill—he only felt the glow of conscious power. He walked about and paused on all the open spots of that high ground, and looked down on the domed and towered city, sleeping darkly under its sleeping guardians, the mountains; on the pale gleam of the river; on the valley vanishing towards the peaks of snow; and felt himself master of them all. That sense of mental empire, which belongs to us all in moments of exceptional clearness, was intensified for him by the long days and nights in which memory had been little more than the consciousness of something gone. That city, which had been a weary labyrinth, was material that he could subdue to his purposes now: his mind glanced through its affairs with flashing conjecture; he was once more a man who knew cities, whose sense of vision was instructed with large experience, and who felt the keen delight of holding all things in the grasp of language. Names! Images!—his mind rushed through its wealth without pausing, like one who enters on a great inheritance."

This passage, taken with those which lead up to it, whether they refer to Bardo or Baldassarre, has the effect of reproducing one great feature in the age of the revival of learning with the finest effect—that sense of large human power which the mastery over a great ancient language, itself the key to a magnificent literature, gave, and which made scholarship then a passion, while with us it has almost relapsed into an antiquarian dry-as-dust pursuit. We realise again, in reading about Bardo and Baldassarre, how, for those times, the first sentence of St. John, "In the beginning was the Word," had regained all its force—to the exclusion, perhaps, of the further assertion that the Word was with God and was God. Man's sense of the great power of language, of which we have now so little, which, indeed, it is the tendency of the present day to depreciate, was in that day full of a new vigour; and to some extent contested with the mysteries of the Gospel the control of great men's souls.

This is the picture which *Romola* makes so living for us. We find here the strife between the keen definite knowledge of the reviving Greek learning, and the visionary mysticism of the reviving Dominican piety. We find a younger generation, represented by Romola, and Dino, and Tito, that has inherited this scholarship, and finds it wholly inadequate for its wants, looking upon that almost as dry bones, which the older generation felt to be stimulating nourishment, and either turning from it, like Dino, to the rapture of mystical asceticism, or using it, like Tito, as a useful sharp-edged tool in the battle of Florentine politics, or trying, like Romola, to turn it to its true purpose, viz. that of clarifying and sifting the false from the true elements in the great faith presented to her conscience by Savonarola. The pride of laborious far-seeing scholarship, gazing with clear, scornful eyes at the inarticulate convulsive ecstasies of faith,—all the powers of language rebelling passionately, as it were, against the deep and fervent passions which transcend the containing powers of language, and boil over its edges, in religious, or even in the opposite animal raptures,—

this is a picture wonderfully painted, and which produces all the more impression, that the minute vivid ripple of the light gossip of the Florentine market-place gives a ground-tone to the book.

This fundamental conflict between the Greek scholarship and the mystical Christian faith which runs through the book is made even more striking by the treacherous character of the man who represents the Greek culture cut adrift from all vestige of moral or religious faith. The fine gradations of social dissimulation so characteristic of Florence in the Mediccan era, ranging from the single politic insincerity of Savonarola, which raises so grand a struggle in his mind, down to the easy-sliding treachery of Tito, bring up before us in another shape the characteristic contrasts of that day between that earnest spirit which revived the old culture because it was *truer* than the degraded current superstitions, —that pliant worldliness which adopted and adapted itself to it, because it was an instrument of finer edge and wider utility,—and lastly, that fervent faith which despised it as substituting the study of a dead past for the great conflict of a living present. Tito's smooth dissimulation is all the more striking a picture, because it comes out as the natural fruit of a mind almost incapable of either strong conviction or strong personal fidelity, gliding about in an age when strong convictions were coming to the birth, and among a race barely redeemed from a spirit of political falsehood (which was just going to be called

Machiavellian) by a proud sense of loyalty to personal and party ties.

Tito is pictured, as the Greeks of that time perhaps deserved to be pictured, not as originally false, but as naturally pleasure-loving, and swerving aside before every unpleasant obstacle in the straight path, at the instance of a quick intelligence and a keen dislike both to personal collisions and to personal sacrifices. His character is, to use a mathematical term, the osculating curve which touches that of each of the others at the surface, and nowhere else— Savonarola's at the point of his external political policy, Romola's in her love of beauty and hatred of the turbid exhalations of visionary excitement, and the scholarly enthusiasm of Bardo only in the apt classical knowledge, by no means in the ardour of his love for it. On Tito's very first entrance to the stage the Florentine artist of the story, Piero di Cosimo, is eager to paint him as a Sinon, not that there is treachery in his face, but that there is in it the softness and suppleness, and gliding ease of movement, and nimbleness of intellect, which, in a time of political passion, seem likely to lead to treachery, because, first, they qualify, both intellectually and morally, for the traitor's part, and next, they serve to mask his play. From this scene, when the fatal ease of the man's manner is first suggested, to the noble scene at the conclusion, in which he sounds, and sounds successfully, Savonarola's too eager statesmanship, with intent to betray him to the Duke of

Milan and the Pope, you see Tito's character grow into the foulest treachery, simply from its consistent desire to compass every pleasant end which suggests itself to him as feasible, without openly facing, if he can help it, any one's severe displeasure.

Nor is anything drawn more finely than the peculiar species of fear which is an essential part of this character,—a fear which, in the last resort, spurs the keen intellect of the man into a certain desperate energy, but which usually remains too cowardly even to understand itself, and lurks on in the character as a kind of unconscious resentment against those who wring from him the exercise of such an energy. A character essentially treacherous only because it is full of soft *fluid* selfishness is one of the most difficult to paint. But whether when locking up the crucifix, which Romola received from her dying brother's hands, in the little temple crowned with the figures of Ariadne and Bacchus, and fondly calling her "Regina mia," which somehow conveys that he less *loves* the woman than passionately admires her,—or buying his "garment of fear," the coat of light chain armour, from the armour-smith,— or faithlessly deceiving the poor little contadina Tessa by the mock marriage at the carnival,—or shrinking before Romola's indignation into that frigid tone of empty affectionateness which is the clearest sign of a contracted heart,—or interpreting the Latin proclamation to the people with a veil of good-nature over his treacherous purpose,—or crowned in the feast at the

Rucellai Gardens, and paling suddenly beneath Baldassarre's vindictive glance,—or petting Tessa and her children in his hiding-place on the hill,—the same wonderful power is maintained throughout, of stamping on our imagination with the full force of a master hand a character which seems naturally too fluent for the artist's purpose. There is not a more masterly piece of painting in English romance than this figure of Tito.

Of Romola it is less easy to say whether one is satisfied or not. The suspicion of hardness of which one is conscious as somewhat detracting from her power, the skill with which the author has prepared us for a mental struggle exactly similar, even in its minutest features, to what might occur to-day between the claims of a sublime faith appealing to the conscience, and a distaste for miracle or vision in its prophet, the striking contrast with Tessa, the ignorant "pretty little pigeon," who thinks every one who is kind to her a saint,—all render it a little difficult to say whether we know her intimately, or whether we have only a very artistic idea of what she is *not*, and what she *is* only by inference and contrast. My own feeling is that Romola is the least perfect figure in the book,—that she is a shade more modernised than the others, several shades less individual, and, after all, though the pivot of her character turns, as it were, on faith, that she does not distinctly show any faith except that which George Eliot owned herself, the faith in rigid honour, in human pity, and partially also in Savonarola's personal greatness and power. I do not say the character is not natural,—I only say it is half-revealed and more suggested than fully painted, though these harder feminine characters always seem to ask to be outlined more strongly than any others.

The portrait of Savonarola produces a greater effect on the first reading than it does on the memory and judgment. It is impressive, but it cannot compare for a moment with Scott's great historical portraits. It does not live in the memory. We are intended to see a large human-hearted Italian Luther, narrower than Luther on some sides, owing to the thin Medicean culture against which he led the reaction, but with a far more statesmanlike and political purpose, and far more fiery imagination,— the same, in fact, whom Mr. Maurice has intellectually delineated with so much delicate fidelity in his history of modern philosophy, and who paints himself in almost everything he wrote, but who yet, even in this book, is hardly so presented as to live before us. But there are passages of great power. Nothing can be finer and more impressive—nothing more difficult to make fine and impressive—than Savonarola's exhortation to Romola to return to the home from which she was flying. You see in it the man's profound trust in God, as the author of all human ties and of all social and political ties, breaking through the fetters of his Dominican order, and asserting the divine order in Nature rather than the divine order out of Nature. This, however, is not the most characteristic side of the study. George Eliot was too sceptical at heart to desire to paint a finer picture of the believer than of the half-believer. And she threw her whole mind into the profoundly pathetic scene in which Savonarola, having in the fervour of his eloquence committed God to working him a miracle at the right moment, is brought to book both by his enemies and friends on the question of the trial by fire, and kneels in prayer that in fact refuses to be prayer, but rises into a political debate within himself as to the policy of seeming to take a step which he knows he must somehow evade. "While his lips were uttering audibly '*cor mundum crea in me*,' his mind was still filled with the images of the snare his enemies had prepared for him, still busy with the arguments by which he could justify himself against their taunts and accusations." The scene is too long to snatch from the context, and is, indeed, closely bound up with the picture of the encounter with Tito which follows. George Eliot rejected apparently the authenticity of the last great words attributed to Savonarola as he is dying on the scaffold, which Mr. Maurice accepts. "The voice of the Papal emissary," says the historian of philosophy, "was heard proclaiming that Savonarola was cut off from the Church militant and triumphant. Another voice was heard saying, 'No, not from the Church triumphant, they cannot shut me out of that.'" It is not surprising that she rejected the evidence for these words. Yet they would have formed a far higher artistic ending to her story than the somewhat feeble and womanish chapter with which it concludes,—the chief blot on the book. Large and genial as was George Eliot's sympathy with Savonarola, she had, of course, no wish to represent his faith as triumphant. Yet Romola's faith in goodness and self-sacrifice, and in little children and "the eternal marriage of love and duty," etc. etc., which the proem tells us is ever to last, would be an idle dream for the world, without a Christ in whose eternal nature all these realities live and grow. George Eliot's conception of the great Reformer probably lost power in consequence of her own deep distrust of religious faith and her reluctance to conceive of it except as a kind of noble self-deception.

Felix Holt contains so little new illustration of George Eliot's genius beyond the fragments of poetry which first taught most of us to understand the poetic side of her imagination, that I will pass it by to speak of *Middlemarch*, which, with its very inferior successor, *Daniel Deronda*, represents her most mature and most characteristic style of art. In *Middlemarch* for the first time George Eliot's deep scepticism may be said to have been openly confessed. At least read by the side of her biography and letters, it is clear that the "prelude" to *Middlemarch* implies a confession that in her belief no Providence guides human destinies. The story itself gains in more respects, I think, than it loses, from this comparative frankness of intellectual purpose. None of George Eliot's tales can compare with *Middlemarch* for delicacy of detail and completeness of finish—completeness as regards not only the individual figures, but the whole picture of life delineated—and for the breadth of life brought within the field of the story. It is, no doubt, as a story, inferior both to *Adam Bede* and to *Silas Marner*, the latter a perfect little gem of its kind, in which the author has done what is so rare with her, sacrificed something of her own deep feeling of the unsatisfactoriness of real life to the ideal demand for "poetical justice," by rounding off the events somewhat more ideally than human lots are usually rounded off, in harmony with the author's and reader's inward sense of moral fitness, and scarcely in harmony with the average teaching of vigilant observation. And yet, even in *Silas Marner*, she has left a certain spring of unhealed and undeserved pain to remind us of the deep unsatisfactoriness of human things; in the catastrophe of *Adam Bede*, we hardly know whether she has not left more rankling pain than satisfaction; and in *Romola*, the sense of foiled aims and wrecked purposes unquestionably predominates, so that we can hardly help thinking she was drawn to the subject of *Romola* by perceiving a certain similarity between the spiritual illusions of the age of the great Dominican heretic and our own—a similarity which enables her to paint a great historical theme in her own favourite melancholy tone, without any violence to nature. Again, in *Middlemarch*, George Eliot set herself, from the very beginning, to illustrate her own profound conviction that the noblest aims, however faithfully and simply pursued, are apt to be wrecked, at least to outward seeming, in this our modern age of distracted life. She set herself to paint by no means a tragedy, but what she herself described as "a life of mistakes, the offspring of a certain spiritual grandeur, ill-matched with the meanness of opportunity." And what she lost in beauty and in grandeur of effect by this deliberate aim she gained in ease, and in the obviously greater accordance between her array of intellectual and moral assumptions, and her artistic treatment of them. We feel that the inmost mind of the writer was reflected, not merely in the criticisms and the casual observations of the tale, but in the tale itself; we feel throughout the painful sincerity which underlies both the humour and the sarcasm; we feel the desolateness of the formative thought as well as the root of its bitterness, and yet we never cease to feel the author's extraordinary fidelity to her own moral aims. *Middlemarch* is, as the preface (unfortunately called a "prelude") pretty plainly confesses, a sort of pictorial indictment of modern society for the crippling conditions it imposes on men and women, especially women, of high ideal enthusiasm. In consequence of the very aim of the tale, it could hardly be a satisfying imaginative whole, either tragic or otherwise; for the object is to paint not the grand defeat, but the helpless entanglement and miscarriage, of noble aims; to make us see the eager stream of high purpose, not leaping destructively from the rock, but more or less silted up, though not quite lost, in the dreary sands of modern life.

The very nature of this conception, while it ensured a certain vein of melancholy and even bitterness in the story, gave George Eliot's genius a fuller play than it had ever had for its predominant realism, and also for that minute knowledge of the whole moral field of modern life which alone tests the strength of a realistic genius. It was impossible to show how ideal aims could be frustrated and overborne by the mere want of room for them, and the crowd of pettier thoughts and hopes in the society in which they were conceived, without a broad canvas and great variety of grouping; and this is exactly where George Eliot excels. To any one who can endure the melancholy which is rather to be read between the lines than ostentatiously paraded, to any one who either does not constantly ask himself how this great author is really conceiving the ultimate problems of faith and duty, or who, if understanding fully the nature of her answer, is steeled against the pain it is liable to give,—the wonderful freshness and variety of the pictures of county character (high and low), the perfect drawing and bold outlines of her figures, and the minute delicacy of the lights and shades, the abundant humour, the caustic philosophy, and the deep undertone of unsatisfied desire, will give, if certainly not pure delight, all the pleasure which can be derived from profound and unaffected admiration. As the object in this tale was to show the paralysis, and the misleading diversions from its natural course, which a blunt and unsympathetic world prepares for the noblest ideality of feeling that is not in sympathy with it, it was essential for the author to give such a solidity and complexity to her picture of the world by which her hero's and heroine's idealism was to be tested and more or less subdued, as would justify the impression that she understood fully the character of the struggle. I doubt if any other novelist who ever wrote could have succeeded equally well in this melancholy design, could have framed as complete a picture of the English county and county-town temper, with all its rigidities, jealousies, and pettiness, with its thorough good-nature, stereotyped habits of thought, and very limited accessibility to higher ideas, and have threaded all these pictures together by a story, if not of the deepest interest, still admirably fitted for its peculiar purpose of showing how unplastic is such an age as ours to the glowing emotion of an ideal purpose.

For melancholy, profoundly melancholy, both in aim and execution, *Middlemarch* certainly is; not that either hero or heroine dies within its limits; on the contrary, the only deaths are deaths of people profoundly indifferent or disagreeable to the reader. And the heroine, though she makes a sad blunder in her first marriage, marries the only man she has ever loved at the end of the tale. Nay, there is another love affair, which eventually prospers well, running through the tale; and the only characters of any moment which are left in a certain cheerless solitude at the close, are those of the young surgeon who has married the woman of his choice, but found the choice a fatal mistake for himself, and of the middle-aged and very Broad Church vicar, who shows to much more advantage in giving up his love than he could have shown in urging it, and who is made the occasion of giving us, perhaps, the only really satisfying emotion which the story excites. The melancholy of the story consists not in the catastrophes of fortune, but in the working out of the design with which the author set out—the picture "of the cygnet reared uneasily among the ducklings in the brown pond, and who never finds the living stream in fellowship with its own oary-footed kind;" in the delineation of what George Eliot (with a sentimentalism and disposition to "gush," of which she is rarely guilty) calls the "loving heart-beats and sobs after an unattained goodness," which "tremble off and are dispersed among hindrances instead of centring in some long-recognisable deed." The object of the book is gained by showing in Dorothea's case that a rare nature of the most self-forgetting kind, and the most enthusiastic love for the good and beautiful, is rather more likely to blunder, in its way through the world, than one of much lower moral calibre — which is probable enough; and also by showing that this rare nature does not find any satisfying inward life to compensate these blunders,

and turn them into the conditions of purer strength
and less accidental happiness—which I should have
thought impossible; and again in Lydgate's case, by
showing that an ardent love for truth—of the purely
intellectual kind—is liable to be betrayed, by the
commonplace good-nature with which it is often
combined, into a paralysing contact with sordid cares
and domestic trials—which, again, is probable enough;
and finally, by showing that this love of truth is not
transmuted into any higher moral equivalent through
the noble and genuine self-denial of the sacrifice made
for another's good—which, again, I should have held
to be impossible. That Lydgate, marrying as he did,
and with his wholesome nature, should before long
have merged the gratification of his disinterested
speculative passion in the necessity of considering
the happiness of his shallow-natured wife, is most true
to nature. That, in pursuing that course from the
high and right motive from which, on the whole, he
pursued it, he should have gained no new power over
either her or himself, but should have become bitter
on his side, and left her as vain and shallow as he
found her, is, I think, not true to nature, but a picture
due to that set theory of semi-pessimism which George
Eliot evidently regarded as the best substitute for
faith. It is only here and there, in the rare glimpses
she gives us of the solitude of Dorothea's heart, that
this radical deficiency of faith is carried, as it seems
to me, into any touch untrue to what we know of
real life. It does so come out, I think, in one or two

descriptions of Dorothea's secret struggles, and in the bitter tone in which the close of Lydgate's career is described. Generally, however, nothing can be more truthful or less like preconceived theory than the pictures of provincial life in this wonderful book. But not the less does this deep distrust of "the Supreme Power," who, in the words of the "prelude" to *Middlemarch*, has fashioned the natures of women " with inconvenient indefiniteness," give a certain air of moral desolation to the whole, and make us feel how objectless is that network of complicated motives and grotesque manners, of which she gives us so wonderfully truthful a picture—objectless as those strange scrawlings on the bare mountain-side which, mistaken when seen from a distance for the handwriting of some gigantic power, turn out when approached to be the mere tracks of old destructive forces, since diverted into other channels—the furrows of dried-up torrents or the grooves of exhausted glaciers.

By far the most remarkable *effort* in *Middlemarch* —I am by no means sure that the success is at all in proportion to the effort, though the success is considerable, and one which only a mind of great genius could have attained—is, of course, the sketch of Dorothea Brooke (as she is at the beginning of the tale), Dorothea Casaubon (as she is throughout its greater portion), Dorothea Ladislaw (as she is at its close). One sees, on looking back over the tale, that it was an essential of George Eliot's purpose to make this high-minded and enthusiastic girl marry twice, and in *neither* case make an "ideal" marriage, though the second is an improvement on the first. The author, indeed, attempted at the close, at least in her original edition,[1] to ascribe the first mistake partly to causes which she had never before indicated, and in so doing made, as I think, a faulty criticism on her own creation. She attenuated Dorothea's own responsibility for her first marriage after a fashion hardly consistent either with the type of the character itself, or with the story as it had been told.

"Dorothea," we are told, "was spoken of to a younger generation as a fine girl, who married a sickly clergyman, old enough to be her father, and in little more than a year after his death gave up her estate to marry his cousin —young enough to have been his son, with no property, and not well born. Those who had not seen anything of Dorothea usually observed that she could not have been 'a nice woman,' else she would not have married either the one or the other. Certainly those determining acts of her life were not ideally beautiful. [They were the mixed result of young and noble impulse struggling under prosaic conditions. Among the many remarks passed on her mistakes, it was never said in the neighbourhood of Middlemarch that such mistakes could not have happened if the society into which she was born had not smiled on propositions of marriage from a sickly man to a girl less than half his own age, on modes of education which make a woman's knowledge another name for motley ignorance,

---

[1] I am much obliged to a correspondent who has called my attention to the fact that George Eliot withdrew the passage I refer to in her one volume edition of *Middlemarch*.

on rules of conduct which are in flat contradiction with its own loudly-asserted beliefs. While this is the social air in which mortals begin to breathe, there will be collisions such as those in Dorothea's life, where great feelings will take the aspect of error, and great faith the aspect of illusion.[1] For there is no creature whose inward being is so strong that it is not greatly determined by what lies outside it. A new Theresa will hardly have the opportunity of reforming a conventual life, any more than a new Antigone will spend her heroic piety in daring all for the sake of a brother's burial; the medium in which their ardent deeds took shape is for ever gone. But we insignificant people, with our daily words and acts, are preparing the lives of many Dorotheas, some of which may present a far sadder sacrifice than that of the Dorothea whose story we know. Her finely-touched spirit had still its fine issues, though they were not widely visible. Her full nature, like that river of which Alexander broke the strength, spent itself in channels which had no great name on the earth. But the effect of her being on those around her was incalculably diffusive; for the growing good of the world is partly dependent on unhistoric acts; and that things are not so ill with you and me as they might have been, is half owing to the number who lived faithfully a hidden life, and rest in unvisited tombs."

Now, the remark as to the world's "smiling on a proposition of marriage from a sickly man to a girl less than half his own age," really has no foundation

---

[1] In the one volume edition of *Middlemarch*, the passage within square brackets reads as follows: — "They were the mixed result of young and noble impulse struggling amidst the conditions of an imperfect social state, in which great feelings will often take the aspect of error, and great faith the aspect of illusion."

at all in the tale itself. When Mr. Brooke, Dorothea's uncle, weakly carries Mr. Casaubon's offer to Dorothea, he accompanies it with as much slipshod dissuasion as it is possible for so helpless a nature to use. Dorothea's sister Celia hears of it with an ill-disguised horror of disgust which bitterly offends Dorothea. If the rector's wife, Mrs. Cadwallader, represents county opinion (and who could represent it better?), the whole society disapproved it. Would George Eliot have had orphan girls protected against the weakness of such uncles as Mr. Brooke by the Court of Chancery, or would she have liked to see a law fixing the maximum difference of ages permissible between husband and wife? I hardly see how Dorothea could have been better protected against her first mistake than the picture which she painted of life in Middlemarch represented her as having actually been protected. I note this point only because I find in this passage a trace that George Eliot was, on reviewing her own work, dissatisfied with her own picture of the "prosaic conditions" to which she ascribed Dorothea's misadventures; and that she tried to persuade herself that they were actually more oppressive and paralysing than they really were. It is obvious, I think, that Dorothea's character was one of much more impetuous self-assertion, of much more adventurous and self-willed idealism, than this passage would suggest. She is painted from the first as groping her way with an imperious disregard of the prevailing conventional ideas,—ideas quite too mean and barren for the guidance of such a nature,—and as falling, in consequence of that imperious disregard, into her mistake —the mistake being due about equally to her hasty contempt for the existing social standards of conduct, and to her craving for nobler standards not supplied. It was rather the ambitious idealism and somewhat wilful independence of Dorothea's nature than any want of a sound general opinion about the matter, which is represented as leading her into the mistake of her marriage with the pedantic bookworm, Mr. Casaubon; and George Eliot was not fair to the life she had so wonderfully portrayed, when she threw the responsibility of Dorothea's first great mistake upon it. In the early part of the tale, George Eliot clearly intended to charge the society around Dorothea with sins of omission rather than sins of commission; with having no noble aims to which such a nature as Dorothea's could dedicate itself with any satisfaction, rather than with failing to have a certain "bottom of good sense," which might have saved her from her blunder, if she could but have shared it without losing anything in ideal purpose by sharing it. But in her final criticism of her heroine the author, in her desire to apologise for her, wavered in her conception, and instead of charging her failure, as at the start, on "the meanness of opportunity," charged it on the positive distortion of the social morality by which she was surrounded—a distortion which in her own picture she had not only forgotten to describe, but had carefully proved not to exist. This little inconsistency is important only as showing that George Eliot had unconsciously, in the course of her story, aggravated the faults of the society against which she brought her indictment both at the beginning and the close—a tendency which attaches more or less to her very negative spiritual philosophy. Faith is wanted in order to make people perfectly candid about the blots in human ideals. A frequent tendency may be noted in those who find no anchor for faith, to throw upon some abstract offender like "society" the faults they see in those who most satisfy their longing for perfection. It is only profound belief in God which prevents us from indulging our moral superstitions about our human ideals, or, as one may almost call them, the idols of one's conscience.

Nevertheless, after all such deductions, the character of Dorothea is very noble, after an original type. She is introduced to us as an enthusiastic girl, with high impulses which were a little unintelligible to the people around her, "a young lady of some birth and fortune, who knelt suddenly down on a brick floor by the side of a sick labourer, and prayed fervidly as if she thought herself living in the time of the Apostles; who had strange whims of fasting like a Papist, and of sitting up at night to read old theological books;" who indulged herself in riding, "in spite of some conscientious qualms;" for "she felt that she enjoyed it in a pagan sensuous way, and always looked forward to renouncing it." She is "open, ardent, and not in

the least self-admiring"; a purist in her dislike of
ornament for herself, but ever eager to indulge her
sister (Celia) in it, though somewhat astonished by
her taste, and obliged to apologise for her to her
own mind by the remark that "souls have com-
plexions" as well as skins, and that "what will suit
one will not suit another." The scene to which I
allude, the first in the book, gives a most skilful
artistic portrait of Dorothea's enthusiastic and mystic
and slightly haughty, though generous nature, and
I must extract a portion at the close, in order to
bring this fresh and ardent character clearly before
my readers :—

"Celia had unclasped the necklace, and drawn it off.
'It would be a little tight for your neck; something to
lie down and hang would suit you better,' she said, with
some satisfaction. The complete unfitness of the necklace
from all points of view for Dorothea made Celia happier
in taking it. She was opening some ring-boxes which
disclosed a fine emerald with diamonds, and just then the
sun passing beyond a cloud sent a bright gleam over the
table.

"'How very beautiful these gems are!' said Dorothea,
under a new current of feeling, as sudden as the gleam.
'It is strange how deeply colours seem to penetrate one,
like scent. I suppose that is the reason why gems are
used as spiritual emblems in the Revelation of St. John.
They look like fragments of heaven. I think that
emerald is more beautiful than any of them.'

"'And there is a bracelet to match it,' said Celia.
'We did not notice this at first.'

"'They are lovely,' said Dorothea, slipping the ring
and bracelet on her finely-turned finger and wrist, and

holding them towards the window on a level with her eyes. All the while her thought was trying to justify her delight in the colours by merging them in her mystic religious joy.

"'You *would* like those, Dorothea,' said Celia, rather falteringly, beginning to think with wonder that her sister showed some weakness, and also that emeralds would suit her own complexion even better than purple amethysts. 'You must keep that ring and bracelet—if nothing else. But see, these agates are very pretty—and quiet.'

"'Yes! I will keep these—this ring and bracelet,' said Dorothea. Then, letting her hand fall on the table, she said in another tone—'Yet what miserable men find such things, and work at them, and sell them!' She paused again, and Celia thought that her sister was going to renounce the ornaments, as in consistency she ought to do.

"'Yes, dear, I will keep these,' said Dorothea decidedly; 'but take all the rest away, and the casket.'

"'She took up her pencil without removing the jewels, and still looking at them. She thought of often having them by her, to feed her eye at these little fountains of pure colour.

"'Shall you wear them in company?' said Celia, who was watching her with real curiosity as to what she would do.

"Dorothea glanced quickly at her sister. Across all her imaginative adornment of those whom she loved there darted now and then a keen discernment, which was not without a scorching quality. If Miss Brooke ever attained perfect meekness, it would not be for lack of inward fire.

"'Perhaps,' she said, rather haughtily. 'I cannot tell to what level I may sink.'

"Celia blushed, and was unhappy; she saw that she had offended her sister, and dared not say even anything pretty about the gift of the ornaments, which she put back into the box and carried away. Dorothea, too, was unhappy, as she went on with her plan-drawing, questioning the purity of her own feeling and speech in the scene which had ended with that little explosion."

Farther on we are told of this generous and buoyant girl that—

"Dorothea, with all her eagerness to know the truths of life, retained very childlike ideas about marriage. She felt sure that she would have accepted the judicious Hooker, if she had been born in time to save him from that wretched mistake he made in matrimony; or John Milton when his blindness had come on; or any of the other great men whose odd habits it would have been glorious piety to endure; but an amiable handsome baronet, who said 'Exactly' to her remarks, even when she expressed uncertainty,—how could he affect her as a lover? The really delightful marriage must be that where your husband was a sort of father, and could teach you even Hebrew, if you wished it."

Now it is the main idea of this book to work out the mal-adaptation, as it were, of this fresh, disinterested, and spiritual-minded girl, to the world into which she was born; to show that instead of giving her a full natural channel for her enthusiasm, and opening to her a career as large as her heart and mind, it, for a time at least, absorbed her great qualities in futile and fruitless efforts, which left hardly any one but herself the better for them; that it made her the victim of a sort of irony of destiny, gave her no chance of marriage with the one man— living in her neighbourhood and in circles where they frequently crossed each other's paths—whom she could perhaps have helped to something great and noble,

and left her, even at the close, in no position better
adapted to her rare qualities than that of a wife
of a clever, mercurial, petulant young politician, not
without good in him, but without any signal need of
the help of such a woman as this, a woman who, as
his wife, came to be "only known in a certain circle
as a wife and mother." Yet no one who knew
George Eliot will suppose that this history is meant to
throw any doubt on the intrinsic value of high moral
qualities. However negative her spiritual creed may
have been, her ethics were always noble. She makes
us feel with increasing force, as the story goes on, the
intrinsic grandeur of Dorothea's capacity for self-
forgetfulness, sympathy, and love. The story does
not end without one signal triumph of the purity of
her unselfish purpose over poorer and meaner natures,
a triumph painted in a scene that deserves to rank
for power beside that in which Dinah wins her victory over Hetty's guilty heart in *Adam Bede*. But
while true as ever to her own passionate love of a
deep and inward morality, George Eliot's main purpose was to show how ill-suited this world is to detect
the highest natures that find their way into it, and
to use them for the highest ends. Dorothea's desire
to devote herself to some one wiser than herself
leads her into marrying the Rev. Edward Casaubon,
a middle-aged, reserved, vain, and dry clergyman,
given to laborious researches into a somewhat vague
science, Comparative Mythology, for the full treatment of which he does not possess the adequate

Oriental learning, nor even access to the German authorities who had made that learning their own. He acts upon Dorothea as a mere moral sponge, to absorb all the finer juices of her nature without being the happier or the better for them—rather, perhaps, the more irritable, and the worse. Her intellectual brightness, her power of perceiving that he himself distrusts his own power for his task, daunts him, and makes him feel under a sort of intellectual surveillance. Her ardent sympathy with his poor cousin, Mr. Ladislaw, and wish to befriend him, make Mr. Casaubon jealous, and dimly conscious of his own narrowness of nature. Her desire to share his deepest life makes him painfully conscious that he has no deepest life to be shared. Her ardour is a reproach to his formalism. Her enthusiasm is bewildering to his self-occupation. They lead together a life of mutual disappointment, in which her self-forgetful compassion for his broken health and his fear of intellectual wreck gradually overpower her own regrets, and she is on the very eve of promising him to carry out after his death, from his voluminous notes, his hopeless intellectual design,—without the slightest remaining faith, on her part, in its value,—when his sudden death relieves her of the necessity of making the fatal promise. Nothing can be finer than the picture of their mutual relations to each other; his reserved pride, her disappointed tenderness; his formal kindness and suspicious vigilance in watching the signs of his wife's distrust of his powers, her sickness of heart when she first begins to understand that his work will come to nothing, and to desire to give him a sympathy he cannot and will not receive. It is a picture such as no one but George Eliot could draw. And the delicate touch with which it is concluded, when she declines, after his death, to carry out his plan according to the "Synoptical Tabulation for the use of Mrs. Casaubon" found in his desk, is one of those signal marks of great genius in which, even taken alone, you would at once discern the master-hand. His "Synoptical Tabulation" she "carefully enclosed and sealed, writing within the envelope, '*I could not use it. Do you not see now that I could not submit my soul to yours, by working hopelessly at what I have no belief in?—Dorothea.*' Then she deposited the paper in her own desk." Here we see that great need of Dorothea for distinctness of feeling, which separates her from so many idealists of the same type. Instead of shrinking from the subject of the trust her dead husband wished to repose in her, and which she could not accept, she felt the need to put down distinctly for him, even though his presence was only imagined, the answer of her heart. She could not leave him without an answer altogether. But she could not but refuse what he had asked. As a whole, the picture, however, is, and is meant to be, one of moral *waste*,—of a rich and generous and buoyant nature wasted on one which was only rendered restless and exhausted by intercourse with her. Nor is the picture of Dorothea's relation to

Mr. Casaubon's young cousin, Mr. Ladislaw, whom her husband forbade her, by his will, to marry on pain of his property going away from her, at all a moral compensation. It is true that his love for her is ardent, though not self-forgetful; but her interest in him is chiefly due to Mr. Casaubon's indifference and apparent injustice, and her love begins only after her attention is painfully called to the subject by the revelation of her husband's suspicions in his will. She lavishes herself on Will Ladislaw as a sort of generous compensation for his own relation's coldness to him; and one feels, and is probably meant to feel acutely, that here, too, it is "the meanness of opportunity," and not intrinsic suitability, which determines Dorothea's second comparatively happy marriage. The world around her is a sponge to absorb Dorothea's great qualities, without profiting by them and without providing any adequate sphere for their expansion and their refinement.

It may be said that in one signal and final instance, George Eliot has given Dorothea the victory over the selfishness of others through the victory over herself; and so, at the end of her tale, has left her beautiful heroine enveloped in the imagination of the reader in a pure and radiant glory. And it is perfectly true that in this one instance she shows a spiritual grandeur *not* "ill-matched with the meanness of opportunity," but, on the contrary, well-matched with the nobleness of opportunity, and so far satisfying, even to the imagination. But even in the instance to which we refer, there is a void which it is impossible not to feel—an intentional and painful void in the background of the picture, which leaves upon us the oppressive sense that Dorothea's fine religious nature had no inward spiritual object on which to feed itself, no object in relation to which its invisible growth would be assured and permanent even when the outward world failed to call into full play her stores of spiritual compassion. But to justify this remark I must say something of the wonderful pendant or companion picture to Dorothea—Rosamond Vincy, afterwards Rosamond Lydgate.

No one has ever so drawn the cruelty that springs from pure thinness and shallowness of nature, and yet given that cruelty so delicate and feminine an embodiment, as George Eliot in her marvellous picture of Rosamond. This exquisitely-painted figure is the deadliest blow at the common assumption that limitation in both heart and brain is a desirable thing for women that has ever been struck. The first impression is of grace, gentleness, propriety, conventional sense, soft tenacity of purpose, and something even that almost looks like tenderness. I refer to the time when Rosamond first falls in love with Lydgate. The reader is even a little disposed at this time to resent the author's evident scorn for Rosamond, and almost to take her part against the critic who seems to have hardened her heart against her own creation. But as the story proceeds, when Rosamond is married, when Lydgate gradually falls into money difficulties, and his graceful wife shows herself not only not able to give him sympathy, but constrained, apparently by her mere poverty of nature, to turn her heart away from him, and even to intrigue against his plans, the picture becomes painfully real and convincing. The reader has no power to doubt its fidelity. The cruelty of a shallow heart in woman has been painted a hundred times on its active side— in its love of power, its delight in admiration, its malicious vivacity. But it has never, as far as I know, been painted entirely in its passive phase, its absolute incompressibility—like the incompressibility of water itself,—its cold aversion to any one, however conventionally dear, who, after being expected to be a source of pride and lustre, turns out to be in need of active sacrifices and of some spontaneousness of sympathy. Rosamond's helpless *finesse*, and mild, but stony-hearted irresponsiveness to her husband's appeals, her unashamed insincerity, her unyielding passiveness, and her perfect confidence in the wisdom of her own wishes in spite of her total inability to understand what is necessary to be understood, make up a startling picture of the unconscious but cruel inexorability of feminine selfishness, and of fair incapacity to understand and feel. The art which has contrasted this picture of Rosamond with that of Dorothea it is not easy to overpraise. The rich spontaneous pity and sympathy of Dorothea are thrown into relief by that poverty of heart of Rosamond which is not even stirred by the most touching appeals of Lydgate's generous self-reproach. The deep, impulsive sincerity of Dorothea is thrown into like relief by that absolute absence of all compunction, of all discomposure, in insincerity, which Rosamond shows in hiding from her husband her counter-plots against his plans. Dorothea's perfect indifference to the world and rank is in striking contrast to poor Rosamond's positive pining after the society of titled people and the little excitements of social esteem. Dorothea's disposition to lavish herself and her means on others is in most curious contrast of all to Rosamond's constant wish to get others to devote their means to her. In short, it is impossible to conceive a finer foil to Dorothea than Rosamond. The realism of the portrait of Rosamond engrosses the imagination even more completely than the noble freshness and living ardour of Dorothea. But though to some extent they cross each other in the story—Rosamond wishing to detach Ladislaw from his love for Dorothea—they hardly meet, in any real contact of mind, till just at the close. And that meeting is a scene of surpassing power. Dorothea, then a widow, assured, as she thinks, of Ladislaw's love for her, is bent on helping Lydgate, who, in the difficulties and false suspicions which have fallen on him, has just given her a glimpse of his wife's inability to understand his position; she has called on Rosamond, and found her own lover, Ladislaw, apparently bending in a lover-like attitude over Rosamond's hand, and has quitted the room, indignant and heart-broken. The night of anguish she passes after this scene, is most powerfully described (though, by the way, with one false note: when did we ever before hear so true and refined a writer as George Eliot gushing about Dorothea's "grand woman's frame," like a sentimental poetaster?); but the victory she gains over herself seems to me a victory that, in such a one as Dorothea at all events, could not have been gained without something more than a bare moral struggle. We have been told indeed that she who used to fall suddenly on her knees on the brick floors of cottages to pray with sick labourers had almost given up praying for herself, but we have not been told that she had been overtaken by any deep speculative doubts; and unless this were so, nay, even if it were so, the conflict of this night could hardly have passed through in the cold moral solitude described; so that there is a painful void, no less artistic than spiritual, to my mind, in reading the following powerful but crippled picture of Dorothea's moral crisis:—

"In that hour she repeated what the merciful eyes of solitude have looked on for ages in the spiritual struggles of man—she besought hardness and coldness and aching weariness to bring her relief from the mysterious incorporeal might of her anguish: she lay on the bare floor and let the night grow cold around her; while her grand woman's frame was shaken by sobs as if she had been a despairing child.

"There were two images—two living forms that tore her heart in two, as if it had been the heart of a mother who seems to see her child divided by the sword, and presses one bleeding half to her breast while her gaze goes forth in agony towards the half which is carried away by the lying woman that has never known the mother's pang.

"Here, with the nearness of an answering smile, here within the vibrating bond of mutual speech, was the bright creature whom she had trusted—who had come to her like the spirit of morning visiting the dim vault where she sat as the bride of a worn-out life; and now, with a full consciousness which had never awakened before, she stretched out her arms towards him and cried with bitter cries that their nearness was a parting vision; she discovered her passion to herself in the unshrinking utterance of despair.

"And there, aloof, yet persistently with her, moving wherever she moved, was the Will Ladislaw who was a changed belief exhausted of hope, a detected illusion—no, a living man towards whom there could not yet struggle any wail of regretful pity, from the midst of scorn and indignation and jealous offended pride. The fire of Dorothea's anger was not easily spent, and it flamed out in fitful returns of spurning reproach. Why had he come obtruding his life into hers, hers that might have been whole enough without him? Why had he brought his cheap regard and his lip-born words to her who had nothing paltry to give in exchange? He knew that he was deluding her—wished, in the very moment of farewell, to make her believe that he gave her the whole price of her heart, and knew that he had spent it half before. Why had he not stayed among the crowd of whom she asked nothing —but only prayed that they might be less contemptible?

"But she lost energy at last even for her loud-whispered cries and moans; she subsided into helpless sobs, and on the cold floor she sobbed herself to sleep.

"In the chill hours of the morning twilight, when all was dim around her, she awoke—not with any amazed wondering where she was or what had happened, but with the clearest consciousness that she was looking into the eyes of sorrow. She rose, and wrapped warm things around her, and seated herself in a great chair where she often watched before. She was vigorous enough to have borne that hard night without feeling ill in body, beyond some aching and fatigue; but she had waked to a new condition: she felt as if her soul had been liberated from its terrible conflict; she was no longer wrestling with her grief, but could sit down with it as a lasting companion and make it a sharer in her thoughts. For now the thoughts came thickly. It was not in Dorothea's nature, for longer than the duration of a paroxysm, to sit in the narrow cell of her calamity, in the besotted misery of a consciousness that only sees another's lot as an accident of its own.

"She began now to live through that yesterday morning deliberately again, forcing herself to dwell on every detail and its possible meaning. Was she alone in that scene? Was it her event only? She forced herself to think of it as bound up with another woman's life—a woman towards whom she had set out with a longing to carry some clearness and comfort into her beclouded youth. In her first outleap of jealous indignation and disgust, when quitting the hateful room, she had flung away all the mercy with which she had undertaken that visit. She had enveloped both Will and Rosamond in her burning scorn, and it seemed to her as if Rosamond were burned out of her sight for ever. But that base prompting which makes a woman more cruel to her rival than to a faithless lover, could have no strength of recurrence in Dorothea when the dominant spirit of justice within her had once overcome the tumult and had once shown her the truer measure of things. All the active thought with which she had before been representing to herself the trials of Lydgate's lot, and this young marriage union which, like her own, seemed to have its hidden as well as evident troubles—all this vivid sympathetic experience returned to her now as a power: it asserted itself as acquired knowledge asserts itself, and will not let us see as we saw in the day of our ignorance. She said to her own irremediable grief, that it should make her more helpful, instead of driving her back from effort.

"And what sort of crisis might not this be in three lives whose contact with hers laid an obligation on her as if they had been suppliants bearing the sacred branch? The objects of her rescue were not to be sought out by her fancy; they were chosen for her. She yearned towards the perfect Right, that it might make a throne within her, and rule her errant will. 'What should I do—how should I act now, this very day, if I could clutch my own pain, and compel it to silence, and think of those three?'"

This picture leaves a sense of want in the mind of the reader that survives even the powerful and pathetic scene of Dorothea's victory over Rosamond, a scene that, as I have already said, challenges comparison with that in which Dinah succeeds in touching Hetty's heart in *Adam Bede*. There is left upon us that for which the previous course of the tale had been preparing us, a conviction not only that Dorothea's life had been crippled by a "meanness of opportunity" sadly ill-matched with her spiritual grandeur, but also that that "meanness of opportunity" had been gradually extending inwards, as well as imprisoning her from outside. There is no such thing as inward "meanness of opportunity" to one who has a life hidden in God as well as a life spent upon the world. That is a resource and a refuge, the grandeur of which is always on the increase, and is sometimes greatest of all when the outward field of opportunity is poorest. With this inward source of joy for Dorothea, one might have left her, even if Will Ladislaw had really failed her, with composure, with that sense of rest which even Greek tragedy, with its far fainter spiritual insights, always gives. But, without it, to know that she married after her first husband's death the young man whom her own generosity had first taught her to love, that she was recognised "in a certain circle as a wife and mother," and that she fascinated all who really came to know her, and even by poor shallow Rosamond was never mentioned with depreciation, is a poor, ungracious, and unhappy close to a delineation of great power. "Meanness of opportunity" does not really win the victory—Dorothea is too noble for that; but it does, in the picture at least, finally circumscribe and cripple a spirit of rare beauty and strength. Dorothea not only fails to express herself in "a constant unfolding of far-resonant action"; we feel that she also fails to reach the constant unfolding of mute but far expatiating faith. She is noble to all whom she closely touches; but she is denied a great life within as well as without. It is true that the Divine Spirit lives in her, but she does not live in Him. She has not the joy, though she has the strength of the spiritual life. She has not the sweetness, though she has the good guidance of the life of purity and self-denial. The "meanness" of external opportunity is, in fact, far more fatal to her than it could be to any equally noble nature with the life of faith freely open before it, for opportunities arising out of her external life are for her the only opportunities; she has no escape from the failing of her heart and flesh to one of whom she can say, "He is the strength of my heart and my portion for ever." The "meanness of opportunity" could have no more cruel triumph.

I must not dwell at the same length on the other parts of this wonderful photograph of provincial life; but it is well to point out the unity of thought which runs through it all, and also the artistic skill to combine with a full expression of love for the noble parts of human nature and an exquisite delineation of them, a pervading impression of the "meanness of opportunity" that besets all noble aims, especially in provincial society in this century. The most elaborate illustration of this, next to Dorothea's history, is Lydgate's. His earnest, though purely intellectual, thirst for scientific truth is far more completely defeated and subjugated by the meanness of opportunity than Dorothea's thirst for goodness, no doubt, *because* it is purely intellectual, and because his moral nature, though manly and generous, has no particularly exalted aims. There are no scenes in English literature so full of power—the sort of power from the excess of which we almost shrink—as those in which Rosamond's thin, unyielding, inexpressible, and incompressible selfishness and worldliness of nature encounters and defeats the strong, masculine, magnanimous, generous struggles of Lydgate to overcome the difficulties caused by an improvident marriage, and to hold fast to his resolve of devoting his life to the higher scientific aims of physiological study, and not merely to winning his bread as a medical specialist. I cannot dwell on the picture, but I cannot leave it without saying that I think here, too, George Eliot put too dark a ground into her canvas, and probably from the same cause as in the previous picture. I quite recognise the fidelity of the conception which makes Rosamond triumph over Lydgate's scientific zeal without even knowing what she is doing. But this final picture is, on its moral side I think, painfully and, at least by what it omits, excessively sombre:—

"Lydgate's hair never became white. He died when he was only fifty, leaving his wife and children provided for by a heavy insurance on his life. He had gained an excellent practice, alternating, according to the season, between London and a continental bathing-place; having written a treatise on Gout, a disease which has a good deal of wealth on its side. His skill was relied on by many paying patients, but he always regarded himself as a failure; he had not done what he once meant to do. His acquaintances thought him enviable to have so charming a wife, and nothing happened to shake their opinion. Rosamond never committed a second compromising indiscretion. She simply continued to be mild in her temper, inflexible in her judgment, disposed to admonish her husband, and able to frustrate him by stratagem. As the years went on he opposed her less and less, whence Rosamond concluded that he had learned the value of her opinion; on the other hand, she had a more thorough conviction of his talents now that he gained a good income, and instead of the threatened cage in Bride

Street, provided one all flowers and gilding, fit for the bird of paradise that she resembled. In brief, Lydgate was what is called a successful man. But he died prematurely of diphtheria, and Rosamond afterwards married an elderly and wealthy physician, who took kindly to her four children. She made a very pretty show with her daughters driving out in her carriage, and often spoke of her happiness as 'a reward'—she did not say for what, but probably she meant that it was a reward for her patience with Tertius, whose temper never became faultless, and to the last occasionally let slip a bitter speech which was more memorable than the signs he made of his repentance. He once called her his basil plant; and when she asked for an explanation, said that basil was a plant which had flourished wonderfully on a murdered man's brains. Rosamond had a placid but strong answer to such speeches. Why, then, had he chosen her? It was a pity he had not had Mrs. Ladislaw, whom he was always praising and placing above her. And thus the conversation ended with the advantage on Rosamond's side. But it would be unjust not to tell that she never uttered a word in depreciation of Dorothea, keeping in religious remembrance the generosity which had come to her aid in the sharpest crisis of her life."

Granted George Eliot's view of Rosamond as one of those persons of whom in this world it is hopeless to expect anything like spiritual growth, except under the rarest and happiest moral influences, which she did not encounter, that touch as to her own view of her second marriage is one of the highest genius. But it is an assumption to which George Eliot herself is hardly quite true, for she does give us one glimpse of Rosamond's reawakening tenderness towards her husband, and makes Dorothea win a complete victory over her; nor is it easy to believe that a nature even so shallow and limited as Rosamond's could have wholly failed to be warmed into something like appreciation of her husband's hasty but generous tenderness. Is there not something of the painter's temptation to deepen unduly the most characteristic lines in a picture in the last touches he gives to it—in order to leave a distincter and stronger effect on the spectator's mind—in this brilliant but bitter farewell to Rosamond? And with regard to Lydgate, though one can easily believe that his final relinquishment of his higher scientific aims might have left such depths of bitterness in him as would break out in the speech about his basil plant, that could hardly have been all. He must have felt even in his solitude that the "meanness of opportunity" which had crushed his ideal ambition in one direction, had opened to him an ideal of an even higher kind in the renunciations he had willingly embraced for the sake of others; and to leave him without a word as to the softer brightness which this humbler but nobler life must have brought him, is to leave him in needless gloom. George Eliot attributes too much moral influence to opportunity, because she ignores the fountain of light which is alone independent of opportunity.

The whole picture both of town and county life in *Middlemarch*, though it is seldom cynical, and often most sympathetic in its portraiture of true nobility of character, is wonderfully vivid in its illustration of the pettiness and of the meanness of the aims generally pursued. Even Caleb Garth, the land-surveyor, a noble figure, with his delight in honest work—which he praises in a phraseology of borrowed Scripture dialect from which the Scriptural ideas have disappeared—only shows his nobility by his benevolence, his integrity, his thoroughness, and his charity, but not by any vision of a life higher than that of the surveyor and land-agent. Though he lives, within his small sphere, up to the full height of Christian purity and charity, his imagination dwells solely on his work of promoting benevolently the thorough cultivation of the land; capable as he is of great self-sacrifices to his own ideal of conduct, the author is anxious to make you see that Caleb Garth's ideal is of the purest secularistic type. Then Mr. Farebrother, a most winning character, is saved from his excusable but not very noble desire to win money at whist to add to his small savings, not by any effort of will, but by opportunity, which gives him a better living. It is true he triumphs manfully over the temptation his love for Mary Garth suggests to him, to let her younger and more favoured lover fall into bad ways without making an effort to save him; and here, for a second time in the story, the "meanness of opportunity" is beaten by the spiritual fidelity of one of its characters. But these endeavours of noble character only bring out, and are intended to bring out, the poverty of the moral circumstances amidst which they move. Again, the whole account

—and most powerful it is—of the illness and death of the old miser, Peter Featherstone, and of the conduct of his relatives, the brilliant if slightly overdrawn picture of the evangelical banker's fraud and crimes,[1] the account of Mr. Vincy's worldly selfishness, the jealousies of the medical men of Middlemarch, the ignorance and meanness of its shopkeepers, the moral vacuity of the country gentry, amongst whom leniency to the tenants and liberality as regards fencing and draining seem to be the highest moral aims of which they have any knowledge, and the clever but petty tittle-tattle of the county society,— are all illustrations of the main idea of the book, that Dorothea's noble, ideal nature had been placed in a world, not indeed of such evil, but of such mean opportunity, that it must have been badly straitened for want of congenial food and air. As poor Dorothea says in one place, "I don't feel sure about doing good in any way now; *everything seems like going on a mission to people whose language I don't know;* unless it were building good cottages, there can be no doubt about that." And the whole tale is founded on this mutual unintelligibility of Dorothea's language of the soul, and Middlemarch's language of the senses.

Indeed, it is the main function of the rich and abundant humour of *Middlemarch* to re-enforce the

[1] When I call it overdrawn I refer to the complete absence of remorse in Mr. Bulstrode's demeanour on the day of the death of his victim. I do not believe that a man who had had such a conflict with his conscience on the previous night could have felt pure relief at the apparent success of his own guilt.

same idea. Richer and more abundant humour there has not been in any book of our own day; but delightful as it is, the general drift of it is to show up the petty moral scale of the life depicted. The most humorous picture in the book is probably that of Dorothea's uncle, Mr. Brooke, with his kindly penuriousness, his fragmentary literary interests, his intellectual shuffle, his dread of going far enough to mean anything, his scraps of reminiscence, and his mode of alleviating disagreeable news by introducing it "among a number of disjointed particulars, as if it would get a milder flavour by mixing." A more humorous picture than that of Mr. Brooke has hardly been produced in all the range of English literature; but it is obvious that its special significance in this story is to illustrate the ideal impotence of the society in which Dorothea was to figure, to give us a vivid impression of the intellectual and moral paralysis of the figures from whom chiefly Dorothea had to look for help and guidance. Then again, the extremely humorous picture of Mrs. Cadwallader, the aristocratic, witty rector's wife, who is always cheapening, not only the commodities she buys, but the minds she encounters in the county life around her, is a perfect instrument for exhibiting the weaknesses and incoherences of the more important figures in *Middlemarch* in a pointed and striking form. Thus, when she tells Mr. Brooke that he is sure to make a fool of himself if he goes speechifying for the radicals, "there's no excuse except being on the right side, *so that you can ask a blessing on your humming and hawing,*" she brings the helplessness of political argumentation before us in the most graphic way, as if it contained no inherent power at all, although, when rightly intentioned, it might be the signal for some miraculous intervention in its favour. And again, when she gives Celia a little advice on marriage, *à propos* of her sister's engagement to Mr. Casaubon, how neatly she manages to make everything and every one she touches—the motives for marriage, household economies, religious petitions, and poor Mr. Casaubon—seem ludicrously small all at once: "We are all disappointed, my dear. Young people should think of their families in marrying. I set a bad example—married a poor clergyman, and made myself a pitiable object among the De Bracys— obliged to get my meals by stratagem, and pray to Heaven for my salad oil. However, Casaubon has money enough; I must do him that justice. As to his blood, I suppose the family quarterings are three cuttle-fish sable, and a commentator rampant." She destroys Ladislaw in the same way, suggesting that Dorothea might almost as well marry "an Italian with white mice," and then comments thus on his genealogy: "It must be admitted that his blood is a frightful mixture! The Casaubon cuttle-fish fluid to begin with, and then a rebellious Polish fiddler or dancing-master—was it? and then an old clothesman." Mrs. Cadwallader is the author's organ of depreciation, and a very powerful organ she is. No

Mephistopheles could illustrate the "meanness of opportunity" more successfully. Indeed, the bold, witty wife of a clergyman, with a flavour of religious phraseology in her mouth, and a keen sarcastic wit, comes as near to the spirit who "uniformly denies" as we could hope to approach in the English society of our own century.

Then again, observe the effect of the humour embodied in the figures of Peter Featherstone's relations, of the horse-doctor and horse-dealer of Middlemarch, and of that exquisitely-drawn hero, the pompous, good-humoured auctioneer, Mr. Trumbull, who is so much comforted by the application of the thermometer to him in his illness, as implying "the importance of his temperature," by the sense that "he furnished objects for the microscope," and by learning many new words suitable to "the dignity of his secretions." The effect of the overflowing humour in all these sketches is the same—to illustrate the narrowness of thought and feeling, the contracted principles, the suffocating social atmosphere of the provincial world in which Dorothea and Lydgate were to struggle, for the most part vainly, after their moral and intellectual ideals. When George Eliot tells us that the kindly Mr. Borthrop Trumbull "would have liked to have the universe under his hammer, feeling that it would go at a higher figure for his recommendation," we almost feel that he might have been right; that the human universe, at all events, in which he lived was small enough to have gained by his recommendation, and was, in any case, full of opportunities so mean, that with them any spiritual "grandeur" whatever, however inadequate to its own standard, must have been utterly "ill-matched." The inexhaustible humour of *Middlemarch* is certainly carefully calculated to enhance the contrast between the greater natures delineated in it and the world of circumstance in which they move.

George Eliot means to draw noble natures struggling hard against the currents of a poor kind of world, and without any trust in any invisible rock higher than themselves to which they can entreat to be lifted up. Such a picture is melancholy in its very conception. That in spite of this absence of any inward vista of spiritual hope, and in spite of the equally complete absence of any outward vista of "far-resonant action," George Eliot should paint the noble characters in which her interest centres as clinging tenaciously to that *caput mortuum* into which Mr. Arnold has so strangely reduced the Christian idea of God,—"a stream of tendency, not ourselves, which makes for righteousness,"—and as never even inclined to cry out, "Let us eat and drink, for tomorrow we die," is a great testimony to the ethical depth and nobility of her mind. And it will add to the interest of *Middlemarch*, and of its very inferior though still remarkable successor *Daniel Deronda*, in future generations, when at length this great wave of scepticism has swept by us, and "this tyranny is overpast," that in pointing to them as registering the low-tide mark of spiritual belief among the literary class in the nineteenth century, the critics of the future will be compelled to infer from them that even during that low ebb of trust in the supernatural, there was no want of ardent belief in the spiritual obligations of purity and self-sacrifice, nor even in that "secret of the Cross" which, strangely enough, survives the loss of the faith from which it sprang.

I cannot leave George Eliot without saying a word of her poetry, though I do not regard her poetry as anything but the attempt of a large but slow imagination to use a medium not really well fitted to her genius. Her verse wants spontaneity. "The Spanish Gipsy," with all its rich colour, and sometimes almost Miltonic stateliness, shows, I think, that George Eliot is far greater when she interprets freely the poetry of real life in her novels and romances than when she submits her imagination to the chains of verse. Verse to her is a fetter, and not a stimulus. In prose she is so free and dramatic that it is a disappointment to find the characters in her "Spanish Gipsy" moving in servile obedience to the intellectual views which the reader at once discovers to have produced them. If I except, perhaps, —and even there I am doubtful,—the Spanish Duke, Don Silva, whose character is certainly finely conceived both in outline and detail, though the general effect is, I think, a little like "the misty Hyades," a haze of moral worlds melting into each other,— the chief characters of the story, including especially the Gipsy chief and the Gipsy heroine, do not leave upon me any impression of dramatic power at all comparable to the leading figures of George Eliot's greater prose works. *Adam Bede* and *Middlemarch* remain much her greatest imaginative efforts, though there is, of course, ample opportunity in the mere form of *verse* for imaginative beauties of a kind inadmissible and unadmitted in her novels.

The intellectual background of the tragedy—for tragedy, with interspersed narrative links, it really is —seems to me the greatest thing about it, and is truly great. The figures which are painted in upon that background, and whose movements are intended to bring it out into relief, are, I think, hardly living and real enough to assert fully their own independent vitality. They betray the intellectual analysis to which they have been subjected, and to illustrate which they were probably created. If I may venture to interpret so great a writer's thought, I should say that "The Spanish Gipsy" is written to illustrate not merely doubly and trebly, but from four or five distinct points of view, her belief that the inheritance of the definite streams of impulse and tradition, stored up in what we call race, often puts a tragic veto upon any attempt of spontaneous individual emotion or volition to ignore or defy their control, and to emancipate itself from the tyranny of their disputable and apparently cruel rule.

You can see the influence of the Darwinian doctrines, so far as they are applicable at all to moral characteristics and causes, in almost every page of the poem. How the threads of hereditary capacity and hereditary sentiment control, as with invisible cords, the orbits of even the most powerful characters,—how the fracture of those threads, so far as it can be accomplished by mere *will*, may have even a greater effect in wrecking character than moral degeneracy would itself produce,—how the man who trusts and uses the hereditary forces which natural descent has bestowed upon him becomes a might and a centre in the world, while the man, perhaps intrinsically the nobler, who dissipates his strength by trying to swim against the stream of his past, is neutralised and paralysed by the vain effort,—again, how a divided past, a past not really homogeneous, may weaken this kind of power, instead of strengthening it by the command of a larger experience,—all this George Eliot's poem paints with a force that answers to Aristotle's fine definition of tragedy, that which "purifies" by pity and by fear.

The heroine of the book, an infant of gipsy birth, as she subsequently discovers, has been adopted by Duke Silva's mother, and when the poem opens the Duke is planning their immediate marriage. The motto of the story might be given in some of Fedalma, the heroine's last words—

> "Our dear young love,—its breath was happiness!
> *But it had grown upon a larger life*
> *Which tore its roots asunder. We rebelled,—*
> *The larger life subdued us."*

At the very opening of the poem the seeds of the constitutional difference of tendency between the free gipsy blood and the deeply-furrowed Spanish pride and honour are beginning to flower. Though the love between the two is perfect, Fedalma frets against the restraints of the secluded Spanish grandeur, and yearns after a larger measure of popular sympathies. On a lovely southern evening she even dances on the Plaza, the public square of Bedmar, the garrison of which Duke Alva commands (for a Moorish force is in the neighbourhood),—and this she does from the mere yearning to express, after the Southern fashion, her spontaneous delight in the harmony of the evening, and her fulness of sympathy with the people who are looking on. This incident is the first made use of by the author to indicate the immense divergence between the inherited natures of the Gipsy and the Spanish Duke,—and this though the difference is purely one of inheritance, for Fedalma has been brought up from her birth in the strict seclusion of a Spanish grandee. Here is her excuse to her lover for the breach of conventional manners of which she has been guilty—

> "Yes, it is true. I was not wrong to dance.
> The air was filled with music, with a song
> That seemed the voice of the sweet eventide—
> The glowing light entering through eye and ear—
> That seemed our love—mine, yours—they are but one—
> Trembling through all my limbs, as fervent words
> Tremble within my soul and must be spoken.
> And all the people felt a common joy

> And shouted for the dance. A brightness soft
> As of the angels moving down to see
> Illumined the broad space. The joy, the life
> Around within me were one heaven : I longed
> To blend them visibly : I longed to dance
> Before the people—be as mounting flame
> To all that burned within them ! Nay, I danced ;
> There was no longing : I but did the deed,
> Being moved to do it."

And on this turns the finest study of character in the poem—that of the Spanish Duke, who has a love in him that overflows the channels of Spanish tradition and convention, and whose wreck of mind, due to the impulse which seizes him to break with those traditions rather than with his love, is the true theme of the tragedy :—

> "A man of high-wrought strain, fastidious
> In his acceptance, dreading all delight
> That speedy dies and turns to carrion :
> His senses much exacting, deep instilled
> With keen imagination's difficult needs ;—
> Like strong-limbed monsters studded o'er with eyes,
> Their hunger checked by overwhelming vision,
> Or that fierce lion in symbolic dream,
> Snatched from the ground by wings and new-endowed
> With a man's thought-propelled relenting heart.
> Silva was both the lion and the man ;
> First hesitating shrank, then fiercely sprang,
> Or having sprung, turned pallid at his deed
> And loosed the prize, paying his blood for naught.
> A nature half-transformed, with qualities
> That oft bewrayed each other, elements
> Not blent but struggling, breeding strange effects,
> Passing the reckoning of his friends or foes.

Haughty and generous, grave and passionate ;
With tidal moments of devoutest awe,
Sinking anon to farthest ebb of doubt ;
Deliberating ever, till the sting
Of a recurrent ardour made him rush
Right against reasons that himself had drilled
And marshalled painfully. A spirit framed
Too proudly special for obedience,
Too subtly pondering for mastery ;
Born of a goddess with a mortal sire,
Heir of flesh-fettered, weak divinity,
Doom-gifted with long resonant consciousness
And perilous heightening of the sentient soul."

This is evidently poetry of the will, but it is not without stateliness. When Fedalma is claimed by her father, the Zincalo (or Gipsy) chief, and called upon by him to break from her Spanish ties and aid him in the task he has set himself of forming his gipsy tribe into an independent nation on the shore of Africa, the struggle between the two natures—the inherited deference to a captain and father of Zarca's free, bold, and commanding nature, and the acquired nature, the passion for her Spanish lover—begins. But in Fedalma it only appears as a struggle which is from the first decided in favour of the stronger nature she has inherited. Her love to the Duke is true and inexhaustible ; but she realises at once that to wrap herself up in the subtle tendernesses of her ducal lover, and leave her father to wrestle alone with his great enterprise on a foreign shore, will make her utterly unworthy even of her own place in life, and so fill her with the conviction that

she is mean and selfish and worthless. If she so
acted she would not be worthy even of the part she
had to play, and would sink in her own and Silva's
esteem. So she goes with her father, broken-hearted,
but firm, and breaks away from Silva.

The Duke, on the other hand, tramples on the ties
of rank, family, and country, for the sake of his love.
He gives up his place as commander of the fortress
to follow Fedalma, hoping to win her back to him.
Finding the Gipsy chief firm, and his daughter in-
exorably resolved to sacrifice her love to what she
thinks her duty, he sacrifices his own place in life
altogether, and swears fealty to the Zincalo chief
rather than lose his betrothed. In the meantime the
latter has to earn his Moorish safe conduct to Africa
by taking the fortress of Bedmar, which Silva had
commanded, and Silva finds, to his unutterable horror
and remorse, that the fortress has been surprised and
all his own dearest companions in arms slain by the
troop of Zincali with whom he had united himself.
In his insanity of remorse he kills Zarca,—Fedalma's
father,—and the tragedy ends with their final separation: she to take, so far as she may, her father's
place as ruler of the Gipsy people on the African
shore; he to get absolved for his sin, and to recover
his knightly name as a Spanish soldier of the Cross.
The point of the tragedy, however, is the contrast
between the moral strength of the Gipsy chief, Zarca,
whose inherited qualities of mind and body and
whole life had been absolutely in harmony, and the

comparative weakness of his daughter, in whom Spanish training and Spanish ties had partly neutralised her gipsy blood, and, again, between both of these and the absolute wreck of character in Silva when he breaks through his whole ancestral traditions, and tries to make a sacrifice of them to love.

The same striking theme is illustrated from several other points of view. Silva's uncle, Father Isidor, the prior of San Domingo, the priest of the Spanish Inquisition, whose nature is all held within the deep-cut channels of Spanish tradition, within the ideas which dominated the Spanish chivalry and the Spanish faith, is the moral foil to his nephew. He stands out —keen, hard, loyal to his own ideas, domineering without hesitation, and crushing without a scruple all even in himself which tends to divide himself— as the model of the morality which acts rigidly and severely, volition and nature being in perfect unison, on a fixed and customary type.

But apart even from these leading characters, perpetually recurring touches throughout the whole poem show how entirely this theme had occupied George Eliot's imagination. Take but as one instance, this, on the inherited forces which form the characters of monkeys *à propos* of the juggler's ape—

"Man thinks
Brutes have no wisdom, since they know not his:
Can we divine their world?—the hidden life
That mirrors us as hideous shapeless power,
Cruel supremacy of sharp-edged death,
Or fate that leaves a bleeding mother robbed?

> Oh, *they have long tradition and swift speech,*
> *Can tell with touches and sharp darting cries*
> *Whole histories of timid races taught*
> *To breathe in terror by red-handed man."*

It is impossible, indeed, to speak too highly of the intellectual basis of the poem, and the finish and power with which many of the ideas are worked out and adorned. Thus, how fine for its purpose is the scene between Don Silva and the Jewish astrologer, Sephardo, who perceives so clearly the scientific limits to astrological prediction, that he refines away and distinguishes till his science is but, as Silva tells him, to pinch

> "With confident selection these few grains
> And call them verity, from out the dust
> Of crumbling error."

This discussion between Silva and the Jewish astrologer on the decaying science of astral influence, and on those contingencies of human life which its clearest visions leave unsolved,—and again, this glimpse of a subtle scientific mind, which, while it had lost confidence in the boasted power of the science, still clung cautiously to the dwindling grain of truth which it still believed that the science contained, are, as it were, poetical glosses and commentaries on the main theme of the story, showing how the past of Europe, in that age of religious inquisition and scientific discovery, was pressing upon the present, how much of it was crumbling away beneath the intellectual solvent of the new thought, and yet how keenly the most vigilant and subtle minds of the age felt the danger of breaking, even intellectually, with the past, and how anxiously, as they cut away the superfluous traditions, they held to everything which had not yet been disproved.

This fading belief, like other fading beliefs, is intended to have its effect on Silva's mind, disposing him to distrust the social and religious traditions in which he had been brought up, and therefore to trust more amply the passion of love in his heart which he knew to be both noble and true. Yet even from the first he, too, cannot keep his mind off the danger of the schism in his life which he feels approaching, and of which his mere love for a nature so untrammelled by tradition as Fedalma's cannot but warn him. In his first love scene with Fedalma he says—

> "Ah yes! all preciousness
> To mortal hearts is guarded by a fear.
> All love fears loss, and most that loss supreme,
> Its own perfection—seeing, feeling, change
> From high to lower, dearer to less dear.
> Can love be careless? If we lost our love,
> What should we find?—with this sweet Past torn off,
> Our lives deep scarred just where their beauty lay?
> The best we found thenceforth were still a worse:
> *The only better is a Past that lives*
> *On through an added Present, stretching still,*
> *In hope unchecked by shaming memories*
> *To life's last breath.*"

While the intellectual ground plan of the tragedy is exquisitely worked out, the characters are faint, misty, imperfectly executed,—and this applies especially to the Gipsy chief and his daughter. The lyrics, too, though one or two are of some beauty, do not interest me like the reflective verse. It is a meditative, hardly at all dramatic work,—its meditation inlaid, as all true meditation must be, with keen and clear observation. Of touches of humour of George Eliot's grave kind there are many. Of wise apophthegms there are still more, and of wholesome sentiment and fancy as much as heart could wish. But as verse it is, I think, less striking than the author's characteristic and sad poem on " The Legend of Jubal." And as a work of imagination it certainly falls far below her greater prose works.

The subject of this latter poem, which I make no apology for analysing, not only as a work of art, but as a doctrinal work,—for so great a writer as George Eliot should be studied as a thinker as well as a painter,—is praise of death, and of the fulness of energy which the dark inevitable fate that awaits us has lent to human life while it lasts. Cain is introduced flying from the wrath of God, and seeking some land where other and kinder gods ruled, who might remit the stern decree of death. He finds such a land as he supposes, and for hundreds of years his descendants grow up around him, without hearing of death, in glad idleness. In some of the most effective lines of the poem we are told how

> "They laboured gently, as a maid who weaves
> Her hair in mimic mats, and pauses oft
> And strokes across her hand the tresses soft,
> Then peeps to watch the poisèd butterfly
> Or little burdened ants that homeward hie.
> Time was but leisure to their lingering thought,
> There was no need for haste to finish aught ;
> But sweet beginnings were repeated still
> Like infant babblings that no task fulfil ;
> For love, that loved not change, constrained the simple
>   will."

Into this world, unconscious of doom, the knowledge of death enters by the accidental death of one of Lamech's children, and Cain is compelled to disclose the fate which remains for all of them by that stern will of Jehovah, which he has hoped, but failed, to escape by his long pilgrimage :—

> "And a new spirit from that hour came o'er
> The race of Cain ; soft idlesse was no more,
> But even the sunshine had a heart of care,
> Smiling with hidden dread,—a mother fair
> Who folding to her breast a dying child
> Beams with feigned joy that but makes sadness mild.
> Death was now lord of life, and at his word
> Time, vague as air before, new terrors stirred,
> With measured wing now audibly arose
> Throbbing through all things to some unseen close.
> Now glad Content by clutching Haste was torn,
> And Work grew eager and Device was born.
> It seemed the light was never loved before.
> Now each man said, ''Twill go and come no more.'
> No budding branch, no pebble from the brook,
> No form, no shadow, but new dearness took
> From the one thought that life must have an end ;

> And the last parting now began to send
> Diffusive dread through love and wedded bliss,
> Thrilling them into finer tenderness.
> Then Memory disclosed her face divine,
> That like the calm nocturnal lights doth shine
> Within the soul and shows the sacred graves,
> And shows the presence that no sunlight craves,
> No space, no warmth, but moves among them all;
> Gone and yet here, and coming at each call,
> With ready voice and eyes that understand,
> And lips that ask a kiss, and dear responsive hand.
> Thus to Cain's race Death was tear-watered seed
> Of various life, and action-shaping need."

The vivifying effect of this knowledge of Death is described especially in relation to the three sons of Lamech—Jabal, who teaches the dumb animals to love and obey him; Tubal Cain, who founds the industrial arts; Jubal, in whom the new sense of limitation breeds the spirit of poetry and music—

> "A yearning for some hidden soul of things,
> Some outward touch complete on inner springs
> That vaguely moving bred a lonely pain,—
> A want that did but stronger grow with gain
> Of all good else, as spirits might be sad
> For lack of speech to tell us they are glad."

Jubal invents the lyre and the art of song, and receives unmeasured glory and gratitude from his kindred for his gift to them of the new faculty, till he grows weary of hearing the echo of his own words, and resolves to seek some distant land where he can find new harmonies and give up his heart to solitary raptures. He journeys on for ages, sowing music everywhere as he goes, till he reaches the sea, and finds himself so utterly unable to render again the music of that "mighty harmonist" that he touches his lyre no more, and longs again for the land where first he realised the power which is ebbing away from him as his "heart widens with its widening home." He returns to find his name famous, and temples built in his praise; but also to find a generation which knows him not and which hardly notices the feeble old man who is the true claimant for these divine honours. Jubal feels a passionate desire to identify himself with the object of all this veneration. A germ of selfishness lurks in him still—

> "What though his song should spread from man's small race
> Out through the myriad worlds that people space,
> And make the heavens one joy-diffusing choir?
> Still, 'mid that vast would throb the keen desire
> Of this poor aged flesh, this eventide,
> This twilight soon in darkness to subside,
> This little pulse of self that, having glowed
> Through thrice three centuries, and divinely strowed
> The light of music through the vague of sound,
> *Ached smallness still in good that had no bound.*"

In other words, the yearning to be personally recognised and identified as the giver of these great gifts to man was the poor alloy still left in Jubal's nature—an alloy which the mere fear of death had, by the way, apparently *stimulated* rather than diminished;

for George Eliot expressly tells us that Tubal Cain at least, and still more, I should think, Jubal,

> ... " wot not of treachery,
> Or greedy lust, or any ill to be,
> Save the one ill of sinking into naught,
> Banished from action and act-shaping thought."

However, Death itself is to purify Jubal from this insatiable longing for personal recognition as the author of that music and song which the fear of Death had generated in him; for Jubal's claim to be the inventor of the lyre is treated as a profanity, and he is beaten and driven away from the temple built in his honour to die alone. Dying, a vision comes to him of the "angel of his life and death," who teaches him that his life had been full enough of blessing without his receiving in his own person the honour due to it,—that

> " In thy soul to bear
> The growth of song, and feel the sweet unrest
> Of the world's springtide in thy conscious breast,"

was itself the greatest of all gifts, far greater than any gratitude which might seem to be due to it. Indeed, it was the very intensity of the light he had radiated which caused his old age to be despised,—as a shrine too mean for a rumour so divine. Nay, it was the final blessing of Death—so I understand the author to teach—that, after stimulating such creative activity as Jubal's, it destroyed the "fleshy self" with all its egotisms, and left him only an impersonal immortality in that human gladness which, in its rejoicings, does *not* recognise the personal origin of its joys—

> "This was thy lot, to feel, create, bestow,
> And that immeasurable life to know
> From which the fleshy self falls shrivelled, dead,
> A seed primeval that has forests bred.
> It is the glory of the heritage
> Thy life has left, that makes thy outcast age;
> Thy limbs shall lie, dark, tombless on the sod,
> Because thou shinest in man's soul a god,
> Who found and gave new passion and new joy,
> That naught but earth's destruction can destroy.
> Thy gifts to give was thine of men alone;
> 'Twas but in giving that thou could'st atone
> For too much wealth amid their poverty."

And with these warnings in his ears Jubal is left at the close of this melancholy legend,

> "Quitting mortality, a quenched sun-wave,
> The All-creating Presence for his grave."

Whether the poetic form is adequate to the thought is questionable. But at all events the thought itself is gravely passionate, expressing a strange depth of gratitude for the power of Death to stimulate energy and give a new keenness of emotion to the race; and finally for Death's power to rob the individual soul of the one selfish husk which clings to all such energy, however disinterested,—the craving for personal recognition.

So I understand the teaching of this legend—a

sort of quasi-Miltonic rendering of Positivism. The deepest part of the teaching, the part of it most likely to strike the imagination and affect the heart of its readers, seems to me profoundly false, and the didactive form of the verse, though sonorous, is, I think, a little leaden. I have already noted the apparent contradiction implied in praising Death for the stimulus it gives to the generally beneficent perhaps, but certainly egotistic desire for immortal fame, and yet praising it *also* for separating the shrivelled, dead husk of the " fleshy self " from the immeasurable life it has engendered in generations to come. But there is a deeper vice still in the doctrine that Death extinguishes that selfish egotism which, as George Eliot so finely says, "ached smallness still in good that has no bound." To extinguish the *power* of selfish feeling is *not* really a victory over selfish feeling; Jubal dies before he has gained any such victory. If he had gained the victory there would have been no praise due to Death, by which he could not have gained it. To be willing to submit to annihilation for the infinite good of others might be a noble and disinterested attitude of mind, but then such willingness is not the gift of Death, but of Life, and he who has it can gain nothing by Death, while the universe loses by it the very flower of its life. The death of the corn of wheat, which, "except it die, abideth alone, but if it die bringeth forth much fruit," is not the death of annihilation, but of transfiguration; and the transfiguration of the highest thing man can know, personal love, involves the retention and development of that highest element, the personality, not its degradation and extinction. If Jubal, instead of being quenched like "a sun-wave" in the "*grave*" of an "All-creating Presence,"—what a paradox is there!—had learnt to renounce the passionate desire to be identified with his own gift to mankind, he would have ceased to "ache smallness still in good that had no bound," in a far higher and truer sense than any in which that can be asserted of "a quenched sun-wave" which has altogether ceased to be. The doctrine of this poem seems to me to come to this: either that Death creates by making us smart under the consciousness of limitation, by stinging self-love into haste and energy, or that purely disinterested creation—creation without the thirst for personal recognition—is not for personal beings like men at all, but is the privilege only of unconscious and impersonal life. But what we do actually experience, in however imperfect a degree, cannot be *impossible* to us,—and the creative power of purely disinterested love has no fascination, indeed, strictly speaking, no *meaning*, for us, if we drop the thought of the personal centre from which it flows. "Love" implies the self-surrender of a conscious being to the wellbeing of others. An unconscious stream of beneficent energy is in no sense "love," and excites none of the moral awe which the display of divine love excites.

Moreover, even the true and undeniable effect of

death in stimulating energy, and making men, by suggesting loss, conscious of the love which otherwise they might hardly know, is more or less conditional on death's being believed to be *not* final. A man with death near at hand will seldom undertake any task unconnected with the life into which he believes himself about to plunge, because it seems hardly worth while. Those who lose their belief in immortality too often sink under the moral paralysis of a creed which leaves so little to be done that it is worth while to attempt. Especially, the loss of faith in immortality usually saps the deepest and tenderest affections of human nature, instead of giving them, as George Eliot intimates, a new tenderness. It is clear that the apprehension of loss cannot *create* feeling; it can and does only bring home to the heart the depth of feeling already cherished there. But the belief in a final death does much more than this: it undermines our respect for the intrinsic worth of a nature so ephemeral, and makes it seem more reasonable—perhaps I should say, makes it *really* more reasonable—to contract our love into better keeping with the short minutes during which alone it can be entertained.

I have analysed this poem, and even criticised its doctrine at some length, because it was one of the few direct confessions of faith which the great critic I am criticising put on record in her lifetime, though indications of similar views are freely scattered through her works; and it is impossible to understand so deep and so thoroughly intellectual a painter without knowing her deepest thoughts and measuring them to some extent by one's own. To me, indeed, George Eliot's scepticism seems one of the greatest of the limitations on her genius. One rises from the study of her works, profoundly impressed with their thoroughness, their depth, their rich colouring, their marvellous humour, their laborious conscientiousness, their noble ethical standard, *and* their weariness,— the weariness of a great speculative intellect which can find no true spring of elasticity and hope, and in vain forces from itself a certain amount of enthusiasm for optimist views of that "wide, gray, lampless, deep, unpeopled world," from which Shelley makes Beatrice Cenci recoil in horror. The only flaw I can see in George Eliot's intellect consists in her rather heavy attempts to conform her mind to facts against which she inwardly rebels. In *The Mill on the Floss* she spoilt her story by endeavouring to paint the physiological attraction of a certain kind of animal character for a nature far above it, as if it were more nearly irresistible than in fact I think it is, and, as far as I can see, only because she had arrived at a conviction that, as physiological attractions exert a great influence in human life, realists should put a certain amount of force on their own dislike to recognise them fully; and, in the poem I have just criticised, George Eliot seems to me to make an extraordinary blunder for so fine and subtle an intellect, in not recognising clearly that Death, if it could really quench the *possibility* of selfish feeling, would in no way carry on and complete the triumph of true disinterestedness, but, on the contrary, would finally prevent that triumph. But, in truth, George Eliot was here making the best of a bad business—trying to discover virtues in inevitable destiny because it is inevitable. It would have been more like her, I think, to admit at once, that while the expectation of Death does actually stimulate finite and selfish men to energy, the hope by which it thus stimulates them is empty air, if Death be all it seems. The laborious enthusiasm in "The Legend of Jubal" seems to me melancholy in disguise,—melancholy striving for a calm and serenity it does not feel.

George Eliot, with a faith like that of her own "Dinah," would, to my mind, have had one of the most effective intellects the world had ever seen. Her imagination would have gained that vivacity and spring the absence of which is its only artistic defect; her noble ethical conceptions would have gained certainty and grandeur; her singularly just and impartial judgment would have lost the tinge of gloom which seems always to pervade it; and her poetic feelings would have been no longer weighed down by the superincumbent mass of a body of sceptical thought with which they struggled for the mastery in vain. Few minds at once so speculative and so creative have ever put their mark on literature. If she could not paint the glow of human enterprise like Scott, or sketch with the easy rapidity of Fielding, she could do what neither of them could do—see and explain the relation of the broadest and commonest life to the deepest springs of human motive. With a quicker pulse of life, with a richer, happier faith, I could hardly conceive the limit to her power.

GEORGE ELIOT'S LIFE AND LETTERS

GEORGE ELIOT'S LIFE AND LETTERS[1]

This sombre book reads like one long illustration of a passage contained in Mr. Myers's essay on George Eliot.

"I remember," says Mr. Myers, "how at Cambridge I walked with her once in the Fellows' Garden of Trinity, on an evening of rainy May, and she, stirred somewhat beyond her wont, and taking as her text the three words which have been used so often as the inspiring trumpet-calls of men,—the words *God, Immortality, Duty,*—pronounced, with terrible earnestness, how inconceivable was the *first*, how unbelievable was the *second*, and yet how peremptory and absolute the *third*. Never, perhaps, had sterner accents affirmed the sovereignty of impersonal and unrecompensing law. I listened, and night fell; her grave, majestic countenance turned towards me like a Sibyl's in the gloom; it was as though she withdrew from my grasp, one by one, the two scrolls of promise, and left me the third scroll only, awful with inevitable fate."

Even to the touch of artificial gloom artistically

---

[1] *George Eliot's Life as related in her Letters and her Journals.* Arranged and edited by her husband, J. W. Cross. With portraits and other illustrations. 3 vols. London: William Blackwood and Sons.

pervading this last sentence, the biography reads like an elaborate illustration of Mr. Myers's reminiscence. Very early in the book all belief in Revelation disappears, the faith in God soon follows, the hope of immortality vanishes almost without a sign that it is gone; but as "night falls" there is more and more straining to enforce the theme of duty, and more and more emphatically are we assured, in vague but anxious asseverations, that it is what we suppose Mr. Myers means to convey by the words "awful with inevitable fate." George Eliot was assuredly a law unto herself, in a sense in which it would be hardly true to say the same of any sceptic or agnostic who ever lived. She ascribed that law to no higher source than her own mind—unless, indeed, she regarded the antecedents which had resulted in her own existence as in some vague sense higher than that existence; and yet she attributed to that law all the absoluteness and exactingness of a power it would be infamy to evade; and she made her life one long strain to show that an interior conception of good may be even more than an equivalent for God—not perhaps so soothing, not so exciting, possibly even justifying a deep tinge of melancholy, but in her opinion all the more enduring, all the more ineradicable, all the more independent of the processes of personal judgment. "The highest 'calling and election' is *to do without opium*, and live through all our pain with conscious, clear-eyed endurance," she wrote in 1860; and it is clear that she regarded the belief in revealed religion and in God as nothing but opium-eating, at least for those who, like herself, could look the origin of religious creeds in the face, and who could dare to pronounce these creeds an illusion of our own fostering, if, as she herself held, an illusion they really are.

To me the character and works of this remarkable woman seem one of the most startling of the moral phenomena of our time; and I opened Mr. Cross's book with the strongest hope that it would throw some new and vivid lights on the paradoxes of her career. To a great extent I have been disappointed. It illustrates her temperament in many ways, but it hardly changes in a single feature the estimate of her mind and character which her books and life had previously suggested. It discloses, I think, that there was much more of straining in her ordinary life and temperament than there was in her genius properly so-called—that the artificial element so strong in her was, if I may be allowed the paradox, *natural* to her, though external to her genius; that she was spontaneous as a novelist, artificial as a woman and a poet; that, strenuous as she was, her strenuousness was too self-conscious to reach the point of positive strength; and that what I may call the pedantically scientific vein in her was not in any way contracted from her association with Mr. Lewes, but was due to her own bias or the circumstances of her education. But though the book supports and strengthens these inferences in a multitude of different ways, they are none of them entirely new to the student of her writings. The Life and Correspondence verify for us what some of those who hardly knew George Eliot personally had previously conjectured, that the richest part of her was almost a secret from herself,— quite a secret till she had reached middle-age,—and that the character known to herself and to the circle of her intimates, the curiously-learned woman, the austere sceptic, the considerately gentle friend, the tenderly-devoted partner, stood to her great genius more in the external relation of a faithful attendant than in the relation of moral substance and essence to the attributes and qualities of that genius.

Still, the spectacle which the Life presents is impressive enough—the spectacle of an industriously regulated career cloven in two by a sudden and striking breach with a moral law which the great majority of men hold to be of the very essence of social purity, and yet a career sustaining itself at a very high and uniform level of ethical principle after that breach as well as before it, and apparently achieving the particular object for which that breach with the commandment was made. It is the spectacle, too, of a woman who was her own God—not in the least in the vulgar and injurious sense of that phrase, not in the least in the sense of worshipping her own nobility and priding herself on her own gifts, but in the better sense that the law of duty, which she regarded as imposed upon her by nothing more elevated than the hidden agencies which had produced her own character, was really a religion to her, and one which she earnestly strove within her own self-imposed limits to obey, and of a woman who endeavoured with all her might to promote the diffusion of these sentiments of "pity and fairness" which she regarded as embracing "the utmost delicacies of the moral life." No one can read the Life without feeling the deepest interest in the presentation of both these paradoxes—the paradox of a woman not only full of enthusiasm for the good, but not to all appearance in the least impulsive, rather singularly painstaking and deliberate in all her decisions, calmly absolving herself from a moral law to which she seems to have attached what we must regard as, for a sceptic, an almost inexplicable sacredness, and, after that grave step downwards, not apparently deteriorating or slipping any lower, but giving us picture after picture of the most impressive kind to illustrate the depth of meaning in true marriage, and the terrible consequences of ignoring that meaning; and next the paradox of a woman who held God to be a mere human ideal, and immortality to be a dream, painfully enforcing in every way open to her the duty of a disinterested and just life, and preaching in season and out of season that men owe as much obedience to an elevated thought of their own as they could possibly owe to any external inspirer of that thought, even though he were also the perfect and concentrated essence of it. Even in an age of paradox such a spectacle is a paradox greater than all the rest. Is there anything in the Life calculated to attenuate it?

In the first place, George Eliot was singularly incredulous of the love and care of others for herself. The most prominent trait which Mr. Cross observes in her, and which is amply illustrated in the Life throughout, is that George Eliot "showed from her earliest years the trait that was most marked in her all through life—namely, the absolute need of some one person who should be all in all to her, and to whom she should be all in all. She had," Mr. Cross goes on to say, "a pre-eminently exclusive disposition." Moreover, she not only needed to feel and to return exclusive devotion, but could not endure deficiency in the external evidence of it. "My affections are always the warmest," she writes to Mr. Bray, "when my friends are within an attainable distance. I think I can manage," she adds jestingly, "to keep respectably warm to you for three weeks without seeing you, but I cannot promise more" (vol. i. p. 146). And, laughingly as this was written, no doubt it represented some feeling of which she was really conscious. In another letter to the same friend she says: "I can't help losing belief that people love me—the unbelief is in my nature, and no sort of fork will drive it finally out" (vol. i. p. 469). And again, in writing to Mr. Bray: "It is an old weakness of mine to have no faith in an affection that does not express itself; and when friends take no notice of me for a long while I generally settle down into the belief that they have become indifferent, or have begun to dislike me. That is not the best mental constitution; but it might be worse—for I don't feel obliged to dislike *them* in consequence" (vol. i. p. 471). In other words, even in her relations to human beings, George Eliot had extraordinary little faith; at least, as regarded the permanence of any feeling for herself. "If human beings would but believe it," she writes, "they do me most good by saying to me the kindest things truth will permit" (vol. i. p. 228). And, undoubtedly, her self-distrust, her doubt that she was of any real importance to others, was so strong that, even *before* she had given up her faith in God, she describes her most painful state of feeling as that in which she seemed to be conscious of dwindling "to a point," and finding herself only a miserable "agglomeration of atoms"; a poor "tentative effort of the *Natur-Princip* to mould a personality" (vol. i. p. 189). It was this deep self-distrust, perhaps, which made her so anxious to be "petted," as she calls it; and since, of course, she must do as she would be done by, to "pet" others. Thus she tells her sisters-in-law, as the phrase which best expresses her tenderness for them, to consider themselves "spiritually petted." Again she declares that after Mr. Lewes's death she had been "conscious of a certain drying-up of tenderness," which was all restored to her by her marriage with Mr. Cross. Hence I read George Eliot's nature as one which, while intellectually, even unduly self-reliant, was very diffident as to the love felt for her by others; not from humility,—for though she appears to have been wholly without vanity, there is no indication of humility, though of diffidence as to her power of inspiring love there is much,—but from deep-rooted hopelessness, and, what may have had the same origin, sheer incredulity as to the existence of that of which she had no plain evidence. If the blessing on those "who have not seen and yet have believed" were the only beatitude touching the secrets of the soul which Christ pronounced, most assuredly George Eliot would be one of the last to come within the wide range of His promises. Doubtless it was not so. There were some of her characteristics which were in the deepest sense Christian; but by this powerlessness to believe that of which she had no immediate evidence before her, whether in things human or things divine, George Eliot was exceptionally distinguished. The "substance of things hoped for" was to her no substance at all; she had no buoyancy in her nature. "The evidence of things unseen" was a shadow—as to the various possible causes of which she could speculate at large with little confidence and no satisfactory result. I attribute to this chronic feebleness of hope and inability to take a strong grasp even of the true significance of past moral experience, a great deal of the ease with which George Eliot surrendered herself to any personal influence which could make an impression on her keen intellect, and the readiness— the precipitation I may almost say—with which she evacuated every stronghold of faith as soon as she saw it seriously attacked.

For, in the next place, nothing strikes me more in this biography than the absence of the least trace of struggle against the rationalistic schools of thought through which George Eliot's mind passed. We are told that on November 2, 1841, she called upon Mr. Charles Bray, the well-known Coventry ribbon manufacturer,—whose crude rationalistic necessitarianism was so thoroughly meat and drink to him that it not only glorified life, but reconciled him to a confident expectation of annihilation,—to try and bring him back to Christianity. Within eleven days from that time she writes to her friend Miss Lewis : " My whole soul has been engrossed in the most interesting of all inquiries for the last few days, and to what results my thoughts may lead I know not ; possibly to one that will startle you ;" and it is perfectly clear that she had all but made up her mind within those eleven days to renounce Christianity, for she thinks it necessary to warn Miss Lewis that a change may take place in her, which might possibly render Miss Lewis—who was at that time, as Miss Evans had been a few days previously, an Evangelical Christian—unwilling to spend her Christmas holidays with her, as had been previously settled ; and so rapidly is the ultimate decision taken, that early in December Mary Ann Evans announced to her father her inability to continue to go to church, and incurred his deep displeasure thereby. Indeed this resolution caused a temporary separation between father and daughter, as well as some alienation of feeling. This sudden change was produced by reading Mr. Hennell's *Inquiry concerning the Origin of Christianity*. Mr. Hennell's book contains the usual arguments, thoughtfully put, for regarding Christ's teaching as just such a product of the age as a man of religious genius and noble character might have been expected to put forth, and for rejecting altogether all that is generally deemed to be supernatural in Christ's life; but to me the remarkable point is that George Eliot felt herself relieved of a burden rather than robbed of a great spiritual mainstay by the change. Not only is there for her no deep paradox in supposing that the life and death of Christ are purely human phenomena, but it is quite clear that Mr. Hennell carried her even more completely with him in the superficial characteristics of his book than in the more serious arguments. She writes some years later :—

"Mr. Hennell ought to be one of the happiest of men, that he has done such a life's work. I am sure if I had written such a book I should be invulnerable to all the arrows of all the gods and goddesses. I should say, 'None of these things move me, neither count I my life dear unto myself,' seeing that I have delivered such a message of God unto men. *The book is full of wit to me. It gives me that exquisite kind of laughter which comes from the gratification of the reasoning faculties.*[1] For instance : 'If some of those who were actually at the mountain doubted whether they saw Jesus or not, we may reasonably doubt whether he

---

[1] The italics are mine, not George Eliot's.

was to be seen at all there, especially as the words attributed to him do not seem at all likely to have been used, from the disciples paying no attention to them.' 'The disciples considered her (Mary Magdalene's) words idle tales and believed them not.' We have thus their examples for considering her testimony alone as insufficient and for seeking further evidence" (vol. i. p. 165).

That passage seems to me to show the remarkable limitation, not the power, of George Eliot's mind. At the time this letter was written, indeed, she put the merit of Mr. Hennell's book on the ground that it was a "message of God to men." But within a few years more she was translating Feuerbach, and endeavouring to prove that fancied messages of God to men are all of them really messages only from men to men; and yet she seems to have attached much the same value to the great thesis of Feuerbach —that God is like the Brocken shadow, which merely reflects on a gigantic scale the gestures of man—which she had previously attached to Mr. Hennell's testimony when she described it as a message from God. Indeed, "the exquisite kind of laughter which comes from the gratification of the reasoning faculties" influenced George Eliot's judgment far too much. She never wrote directly on the great subjects on which she had translated so much from the German, but you can see in all that she says indirectly on these subjects that irony, of the kind which she quotes from Mr. Hennell, was one of the chief instruments that had undermined her faith. Yet a mind of any capacity can use irony, and use it effectively, against almost any convictions or any doubts; so that irony, as such, should, I think, weigh little or nothing in the scales of a wise judgment. It seems to me, for instance, that the simplicity with which the first evangelist tells us that when the risen Christ met His eleven apostles in Galilee "they worshipped him, but some doubted," though it would have justified Mr. Hennell's sarcasm if that had been the end of the Christian story, throws a very different light upon the actual issue. If we know any historical fact in this world, we know that this frankly confessed doubt of the apostles was extinguished in the most fervent and practical conviction,—a conviction absorbing the whole existence of lives of labour and pain,—and therefore it becomes a matter of the utmost importance to us to know that the doubt *had* been felt, and had been openly declared, that both in the first gospel and in the fourth the existence of this doubt, even after the day of Resurrection, had been plainly avowed. A fanatical conviction is not one which surmounts doubt, but one which is from the first incapable of doubt. It seems to me that, looking at the matter from the broadest point of view, the evidence that doubt once existed is at least as important for the purposes of an historical estimate as the still more unequivocal evidence that doubt soon ceased to exist. A reasonable man's faith in Christ *now* does not depend on the exact kind or amount of evidence by which the witnesses of the resurrection were convinced of its truth, but on the broad fact that though these witnesses had once given up all for lost, and though they had been hard of belief, even after they had begun to hope again, those who had everything to lose if the resurrection were a dream, and everything to gain if it were a fact, were actually so profoundly persuaded of their Master's resurrection that they spent their lives, and often came to their deaths, in publishing the truth, and in building up the Church founded on that truth. And I cannot help thinking, therefore, that the sensitiveness which George Eliot displayed in this case, as in many other cases, to the power of a rather minute and petty irony, showed that her intellectual keenness was far in advance of her intellectual grasp and strength.

Now one sees easily how George Eliot came to use irony so freely and confidently, and to regard Christian convictions, of which she found it so easy to make light, as intrinsically valueless. She had a great dramatic power of interpreting vividly the petty motives of mankind, and it was no easy matter to use this dramatic power freely, and not to be shaken as to the depth of a great many apparently solemn convictions. She delighted to observe how people with a meagre lot, and no influence of any importance in this world, reconciled themselves to their obscurity by embracing some peculiar faith which enabled them to feel themselves "in secure alliance with the unseen but supreme" power. She liked to discern in prosperous people a preference for "such a view of this world and the next as would preserve the existing arrangements of English society quite unshaken, keeping down the obtrusiveness of the vulgar and the discontent of the poor." She liked to observe how "when the Black Benedictines ceased to pray and chaunt" in a particular church at the time of the Reformation, and, "when the Blessed Virgin and St. Gregory were expelled, the Debarrys, as lords of the manor, came next to Providence, and took the place of the saints." And to a mind loving such bits of dramatic insight as this, it is evident how difficult it must have been to regard creeds, if once her faith had been greatly shaken, as representing anything but the various aspects of human desire, some of them no doubt charitable and noble, but some of them vulgar and selfish desires, and all of them of human origin. To a mind alert as hers the very fact that she saw clearly how much of irrelevant or even unworthy motive is mingled consciously or unconsciously in the profession of the most sacred and momentous beliefs—and this she did see—must have disposed her to accept the key to religious belief which Feuerbach offered her,—the explanation which traces it back simply to human desire or need. I feel no doubt that to a dramatic genius like hers this explanation must have seemed far more adequate and satisfactory than it really is. Feuerbach's book suggested that the whole history of religious belief is nothing but a history of human fears, wishes and hopes asserting their own fulfilment, declaring dogmatically their own realisation. And at this solution

George Eliot, who had already resolved the most authoritative of all the professed revelations of God into a myth, eagerly grasped, as resolving the deepest religious problem of all on the same lines with Strauss's solution of the questions involved in the origin of Christianity. Feuerbach's is indeed an ironic explanation of the religions of the world, and it was as an ironic explanation of the religions of the world that George Eliot, as I interpret her, so eagerly embraced it. Possibly she would not herself have called it ironic. She would have said that, though this solution of the objective truth of religious creeds discards God, it leaves the nobler orders of human feeling and motive, which had been falsely attributed to an external being, as much superior to the ignobler orders of human feeling and motive as any divine law or revelation could have made them, and in so speaking she would have been perfectly serious. None the less, this explanation of religion—this bold assertion that man's temporary and evanescent feelings have been the true origin of the supposed eternity and immutability of the divine character and volitions —is unquestionably an ironic explanation, which makes the most momentous factor in the history of the world to consist in a grand procession of pure illusions; and, unless I greatly misread both George Eliot's works and her letters, it is the ironic aspect of this solution which constituted for her one of its chief fascinations, if not absolutely its greatest charm. No one can study her carefully without seeing how deeply ingrained in her is the belief that you must make men feel small, before you can make them modest enough to attempt only what they have some chance of achieving. To this end she uses irony in season and out of season, with good taste and bad taste, on small subjects and great subjects— her real belief evidently being that pure religion is pure idealism, and that every attempt to represent ideals as actually existing in any world has led to the blunders and follies which make men rely solely on another world for help which they ought to find, and would otherwise find, for themselves. Thus she says in a letter to Mr. Bray, written in 1853, about the time of her Feuerbach studies: "I begin to feel other people's wants and sorrows a little more than I used to do," and then she explains why; the reason is that, as there is nothing in existence which is not more or less mingled with want and sorrow, if we don't help each other, there is no help at all to be found. For she goes on: "Heaven help us, said the old religion; the new one, *from its very lack of that faith*,[1] will teach us all the more to help one another" (vol. i. p. 302). And in a letter to Miss Sara Hennell she reiterates the same conviction: "I wish less of our piety were spent in imagining perfect goodness, and more given to real *im*perfect goodness" (vol. i. p. 392). And again, still more emphatically: "My books have for their main bearing a conclusion . . . without which I could not have cared to write any

---

[1] The italics are mine, not George Eliot's.

representation of human life—namely, that the fellowship between man and man, which has been the principle of development, social and moral, is not dependent on conceptions of what is not man; and that the idea of God, so far as it has been a high spiritual influence, is the ideal of a goodness entirely human (*i.e.* an exaltation of the human)" (vol. iii. p. 245). In other words, George Eliot held that ideals affect us only so far as they persuade us to adopt them into our own principles of conduct, that the fear of God is idle and mischievous, that the trust in His doing for us what we cannot do for ourselves is vain, and makes the heart sick by hope deferred; and that all which is operative in faith is the attractiveness which makes us embody our own ideal in our own thoughts and actions. And I think that, as I have already suggested, a great deal of her persistent effort to make men feel the poverty of their own lives was due to the belief that thereby she would render them more disposed to aim at what was within their reach, and more likely to secure what they aimed at. By exposing, as she believed, the illusory ambitiousness of human creeds, she thought to concentrate men's attention on the little they could really do to embody in their own lives the conceptions of righteousness which religious people had so often contented themselves with glorifying in God without any attempt to transfer them to their own conduct.

But then, how did this humanised view of religion

affect George Eliot herself? I think the Life gives ample evidence that it affected her gravely, and very far indeed from happily. It is impossible to hold that there is no spiritual judge of human conduct outside man, without a doubly mischievous effect resulting to all proud, self-reliant, but otherwise noble natures. First, there is a readiness to absolve yourself more easily from any self-accusation of moral declension on great occasions; for where you hold that there is no spiritual judge by whom your own absolution of yourself will be revised, you run a great risk of mistaking a final resolve for a final conviction. Next there is a tendency to be always holding yourself in hand, so as to fall into an artificially painstaking and self-conscious groove of life; for if you believe that, when you do not spur yourself on to due effort, there is no other power in creation which can be relied on to spur you on from within, you are pretty certain to apply the spur, if there is any nobility in you, too frequently and too energetically. I know it will be said that these objections answer each other; that it is self-contradictory first to look for too easy a sentence of self-absolution in relation to conduct which, if you believed in an external spiritual judge, you would probably condemn, and then to assert that the same absence of belief in an external judge will make you too scrupulous and even fastidious a critic of your own actions. Nevertheless, to any one who knows human nature, there is nothing but what is justified by experience in the apprehension of this double mischief; and I think I see the clear evidence of both in George Eliot's life. She certainly took the moral law into her own hands with very unhappy results in forming what is euphemistically called her "union" with Mr. Lewes; and warmly as she protests against any imputation that she secretly condemned herself for that step, or ever repented it, it is clear to me that, on the whole, she intended her work as an authoress to be expiatory of, or at least to do all that was possible to counterbalance, the effect of her own example. She almost says as much in her letter to Miss Hennell, in which she promises herself that, "If I live five years longer, the positive result of my existence on the side of truth and goodness will outweigh the small negative good that would have consisted in my not doing anything to shock others" (vol. i. p. 461). And though she adds immediately, "I can conceive no consequences that can make me repent the past," she has already admitted that the example of her life would need "outweighing" by the influence of her books. Nor did she remember, apparently, that the higher the estimate formed of her books, and the higher their moral tone, the more weighty would be the personal authority of the woman who had written such books, and the more effective, therefore, would be the shield which her example would cast over those who guided themselves by her practice rather than by the moral drift of her fictions. But even in the very remarkable letters in which George Eliot

defends herself to Mrs. Bray and Mrs. Peter Taylor
for what she has done, she explicitly rests her defence
on grounds which practically condemn her conduct.
"Light and easily broken ties," she writes to Mrs.
Bray, "are what I neither desire theoretically, nor
could live for practically; we are working hard to
provide for others better than we provide for ourselves,
and to fulfil every responsibility that lies upon us"
(vol. i. pp. 327-328). And to Mrs. Peter Taylor she
writes in 1861: "For the last six years I have ceased
to be 'Miss Evans' for any one who has personal
relations with me, having held myself under all the
responsibilities of a married woman" (vol. ii. p. 294).
Probably there is not one woman of the smallest
nobility of character—unless it were George Sand—
who ever entered into such relations as George Eliot's
with Mr. Lewes, who would not have echoed George
Eliot's words, though it may not have been eventually
in the power of such women, as it actually proved
to be in George Eliot's, to carry out her intention
without the help of any legal tie. But the woman
who sets the example of dispensing with that tie
in her own case, sets the example of entering upon
relations which no good intentions on either side,
nor even mere good intentions on both, can secure
by giving to these relations the seriousness and
permanence which George Eliot so justly valued.
And yet it can hardly be said that she valued even
seriousness and permanence *enough*, for in the letter
which she wrote concerning Miss Brontë's *Jane*

Eyre, a letter written in 1848, years before her own deplorable course was taken, she assails Miss Brontë's heroine, as we understand it, for thinking it a needful self-sacrifice to abandon a man who could not marry her, only because his wife was living and a lunatic. "All self-sacrifice," she says, "is good, but one would like it to be in a somewhat nobler cause than that of a diabolical law which chains a man soul and body to a putrefying carcase" (vol. i. p. 191). For putrefying carcase, read here an insane wife. There is clearly not the highest "seriousness or permanence" about George Eliot's view of a relation which, in her opinion, ought to be dissolved by such a calamity as alienation of mind supervening on either side. The "seriousness and permanence" which George Eliot claimed for the relation of marriage, and which she thought ought to be regarded as the moral equivalent of marriage even where no legal tie was possible, were certainly not very profound, if she held a law to be "diabolical" which does not dissolve the relation whenever the greatest of earthly calamities falls upon either of the parties. And it is still clearer that such "seriousness and permanence" would soon become a dream, if good men and women thought themselves at liberty to follow her own example. And so I verily believe she herself felt, even if she did not consciously *think* so, for I look upon most of her novels as written in great measure to impress on others the depth and significance of a tie, the sacredness of which her own example will do much to undermine. Moreover, I very much doubt whether, if George Eliot had continued to believe in the spiritual Judge of all men, she would have found it so easy to absolve herself from the provisions of the moral law of marriage as she did find it. To a very proud and self-reliant intellect like hers it must certainly be easier to take a final resolve which sets social traditions at defiance, if it disbelieves in any true spiritual censorship, than it can be when it regards its own decisions as liable to be scrutinised and reversed by a perfect and omniscient Judge. The mere belief in the existence of a Court of Moral Appeal is a great security for care and humility in most natures.

Now of care there is enough and to spare in George Eliot. She is nothing if not careful, and nothing if not anxious to increase the store of pity and fairness in human life. But of humility, which seems to me so essential to the moral life of such "beings as we are," there is a remarkable deficiency in her judgments. It was not so much that she was proud—though all who knew her seem to speak of her as "proud and sensitive" in a manner peculiarly her own—but that her "fastidious, yet hungry ambition" (vol. iii. p. 125), as she herself described the side of her nature which caused her a perpetual melancholy, made her an easy prey to all those multitudinous doubts of which intellectual criticisms and intellectual subtleties are the source. She was reproached once by a friend at Geneva with having "more intellect than *morale*," and says that the remark was "more true than agreeable" (vol. i. p. 223). It is very doubtful, however, how far this was true. It was certainly not true at all, if it meant that she had more *sympathy* with intellectual people than she had with moral enthusiasts. But it is true that her ambition always took an intellectual form, that she despised the moral judgments of those who were not intellectual, and never showed a trace of sympathy with the Christian principle that "God hath chosen the foolish things of the world to confound the wise, and the weak things of the world to confound the things which are mighty, and base things of the world and things which are despised hath God chosen; yea, and things which are not, to bring to nought things that are." George Eliot had absolutely none of this feeling; she was always aiming at being even more intellectual than she really was, and this gives the touch of pedantry to her writings, and the large vein of pedantry to her letters. "It would really have been a pity to stay at Plongeon," she writes from Geneva, though all the people at Plongeon had been most kind and attentive to her, "out of reach of everything and with people so little worth talking to;" and that was always her attitude towards non-intellectual people. This is indeed the one flaw in her intellect, that she values every indication of intellect too highly, and so is often grandiose when she might have been great. She loves to write of "schematic forms," of a "terrene destiny," of "centripetal" and "centrifugal" forces that would carry her to or from her friends, the Brays;

she is pleased with herself for suggesting that man is "an epizoon making his abode in the skin of the planetary organism," where Cobbett would have called him a tick or a harvest-bug; and she even describes her marriage as "something like a miracle-legend," though it certainly requires a good deal of intellectual grandiosity to detect the resemblance. Unquestionably, the one defect of her intellect was her utter inability to see that simplicity, not strain, is the token of true mastery. So far as I can judge, she really thought the elaborate theories by which Strauss and Feuerbach attempted to replace the supposition of the truth of Christianity and of Theism by certain purely subjective illusions more, not less, likely to be true for their elaboration and far-fetchedness and surprising ingenuity. With her wonderful dramatic power she could be simple enough when she had a simple character to interpret. Her children are admirably drawn, though she is not very fond of drawing them. But when she writes about children in her own person, how stiff and unnatural she is! Mr. John Morley, whose estimate of George Eliot seems to me in general a very accurate one, has quoted as the best specimen of her letters one written (vol. iii. p. 323) to cancel an invitation to the children of her friend, Mr. Burne Jones, to spend Christmas Day with them; and it seems to me hardly possible to exaggerate the artificiality of that letter's pleasantry. Here it is:—

"LETTER TO MRS. BURNE JONES.

"*3d December* 1877.

"I have been made rather unhappy by my husband's impulsive proposal about Christmas. We are dull old persons, and your two sweet young ones ought to find at Christmas a new bright bead to string on their memory, whereas to spend the time with us would be to string on a dark shrivelled berry. They ought to have a group of young creatures to be joyful with. Our own children always spend their Christmas with Gertrude's family; and we have usually taken our sober merry-making with friends out of town. Illness among these will break our custom this year; and thus *mein Mann*, feeling that our Christmas was free, considered how very much he liked being with you, omitting the other side of the question— namely, our total lack of means to make a suitably joyous meeting, a real festival for Phil and Margaret. I was conscious of this lack in the very moment of the proposal, and the consciousness has been pressing on me more and more painfully ever since. Even my husband's affectionate hopefulness cannot withstand my melancholy demonstration. So pray consider that kill-joy proposition as entirely retracted, and give us something of yourselves only on simple black-letter days, when the Herald Angels have not been raising expectations early in the morning."

That seems to me just one of the elaborately playful letters which it sets one's teeth on edge to read,—a mosaic of genuine tenderness for children and intellectual contempt for their credulous attitude of mind.

But it was this ardent belief in intellectuality, this complete failure to regard humility as in any sense whatever a true guide to truth, which, as it appears to me, greatly increased that moral tension so vividly present to the mind of Mr. Myers, as he listened to her remark that the less you believe in God the more peremptory becomes the personal authority of duty. Now I quite admit that this conception of an ideal to which George Eliot felt herself absolutely bound to approximate as closely as she could, and to which she did not believe that any one but herself could effectually urge her, pervades her whole correspondence. But I think that, eager as her devotion to the ideal is, it constrained, even if it stimulated, the fibre of her character. Undoubtedly, as I have said before, George Eliot was in the *highest* sense her own God, *not* the object of her own worship, but her own moral Providence, her own conscience, her own lawgiver, her own judge, her own Saviour. This is, as it seems to me, what makes the sense of strain in her life grow greater towards the close. There never was much spontaneousness in her, but what there was at first grows rapidly less and less. She tried to do for herself all that religious people rightly leave to God, as well as all that religious people rightly do for themselves. Of course, George Eliot thought this the great advantage of her scepticism. It secured her, she held, from expending piety on "imaginary perfection," and required her to spend it on "real imperfection." But whatever her own view of this economy of force may have been, I think it plain that her genuine anxiety to be a law to herself, though it broke down at a very critical moment, usually made her painfully eager to assume

the right moral posture, and to assume it with
emphasis. A human being of strong ethical convictions, who thinks that God is to be replaced by his
own moral thoughtfulness, must be always exerting
himself to be more and more morally thoughtful, and
must injure himself by giving to his moral thoughtfulness a highly artificial character, and that seems to
me exactly George Eliot's case. "I am better now,"
she writes in 1852 to Mrs. Bray; "have rid myself
of all distasteful work, and am trying to love the
glorious destination of humanity, looking before and
after." What can be worse for any mind than
"trying to love the glorious destination of humanity,
looking before and after?" and this, though George
Eliot, of course, confessed to herself, that in the
absence of any faith in God, she could only judge by
the most doubtful criteria what that destination was
likely to be. For my part, I wonder that she did
not feel worse instead of better for that Quixotic
endeavour to love the ambiguous destiny of a father-
less race. Again, in 1870 she writes to Mrs. Robert
Lytton (now Lady Lytton): "I try to delight in the
sunshine that will be, when I shall never see it any
more, and I think it is possible for this sort of
impersonal life to attain great intensity—possible for
us to gain much more independence than is usually
believed of the small bundle of facts that make our
own personality." Can any one conceive a more
artificial strain than an endeavour to delight in "the
sunshine that will be" after we are dead? That

seems to me a vain endeavour to make up for the void with which George Eliot has in imagination replaced God, by craning eagerly into an as yet non-existent universe, and blessing it in her own person. A fine nature stripped of faith will put itself through all sorts of painful gymnastic efforts in the attempt to supply to bereaved humanity the place of Him who is the same "yesterday, to-day, and for ever."

One of the finest touches in this book is contained in that letter to Madame Bodichon from which I have already quoted, where George Eliot, after stating that she has full faith "in the working out of higher possibilities than the Catholic or any other Church has presented," goes on to say that "those who have strength to wait and endure, are bound to accept no formula which their whole souls—their intellect as well as their emotions—do not embrace with entire reverence. The highest 'calling and election' is to *do without opium*, and live through all our pain with conscious, clear-eyed endurance." I heartily agree. The sceptic, however great his hunger of soul, *is* bound not to make-believe that he thinks what in his real inner mind he does not think, for the sake merely of the satisfaction of a little sympathy and warmth. Doubtless there is such a thing as opium-taking in the shape of entertaining in the mind soothing beliefs which are not really held with inward conviction. But it seems to me that George Eliot had not the strength to act up to her own principle. Minute doses of opium in the shape of soothing but thoroughly unreal assuagements of the pain of her own incapacity to help her friends when in trouble, she certainly did take. It is no doubt very painful to hear of the anguish of a friend and to have nothing further to say than that the knowledge of that anguish gives you pain. And there are no dismaller letters than the letters in which George Eliot tries to make believe very much that she has something more than this to say. For example, on such an occasion she writes to Mrs. Bray, justly enough from her point of view: "There is no such thing as consolation when we have made the lot of another our own;" but the words are hardly written before she makes an attempt at consolation, and, as it appears to me, a most unhappy one, which may have imposed on herself, but cannot have imposed on her friends:—

"I don't know whether you strongly share, as I do, the old belief that made men say the gods loved those who died young. It seems to me truer than ever, now life has become more complex, and more and more difficult problems have to be worked out. Life, though a good to men on the whole, is a doubtful good to many, and to some not a good at all. To my thought it is a source of constant mental distraction to make the denial of this a part of religion—to go on pretending things are better than they are. To me early death takes the aspect of salvation, though I feel, too, that those who live and suffer may sometimes have the greater blessedness of *being* a salvation" (vol. ii. p. 400).

I think this is hardly opium—at best it is make-believe opium; but it is curiously unreal all the same.

If the early extinction of life—for that is what George
Eliot means by death—is in any sense a matter for
rejoicing, it must clearly be, as she implies, simply on
the ground that longer life would involve a preponderance
of evil; but how escape by extinction from
a preponderance of evil can, in any real sense, be
called a "salvation,"—a making whole,—and that,
too, in the very same context in which such salvation
or making whole as the good procure for those on
whose behalf they suffer, is appreciated at its true
worth, it is simply impossible to conjecture. The truth
is, that salvation is a conception which George Eliot,
with her creed, was bound to reserve exclusively for
the healing of the moral maladies of the *living*. To
talk of salvation as secured by the dead was playing
fast and loose with her own convictions in the supposed
interest of those who were suffering under
some keen grief. So again in writing to another
friend she says: "I have had a great personal loss
lately, in the death of a sweet woman to whom I have
sometimes gone, and hoped to go again, for a little
moral strength. She had long been confined to
her room by consumption, which has now taken her
quite out of reach except to memory, which makes
all dear human beings undying to us as long as we
ourselves live" (vol. ii. pp. 377-378). In other
words, as there is no real compensation for the loss
we suffer in the death of our friends, to those who
believe that death is final, and as it is intolerable to
confess this to ourselves "with conscious, clear-eyed

endurance," we must *talk* of memory making the dead undying to us as long as we ourselves live, though there is no meaning in the phrase, since memory does not begin when our friends die, but, on the contrary, rather begins then to grow less vivid. Still more unreal appears to me to be the consolation offered to a widowed friend: " You will think of things to do such as he would approve of your doing, and every day will be sacred with his memory—nay, his presence. There is no pretence or visionariness in saying that he is still part of you." Certainly there is no pretence or visionariness in saying so, if you only mean it, as George Eliot only meant it, in a very inferior sense to that in which you may say that your ancestors are still part of you. But as there is no particular consolation in thinking of that —and certainly it would not justify you in saying that they are *present* with you—it is surely a very make-believe consolation to tell a widow that her husband is present with her, when you mean only, and she knows that you mean only, that you want to say something which sounds comfortable, though it has no comfort in it. *That* surely is not "living through all our pain with conscious, clear-eyed endurance." And when it came to experiencing the same trouble herself, George Eliot did not find much consolation in reflections of this kind. On the contrary, she says, " I had been conscious of a certain drying-up of tenderness in me," and she took refuge, not in amusing herself by imagining the " presence" with her, in a non-natural sense, of him whom she had lost, but in the speedy formation of new ties. The moral strain under which she lived, in the effort to be a law to herself, did not fail to distort her intellect into very unnatural postures, which she herself even found to be hollow and unmeaning when she came to test them for herself.

George Eliot's letters are at their best when she sets herself to persuade a correspondent, who had apparently been turned into something like a misanthrope by the philosophy which rejects God, immortality, and moral freedom, that she is quite unreasonable in allowing any deeper insight into the lot of man to alienate her sympathies from man. I have already quoted the first few sentences of this letter to Lady Ponsonby, in which George Eliot declares her belief that the idea of God has only influenced men for good, so far as it has contained a true ideal of human goodness. The remainder of the letter is devoted to showing that *more*, not less, pity ought to be felt for mere mortals, than for immortals with a future in reserve; that no belief in the necessarian or determinist theory of human action ought to affect any one's resolve to take the proper means for becoming just, tender and sympathetic; and that to plead the petty scale of human life as a reason for ignoring the difference between happiness and misery is to use an argument to which no one would be in the least disposed to grant any validity, if it were brought to bear on his own lot. The letter seems to me on the whole so much the ablest which these volumes contain, and so full of the kind of determination to make the best of a bad business which constituted George Eliot's philosophy of human life, that I must give the remainder of it in full. Nothing can express better her absolute disbelief in what seems to me the noblest elements of the human character, and the grave fortitude with which she braced herself and her friends up to the task of attenuating the miseries of a lot thus discredited :—

"Have you quite fairly represented yourself in saying that you have ceased to pity your suffering fellow-men, because you can no longer think of them as individualities of immortal duration, in some other state of existence than this of which you know the pains and the pleasures ? —that you feel less for them now you regard them as more miserable ? And, on a closer examination of your feelings, should you find that you had lost all sense of quality in actions—all possibility of admiration that yearns to imitate—all keen sense of what is cruel and injurious—all belief that your conduct (and therefore the conduct of others) can have any difference of effect on the wellbeing of those immediately about you (and therefore on those afar off), whether you carelessly follow your selfish moods or encourage that vision of others' needs which is the source of justice, tenderness, sympathy, in the fullest sense ? I cannot believe that your strong intellect will continue to see, in the conditions of man's appearance on this planet, a destructive relation to your sympathy : this seems to me equivalent to saying that you care no longer for colour, now you know the laws of the spectrum.

"As to the necessary combinations through which life is manifested, and which seem to present themselves to you as a hideous fatalism, which ought logically to petrify your volition—have they, *in fact*, any such influence on your ordinary course of action in the primary affairs of your existence as a human, social, domestic creature? And if they don't hinder you from taking measures for a bath, without which you know that you cannot secure the delicate cleanliness which is your second nature, why should they hinder you from a line of resolve in a higher strain of duty to your ideal, both for yourself and others? But the consideration of molecular physics is not the direct ground of human love and moral action, any more than it is the direct means of composing a noble picture or of enjoying great music. One might as well hope to dissect one's own body and be merry in doing it as take molecular physics (in which you must banish from your field of view what is specifically human) to be your dominant guide, your determiner of motives in what is solely human. That every study has its bearing on every other is true; but pain and relief, love and sorrow, have their peculiar history which make an experience and knowledge over and above the swing of atoms.

"The teaching you quote as George Sand's would, I think, deserve to be called nonsensical if it did not deserve to be called wicked. What sort of 'culture of the intellect' is that which, instead of widening the mind to a fuller and fuller response to all the elements of our existence, isolates it in a moral stupidity?—which flatters egoism with the possibility that a complex and refined human society can continue, wherein relations have no sacredness beyond the inclination of changing moods?— or figures to itself an anæsthetic human life that one may compare to that of the fabled grasshoppers who were once men, but having heard the song of the Muses could do nothing but sing, and starved themselves so till they died and had a fit resurrection as grasshoppers; 'And this,' says Socrates, 'was the return the Muses made them.'

"With regard to the pains and limitations of one's personal lot, I suppose there is not a single man or woman who has not more or less need of that stoical resignation which is often a hidden heroism, or who, in considering his or her past history, is not aware that it has been cruelly affected by the ignorant or selfish action of some fellow-being in a more or less close relation of life. And to my mind there can be no stronger motive than this perception, to an energetic effort that the lives nearest to us shall not suffer in a like manner from *us*.

"The progress of the world—which you say can only come at the right time—can certainly never come at all save by the modified action of the individual beings who compose the world; and that we can say to ourselves with effect, 'There is an order of considerations which I will keep myself continually in mind of, so that they may continually be the prompters of certain feelings and actions,' seems to me as undeniable as that we can resolve to study the Semitic languages and apply to an Oriental scholar to give us daily lessons. What would your keen wit say to a young man who alleged the physical basis of nervous action as a reason why he could not possibly take that course?

"As to duration and the way in which it affects your view of the human history, what is really the difference to your imagination between infinitude and billions when you have to consider the value of human experience? Will you say that since your life has a term of threescore years and ten, it was really a matter of indifference whether you were a cripple with a wretched skin disease, or an active creature with a mind at large for the enjoyment of knowledge, and with a nature which has attracted others to you.

"Difficulties of thought—acceptance of what is, without full comprehension—belong to every system of thinking. The question is to find the least incomplete."

It is a strange and yet a most characteristic state of mind, which insists that the more insignificant man really is, the more miserable he is, and there-

fore the more deserving of pity, for if that were so,
the ephemera would thereby be proved more miserable and pitiable still. But it was very characteristic
in her to accept without a murmur a pessimistic
estimate of man's nature and capacities, and then to
strain to the utmost all her powers to show that the
worse his condition the more imperative is the duty
to mitigate its miseries. That is George Eliot all
over—the low-spirited acquiescence in a depreciating
estimate of human nature, and the obstinate resolve
to take the more pity on it, the more dismal is its
plight. It never occurs to her that perhaps it would
be the truest pity to look deeper into the question
why man is so pitiable;—whether it is possible that
a mere creature of circumstances and of the hour,
without the capacity for either true responsibility or
true guilt, could be deserving of so much pity as she
bestowed on him, or could be even capable of feeling
so much pity as she herself felt. She told herself
truly enough that she did not admire colour the less
for understanding the laws of the spectrum, but then
she forgot to add that there is nothing in the laws
of the spectrum to lower the significance commonly
attached to colour, while there is a great deal in her
fatalist philosophy of human conduct to extinguish
the significance commonly attached to responsibility,
to virtue, and to guilt. It was very characteristic in
her to urge that it is just as silly to ignore the fittest
incentives to virtue, if you want to be virtuous, as it
is to ignore the proper steps for learning Hebrew, if

you want to learn Hebrew. But it is equally characteristic in her to pass by the consideration that, if you *don't* want to be virtuous, the fatalist can always omit the requisite incentives to virtue, and attribute the omission to the defective conditions under which his character was formed, and console himself by remembering all the time that it is not he, but the conditions under which he acts, which are to blame. The whole letter shows George Eliot acquiescing, almost eagerly, in the poverty of human nature, yet none the less obstinately set on teaching the world that, even though we have to deal with wretched materials in our effort to improve mankind, we are bound to make the condition of men better than we found it, and that we have the means of doing so if we will. This resolve is noble enough; but it seems strange that she did not infer from it that, after all, she had misunderstood the nature which was thus tenacious of its ground, and which, though believing the odds to be all against it, fights on all the same.

To me, George Eliot's whole career seems to be all of a piece;—She conceded everything to doubt; she conceded too much to temptation, perhaps rather from a strong sense of the hopelessness of holding high ground than from any inability to maintain her ground when once she had taken it; but after all these concessions were made, and partly in the pride of these concessions, as though she had yielded everything which the most severely intellectual view of human nature could demand, she fought on in gloom and dejection as strenuous a fight for a pitiful demeanour towards the human race as it is in man to maintain. Her own position was, by her own choice, one of serious moral disadvantage; her philosophy made that position of moral disadvantage one of intellectual disadvantage also; her dramatic insight showed her very vividly how petty and illusory human motives frequently are; but none the less she struggled on, often in gloom, sometimes in despair, to convince mankind that their one clear duty is to be more pitiful to each other's sufferings, and more fair to each other's faults. "Pity and fairness—two little words which, carried out, would embrace the utmost delicacies of the moral life—seem to me not to rest on an unverifiable hypothesis, but on facts quite as irreversible as the perception that a pyramid will not stand on its apex" (vol. iii. p. 317). There is George Eliot's philosophy compressed, and a very inadequate philosophy indeed it is; for "pity and fairness" at their best will only teach us to treat others as we treat ourselves, and will not teach us to treat ourselves as we ought. But with a languid temperament, with no faith worthy of the name, and an artificial and enervating theory of human nature, George Eliot yet used her vigorous and masculine imagination in the service of "pity and fairness" with a strenuousness and even a passion which we might most of us emulate in vain. Still this Life seems to me to serve rather as a dusky background against which we see more clearly the true moral of her works, than as any enhancement of the pleasure which these works give us. Instead of enlarging the suggestions of those striking works, it rather makes them a greater mystery than ever.

Two grave disappointments certainly the book has for me. The first, that it seems rather to conceal, as under a mask and domino, the vivacity and fertility which one naturally ascribes to the great author who understood labourers and butchers and farriers and sporting clergymen and auctioneers and pedlars better even than she understood scholars and poets and metaphysicians. The second and still greater disappointment was to find that, so far as I can judge from these letters, her heart never seems to have rebelled against her own dim creed—a creed for pallid ghosts rather than for living and struggling men. In the last few months of her life she visited the Grande Chartreuse, as Mr. Arnold had done many years before her; nor have we any indication in her brief notice of enjoyment that she shared those sad feelings which the most sceptical of our Oxford poets has depicted as his experience there. But to the reader of her Life nothing seems to express better its joyless and yet laborious attitude towards the world of faith than Matthew Arnold's touching lament that he could neither believe with the Carthusians nor rejoice with the so-called leaders of Western progress:—

> "Wandering between two worlds, one dead,
> The other powerless to be born,
> With nowhere yet to rest my head,

Like these, on earth I wait forlorn.
Their faith, my tears, the world deride,
I come to shed them at their side.

"Oh hide me in your glooms profound
Ye solemn seats of holy pain !
Take me cowl'd forms and fence me round
Till I possess my soul again ;
Till free my thoughts before me roll
Not chaf'd by hourly false control."

For this is, to my mind, the secret of a character which through all its years waited "forlorn" for a faith which the "hourly false control" of a powerful but disintegrating intellect withheld to the very last.

VI

FREDERICK DENISON MAURICE

FREDERICK DENISON MAURICE [1]

This book must read like the story of a shadow in a dream to those who think that there is no eternal world at all. Nothing illustrates better the fidelity and skill with which Colonel Maurice has pictured for us his father's life—chiefly, as he himself tells us, in his father's own words—than the force with which from beginning to end it impresses on us the conviction that here was a man living, and living eagerly, in time, for ends which mere creatures of time cannot either measure or apprehend. It is not surprising, therefore, that the Life of Maurice is not what any one would think of calling a popular book. And yet it has already awakened a kind of interest which no popular book would awaken, for it is one of the most striking testimonies to the existence of an eternal life, in Maurice's own sense of the word, that was ever yet given. Throughout these twelve hundred closely printed pages one cannot come on the trace of a day

---

[1] *The Life of Frederick Denison Maurice, chiefly told in his own Letters.* Edited by his son, Frederick Maurice. With portraits. In two volumes. Macmillan and Co.

of Maurice's life that was not chiefly lived in the light of eternity. I don't, of course, mean that he lived always as he himself would have desired to live; for one of the chief notes of this remarkable book is the profound sense, not merely of humility, but of almost extravagant humiliation which marks it. I only mean this, that whether Maurice lived as he would have desired to live or not, every day of his life seems to have been scored and furrowed either with the passionate desire so to live, or an almost unreasonable self-reproach for not having so lived. It has been said that his life was one long pursuit of "unattainable ends" by "inappropriate means." If Maurice's ends were really unattainable it does not require much literary acuteness to perceive that any means he took to gain them must necessarily have been inappropriate, so that the epigram, like most epigrams, over-reaches itself. But I think it would be much truer to say that he lived to pursue ends which he actually attained with much more marvellous success than ends of that kind are usually attained, by means which often seemed, and sometimes were, clumsy, and more or less inappropriate for the end he had in view. There was nothing of the genius of delicate adjustment about Maurice. The ends which he attained he attained often with a great waste of power, and partly, perhaps, by showing how indifferent he was to the wasting of himself upon them, if only he might somehow gain them even partially at last. What Cardinal Newman once wrote in reference to St. Gregory Nasianzen has often seemed to me curiously applicable to Maurice :—

> "So works the All-wise! our services dividing
>   Not as we ask :
> For the world's profit, by our gifts deciding
>   Our duty-task.
> See in kings' courts loth Jeremiah plead,
> And slow-tongued Moses rule by eloquence of deed.
>
> "Yes, thou bright Angel of the East didst rear
>   The Cross divine,
> Borne high upon thy liquid accents where
>   Men mocked the sign ;
> Till that wild city heard thy battle-cry,
> And hearts were stirred and deemed a Pentecost
>   was nigh !"

So it was that London heard Maurice's battle-cry. And yet a great deal of his work was undoubtedly tentative, awkward, "inappropriate." But the persevering and redundant laboriousness with which, when needful, it was all done over again, produced an effect which could hardly have been produced by the highest genius for adapting means to ends. There was the lavishness of the eternal world in all his efforts, though there was all the humiliation of human inadequacy too. "We have this treasure in earthen vessels, that the excellency of the power may be of God and not of ourselves," might be the motto of Maurice's career, so little did he feel the brightness of success, and so much nevertheless did he really attain.

And the present Life of Maurice only echoes, alike

in its evidence of failure and in its evidence of success, the impression produced by the career of the living man. It is about forty years since my most intimate friend, the late Walter Bagehot, who was then a student of Lincoln's Inn where he was afterwards called to the bar, took me to hear one of the afternoon sermons of the chaplain of the Inn. I remember Bagehot's telling me, with his usual caution, that he would not exactly answer for my being impressed by the sermon, but that at all events he thought I should feel that something different went on there from that which goes on in an ordinary church or chapel service; that there was a sense of "something religious"—a phrase Maurice himself would hardly have appreciated—in the air which was not to be found elsewhere. I went, and it is hardly too much to say that the voice and manner of the preacher—his voice and manner in the reading-desk at least as much as in the pulpit—have lived in my memory ever since, as no other voice and manner have ever lived in it. The half-stern, half-pathetic emphasis with which he gave the words of the Confession, "And there is *no* health in *us*," throwing the weight of the meaning on to the last word, and the rising of his voice into a higher plane of hope as he passed away from the confession of weakness to the invocation of God's help, struck the one note of his life—the passionate trust in eternal help—as it had never been struck in my hearing before. There was intensity—almost too thrilling—and something, too, of sad exultation in every tone, as if the reader were rehearsing a story in which he had no part except his personal certainty of its truth, his gratitude that it should be true, and his humiliation that it had fallen to such lips as his to declare it. This was what made his character present itself so strongly to the mind as almost embodied in *a voice*. He seemed to be the channel for a communication, not the source of it. There was a gentle hurry, and yet a peremptoriness, in those at once sad and sonorous tones, which spoke of haste to tell their tale, and of actual fear of not telling it with sufficient emphasis and force. "They hurried on as if impatient to fulfil their mission." They seemed put into his mouth, while he, with his whole soul bent on their wonderful drift, uttered them as an awestruck but thankful envoy tells the tale of danger and deliverance. Yet though Mr. Maurice's voice seemed to be the essential part of him as a religious teacher, his face, if you ever looked at it, was quite in keeping with his voice. His eye was full of sweetness, but fixed, and, as it were, fascinated on some ideal point. His countenance expressed nervous, high-strung tension, as though all the various play of feelings in ordinary human nature converged, in him, towards a single focus—the declaration of the divine purpose. Yet this tension, this peremptoriness, this convergence of his whole nature on a single point, never gave the effect of a dictatorial air for a moment. There was a quiver in his voice, a tremulousness in the strong deep lines of his face,

a tenderness in his eye, which assured you at once
that there was nothing of the hard, crystallising character of a dogmatic belief in the Absolute in the faith
which had conquered his heart; and most men recognised this, for the hardest voices took a tender and
almost caressing tone in addressing him. The more
Maurice believed in Christ, the less he confounded
himself with the object of his belief, and the more
pathetic was his distrust of his own power to see
aright, or say aright what he saw. The only fault,
as most of his hearers would think, of his manner,
was the perfect monotony of its sweet and solemn
intonation. His voice was the most musical of voices,
with the least variety and play. His mind was one
of the simplest, deepest, humblest, and most intense,
with the least range of illustration. He had humour
and irony,—usually faculties of broad range,—but
with him they moved on a single line. His humour
and irony were ever of one kind—the humour and
irony which dwell perpetually on the inconsistencies
and paradoxes involved in the contrast between human
dreams and divine purposes, and which derive only a
kindlier feeling for the former from the knowledge
that they are apparently so eager to come into painful
collision with the latter. As an intimate friend very
truly remarked, his irony was rather the irony of
Isaiah than the irony of Sophocles, but it was gentler
and less indignant. The most bitter flight of irony
that I can recollect is a very fine passage in one of
the Lincoln's Inn sermons, wherein Mr. Maurice,

speaking of the travesty which the popular theology makes of Revelation, in that it starts from the fundamental assumption of original sin rather than from God, suggested the clauses of an imaginary Te Diabolum Laudamus, in honour and propitiation of the powers of darkness, as the psalm which, if it only rightly knew itself, the modern theology ought to substitute for the great song of Christian thankfulness. It could not but have suggested to many who heard it Isaiah's grim irony against the idolaters who, after using some of their timber to cook their dinner, " with the residue thereof made them a god." But Mr. Maurice's irony was not often so keen. Generally it was mixed with sweetness, and almost always double-edged, with one edge for himself and only one for his opponent. Sometimes, perhaps, he a little overdid the irony intended to be at his own expense. He was not insensible to the pleasure which some men find in under-rating their own influence and power. His humility was as sincere as it was profound; but he seems to me to have derived something of fresh assurance for the great truths of which he was most sure, through unduly exaggerating the extent of his own personal shortcomings in setting them forth.

His life, indeed, was a sort of chaunt, rich, deep, awestruck, passionately humble, from beginning to end. And it was this in more senses than one. No man, as I have said, ever was more anxious to use words in their simplest, most straightforward, most obvious sense. No man was ever more indignant at the pretensions of journalists and others to speak for a class, when they really only expressed the convictions of an individual. No man was ever more explicit in making people understand that what he said he said only for himself, that he expressed nothing in the world but the faith, or the hope, or the opinion, or the surmise, as the case might be, of a single and very humble mind. Yet, as a matter of fact, no man's thoughts ever fell more into the forms of a kind of litany than Mr. Maurice's. You can hardly interpret him fairly if you treat all his avowals of "shameful" failure, of humiliating inferiority to everybody with whom he acted, of suspected dishonesty lurking at the root of his best thoughts, of "hard and proud words" used when he ought to have been gentle and forbearing, as if they were strictly individual confessions limited to individual memories. They were, as I believe, nothing of the kind. He had a strange power of sympathy with others, especially, I think, with their weaknesses; and when he felt this sympathy, he imputed it to himself as a fault that he had felt it, even though in the next minute he would be ready to declare that he had felt too little sympathy, and had alienated those whom he might have helped by his own hardness of heart. Thus it happened that the tenderness of his moral sympathies gave him a double ground for self-reproach and self-abasement. He thought himself guilty of the guilt into the depths of which he had pierced, and he thought himself equally guilty of not having entered into its pangs more generously, and with more healing power. His confessions, then, were a kind of litany, poured forth in the name of a human nature, the weakness and sinfulness of which he felt most keenly, most individually, most painfully, but which he felt at least as much in the character of the representative of a race by the infirmities of which he was overwhelmed, as on his own account. For example, in one letter he writes: "I wish to confess the sins of the time as my own. Ah, how needful do I feel it, for the sins of others produce such sin in me, and stir up my unsanctified nature so terribly." That passage reveals accurately the secret of the matter. Maurice's confessions of profound unworthiness are as simple and genuine as confessions can be, but they are confessions at least as much due to his consciousness of being able to enter to the full into all the evil of the social life to which he belonged, as to any experience that could be called strictly individual. In one who does not catch the wonderful depth of his social nature, his curiously profound sense of shame at noticing that the evil of others produced a sort of reverberation in his own heart, his constant chaunt of self-depreciation, looks unreal. When, however, you catch that he feels—as all the deeper religious natures have always felt—a sort of self-reproachful complicity in every sinful tendency of his age, you feel that the litany in which he expresses his shame, though most genuine, nay, most piercing in its genuineness, is not so much morbid self-depreciation as a deep sense of the cruel burden of social infirmity and social sin, which he laid down on behalf of all men in whose infirmities and sins he could perceive echoes of his own, at the feet of his Saviour. Thus, in one of his books, after criticising what is wrong in others, he adds: "If I have any occasion to speak against them, I will add that I do not hold them to be worse men than I am, and that I am satisfied they have a better and nobler spirit in them, which is aspiring to the true God, and rendering, probably, a more acceptable homage to Him than I render. I will say this, because I hold it to be true, and because I ought to say it," though he expects to be charged with hypocrisy for saying it. That means, what I believe to be the exact truth, that Mr. Maurice's many and strong expressions of inferiority to all the rest of the world were really as much due to the sense of shame and confusion with which the perception of other men's weaknesses and sins came home to him when he recognised kindred feelings in his own nature, as to the urgency of those feelings in his own individual experience. His confessions must be taken as the outpourings of the conscience of a race rather than as the outpouring of the conscience of an individual, or they will seem artificial and unreal. Once catch the perfect simplicity with which he pours out the humiliation of the heart of man, rather than the humiliation of the heart of an individual man,— though, of course, it is the experience of the individual man which justifies him in that confession,—and you see how truthful and genuine it is, and how wonderful was the ardour with which Maurice entered into the social tendencies of his day.

Yet a simpler and homelier man there never was in this world; indeed, he was one who, though he could hardly speak without showing that his mind was occupied with invisible realities, had a quite pathetic sense of his own inadequacy to do what he desired to do, and the tenderest possible sympathy with the like incapacities of others. His own idea of himself was curiously unlike the truth. He felt deeply his own want of sympathy with most human enjoyments, and tells Mr. Kingsley that he is a "hard Puritan, almost incapable of enjoyment; though I try," he adds, "to feel no grudge against those who have that which my conscience tells me it is not a virtue but a sin to want."

The sin of which he thus accused himself was his joylessness, and his envy of the joyousness of others; and also the tendency which the sight of evil in others had to provoke anger in himself of a kind which he could not justify, and which he told himself was Pharisaic. Any man less like a Pharisee probably never lived, and it has often been a puzzle to me how he even suspected himself of that species of arrogance and hardness. I think he mistook the monotone of his religious feeling, when he compared it with the liveliness and flexibility of others, for evidence of aridity and dogmatism. And yet so subtle was his religious feeling that he was sometimes thankful for his own hardness, because it helped him to ascribe more genuinely all that was not hard in him to God. His theory of himself obviously was that he was deficient in human feeling, but that this consciousness of deficiency in human feeling was good for him, because it enabled him to refer to the divine love alone all the consciousness he had of being able to stir the hearts of others. In a most characteristic letter to myself which Colonel Maurice has published he says: "The sense of our substantial union as men with Christ, and of His union with the Father, sometimes comes to me with overpowering conviction, not of delight such as a Santa Theresa or Fénélon may have felt, but of its stern, hard, scientific reality, which makes me long that I had the fervour and earnestness in making my belief known, which I admire and ought not to envy in other men. But at other times I can thank God for having granted me a cold, uncordial temperament and constitution, on purpose that I may refer all love, and all power of acting upon the reason and the conscience and the heart to Him. Some day I hope our tongues may be loosed, and that we may as earnestly speak of what we feel to be deep and universal, as we drop what we find to be only transitory and for a few." What he chiefly found fault with in himself was his spiritual rigidity, his deficiency in keen human emotions and sympathies, though this deficiency was a mere inference of his own from his want of a vivid perceptive and sensitive life, such as he saw with admiration, for instance, in his close friends Charles Kingsley and Tom Hughes. Whether he really felt, as he so often implies that he did, the temptation of the Pharisee to judge harshly the sins of others, more powerful within him than very inferior men feel it, it is of course impossible to say. But if he did, no one ever contended against that temptation more successfully, or warned the world so well of its own Pharisaic bias. But it is true, I think, that Maurice did feel so strongly upon him the spell of the eternal and invisible will that he had some reason to dread the temptation to identify it with himself, and to speak as if that which he discerned outside him were really part of him. Certainly he dreaded this temptation much more than he dreaded the ordinary weaknesses to which he was liable. He had a warm temper, and accused himself freely of having indulged it, but he never accused himself of that with half the same bitterness with which he accused himself of Pharisaically judging others. He knew the extent of the one danger, but he never seemed able to measure for himself the extent of the other. Bearing witness, as his whole nature did, to the eternal world, he was always, he thought, in danger of imagining that what he judged to be evil God must judge to be equally evil; and consequently there was no sin on which he passed such vehement and stern sentences, for he always believed that those vehement and stern sentences were passed virtually upon himself. Colonel Maurice gives us one very curious illustration of this in the interesting chapter on the controversy with Dr. Mansel. Maurice had always accused himself of not having been tender enough in dealing with the sceptical leanings of Sterling, of having shown dogmatic hardness towards Sterling's doubts. He refers to this in his remarks on the agnostic theory of Mansel with the same poignant self-reproach that he had always felt, saying that " the remembrance of hard and proud words spoken against those who were crying out for truth will always be the bitterest" of remembrances for one who holds that the Bible testifies, from its first page to its last, that God does implant and does satisfy the yearning for truth, and does satisfy it by unveiling Himself to all who really seek Him. Dr. Mansel, in his profound ignorance of Maurice's general drift, style, and character, was blind enough to suppose that this was a sneer directed against *him*, though the whole drift of his own book, against the teaching of which Maurice was protesting, had been to prove that God does not and cannot so unveil Himself to men as Maurice believed, but can only give us " regulative " hints, carefully-adapted rules of action —working hypotheses concerning Himself—on the assumption of which He directs us for all practical purposes to proceed. This blunder of Dr. Mansel's exactly illustrates the frequent inappropriateness of Maurice's language for the purpose of conveying his meaning, even when that meaning was nearest his own heart. In the intensity of his earnestness he wrote on as if in soliloquy, without clearly representing to himself either the class of people or the individual person for whose immediate benefit he was writing, and expressing himself much as he would have expressed himself to the most intimate friend who perfectly understood the reserves and illusions by which he qualified almost all his teaching. The great waste of energy of which I have spoken was probably never better illustrated than in his answers to Dr. Mansel, full of noble truth and passion as they were. The Dean did not catch his drift at all, indeed but few of the theologians of the day caught his drift; it was only those who had got the key to his mind from the study of many previous writings who really understood what he meant. And yet what he meant was intrinsically lucid as well as true, and was marked by large intellectual grasp. There was no economy of spiritual power possible to him.

Again, the biography shows us quite frankly where Maurice's own light failed him. For example, he always held the language that the whole race has been and is redeemed by Christ once and for ever. Hence, in his correspondence with Mr. Kingsley (vol. ii. pp. 272-274), he admits that the Baptismal Service which speaks of the infant as "made" the child of God in baptism—instead of simply being *declared* so —is not entirely satisfactory to him; and he explains it away after a fashion, as it seems to me, not at all different from similar explanations in "Tract 90." In another place Colonel Maurice gives us, as I think, quite clearly, the origin of a certain very gross misunderstanding of his father, with which however, when he meets with that misunderstanding in Principal Shairp's account of Mr. MacLeod Campbell's conversation, he is greatly shocked. Mr. MacLeod Campbell's statement was that, according to Maurice and his friends, " there is nothing real in the nature of things answering to this sense of guilt. The sense of guilt becomes a mistake, which further knowledge reverses. All sin is thus reduced to ignorance." Doubtless this is a gross misunderstanding of the general tenor of Maurice's writings, where the sense of guilt is profoundly, deeply, oppressively apparent from beginning to end. But surely there was much in his language at times to excuse the misunderstanding. If the only difference between sin and righteousness is that men living in sin do not recognise their accomplished redemption, while men living in faith do, the sin would appear to be a sin of ignorance rather than of will. And in exact agreement with this view, Maurice says, in a remarkable letter to Miss Barton (vol. i. p. 233), that he wishes to treat evil "as though it were not, for in very truth it is a falsehood. It has no reality, and why should not we treat it as having none?" If Mr. MacLeod Campbell had come upon that sentence alone, —and there are a good many partially analogous statements to be found here and there in Maurice's writings,—surely he might be excused for supposing that Maurice regarded sin as a purely negative and unreal affair. For my own part, I have never been able to reconcile Maurice's profound and deep sense of the awful reality of sin—expressed hundreds or thousands of times in these volumes—with his language as to the absolute completeness of redemption even as regards those who have not been rescued from a life of sin; nor with his language here and there—language which I believe he holds in common with the Roman Church—as to the purely negative and unreal character of sin. But it is Colonel Maurice's great merit that he conceals nothing. He weaves together with great art, and in a fashion that must have cost continuous labour carried on through a great portion of twelve years since his father's death, passages of Maurice's letters revealing his thoughts and hopes as to all the main events of his life, inward and outward, and interpreting them, when they need interpretation, by the light of his own deep insight into his father's works and his own profound reverence for his father's character.

Maurice was always lavish of himself. That is why he influenced those who once fell under his spell so much, for it is this wealth of energy, which is unable to economise itself, that exerts the greatest effect when it produces an effect at all. When he was still a young man of twenty-five, Arthur Hallam, the subject of "In Memoriam," wrote to Mr. Gladstone: "I do not myself know Maurice, but I know many whom he has moulded like a second nature, and these, too, men eminent for intellectual powers, to whom the presence of a commanding spirit would, in all other cases, be a signal rather for rivalry than reverential acknowledgment. The effect which he has produced on the minds of many at Cambridge by the single creation of that society of the Apostles (for the spirit though not the form was created by him) is far greater than I can dare to calculate, and will be felt both directly and indirectly in the age that is upon us." Archdeacon Hare, one of the authors of the *Guesses at Truth*, told Mr. Llewelyn Davies that, in his belief, "no such mind as Maurice's had been given to the world since Plato's." And though there was no trace in Maurice of that exquisite imaginative grace which makes Plato's philosophy so much more fascinating than the philosophy of any other human thinker, there is no doubt that he had more of Plato's eye for discerning the evidence of a superhuman origin of truth, and of the complete incapacity of our minds to originate the highest truths which it is given us to perceive, than any Englishman of our century, Coleridge himself—to whom he owed so much—not excepted. There has probably never been a thinker who has more perfectly realised himself, and more successfully compelled others to realise, that the truth and our knowledge of the truth are of very different orders of importance; that needful as it often is for us to know the truth, the truth itself produces its most potent effects whether we know it or not; the only consequence of our ignorance of it being, that when ignorant of it we often stumble up against it and lame ourselves, whereas if it could cease to be, we should cease to be with it. This being Maurice's profound conviction, he naturally held that Revelation —the truth concerning His own being voluntarily communicated to us by Him who is the truth—must be infinitely the most important part of all truth, though it cannot of course be separated for a moment from the truths concerning our condition which God has enforced upon us by the gradual training of our minds and bodies. This was what made Maurice a theologian. He could not read the history of the Hebrew people without feeling assured that God had trained that particular race for the express purpose of manifesting His own nature through it to men; and this he regarded as the great complement and key to the lessons which in all other races man had been taught concerning the significance of human nature, and of the otherwise inexplicable yearnings and wants by which that nature is penetrated.

Miss Wedgwood, in the very striking paper on Maurice which she contributed to the *British Quarterly Review*, has contested Maurice's reverence for facts on the ground that there were a good many facts to which he could not even persuade himself to pay attention. She refers to the facts from which scientific men are supposed to deduce almost all their general views of the meaning of the universe, and I have no doubt that, if challenged, she could also illustrate her meaning by the utter indifference which Maurice showed to such criticisms as those of Bishop Colenso on the historical accuracy of the Pentateuch, through his inability to conceive that the kind of inaccuracy in the Bible for which Bishop Colenso contended, had any relevancy at all to his own conviction that the Bible contains the key to human history and destiny. Yet I cannot think that Miss Wedgwood is right in regarding Maurice's indifference to these facts as significant of a want of reverence for fact in general. So far as I can judge, it never occurred to him that either physical science or historical criticism, whatever might come of either, could possibly break down either the truth or the importance of revelation. He did not meddle very much with either, because he did not think himself well fitted to do so with effect, and he had the humblest possible opinion of his own powers whenever he travelled out of the range of truths pressing closely upon his own mind. But though I have often regretted that he did not pay more attention to the methods of physical science and of historical criticism, I cannot say that I think his neglect to do so betrayed the smallest want of reverence for fact. What it did betray was a great want of reverence for theories which he regarded as unintelligible and unjustifiable generalisations from facts which he was eager to acknowledge. He had no more belief that the discovery of uniform laws of phenomena could disprove the possibility of the supernatural facts recorded in the Bible, than he had that the discovery of a mass of inaccurate figures in the Pentateuch could disprove the truth that Moses had been led by God when he guided his people through the wilderness to the borders of the promised land. Indeed he had never entered into the minds of the men who began life without any belief except in the uniformity of the outside world, or the minds of the men who supposed that the first guarantee of divine revelation must be the perfect accuracy of all the figures and minute incidents with which the memory of that revelation was mixed up. It is a pity, I think, that he did not more earnestly endeavour to master both states of mind, and to say exactly what one who had entered into those states of mind, but who held his own faith, might have said. But his neglect to do so was, I believe, due much more to an excessive indifference to theory than to the smallest indifference to fact. I should say that whenever he thought any fact established by history, he was disposed even to over-estimate its importance. Consider, for instance, his frank surrender of his own—to me unintelligible—attachment to the practice of subscription at the universities, and to the practice of reading the Athanasian Creed in churches, so soon as he saw that it was simply impossible to make men in general accept his own view of the meaning of these practices. Consider again his ardent political constitutionalism, which was wholly founded on his reverence for institutions which had proved their strength. Consider further his extreme prudence in directing the co-operative societies to which he devoted so much of his time, and the anxiety with which he strove to keep out all innovations for which the theorisers or dreamers amongst his companions contended. Again, to me the charm at once of such books as *The Prophets and Kings of the Old Testament*, and of such books as his *Metaphysical and Moral Philosophy*, depends almost entirely on the love for fact shown in both, the naked realism with which he accepts such histories as Jehu's, and the characteristic fidelity with which he recounts the teaching of Hobbes or Spinoza, and connects it with the facts of their external lives.

The admiration Maurice always felt for men who openly confessed themselves in the wrong—as Mr. Gladstone, for instance, did on the Maynooth question—was, I believe, really founded, as he himself said that it was, on his belief that facts are "angels of the Lord," against which it is useless and impious to struggle. No doubt, like most idealists, he made at times a long struggle for opinions of his own, which he had taken for something more than opinions; but I do not think he ever once realised the relevancy of a fact on any subject without endeavouring to ascertain its full significance and bearing, with a humility all his own. "The vesture of God's own ideas must be facts," he writes to a son, who had told him how he had heard it argued that a Christian legend which appealed to the conscience might produce the same result as a fact. "If He reveals His ideas to us, the revelation must be through facts. . . . I believe the modern process of idealising tends to destroy ideas and facts both, and to leave nothing but a certain deposit of both. The sensation novel is the appropriate sink or cesspool for this deposit.

All historical criticism is good, it seems to me, just so far as it tests facts, in love and reverence for facts and for what facts contain; all is bad and immoral which introduces the notion that it signifies little whether they turn out to be facts or no, or the notion that their reality as facts depends on certain accidents in the narration of them." I think Maurice's reverence for facts was profound, but that the facts which he regarded as "the vesture of God's ideas," and not the facts which he regarded as "the accidents of the narration," were those to which he accorded this reverence. And often, no doubt, he put by as an unimportant "accident in the narration," what another may have held to be of its essential character. Now, of course, the most sincere believer in the sacredness of facts as "angels of the Lord" must select for himself which facts are cardinal and which are not. To the man who believes that he has to *establish* the credit of the Bible, before he even thinks of guiding himself by it, the cardinal facts will be the small consistencies or the small inconsistencies of the narrative, and he will postpone all question of learning from it the mind and character of God, till he is quite sure that all the human joints and seams are in perfect order. To Maurice, who never dreamt of thinking about the Bible from this point of view, and who certainly held that the revelation it contained was proved at once by the strong light it shed on human nature, and by the fresh power it bestowed on human nature, the stress laid on numerical blunders, and on petty historical inconsistencies, or on the minutiæ of the sacred literature generally, was not intelligible. While Colenso thought Maurice hardly candid, Maurice thought Colenso hardly sober and serious, and too much inclined to weigh grains of dust against the testimony of the soul. How different were their standards of fact may be gathered best, perhaps, from the letter in which Maurice declares that to him the Book of Isaiah seems lucidity itself compared with Lord Mahon's *Life of Pitt;* the difference, of course, being that in Isaiah the reference of everything to the divine standard is plain, and only the implied human events obscure, while in Lord Mahon's *Life of Pitt* the human events are pretty clearly determined, and only the standard to which his policy was referred is wholly obscure and ambiguous. After all, were not Maurice's "facts" the more important class of facts of the two? Events, without their moral motives and their spiritual influences, are hardly facts, and are certainly unintelligible facts. The existence of moral motives and the prevalence of great spiritual influences are facts, and facts of the first order, even where the precise events which proceeded from those motives and exerted those influences are more or less ill-defined and left in shadow. In one of Sir Edward Strachey's very interesting letters he tells his correspondent that "Maurice said the other day that if we ignore facts we change substances for suppositions; that which really does stand under an appearance for that which we put under it by our imaginations." No more weighty or more scientific remark could be made; but, of course, the question remains as to the criterion by which we are to distinguish the trustworthiness of the appearance. Colenso thought he could distinguish the untrustworthiness of a history sufficiently by bringing to light a great number of minor discrepancies in it. Maurice thought he could distinguish its trustworthiness as regarded its main features by comparing the moral and spiritual antecedents in one page of the history with the moral and spiritual consequents in another, and showing how truly they corresponded to each other, and how full of human nature, and how fully verified by our own experience, was the connection between the different stages. For my part I believe that both are right up to a certain point, but that Maurice had got hold of immeasurably the more important criterion of the two.

Perhaps those who have written upon Maurice have not given enough prominence to the militant side of his nature. He was essentially a spiritual knight-errant, and this was the side of his nature which led him into extravagance. Such expressions as those which were called forth from him by a narrowly denominational meeting of "the National Society" are not unfrequent in his life, and are quite Quixotic in their vehemence. "The National Society will either become a mere dead log or it will be inspired with a false demoniacal life by a set of Church clubs, which I do believe will, ten years hence, have left the Jacobin Club, and every other, at an immeasurable distance behind them in the race of wickedness. I speak what I feel—would that I trembled ten times more than I do at my own prophecy." And again, in reference to a pamphlet of his own on the Sabbath day: "The working men, and many of my friends, will suppose that I write it to please the religious world, which I hope will hate me more and more, and which I hope to hate more and more." Such passages abound, but though they express Maurice's very serious conviction that men often do worse things under the plea of what they call fidelity to their religious, or, for that matter, to their irreligious, opinions than they would ever dare to do simply on their own responsibility, yet I cannot but think that the whole of his horror of clubs, leagues, sects, denominations, irresponsible associations of every kind, is expressed much more in the spirit of a knight-errant who has had to fight against them, almost unaided, than in the spirit of sober judgment. He had learnt from the Bible to fight boldly, and the spirit of the soldier ran through his whole life. No man was a more generous enemy when he knew his antagonist. But no man was a more vehement foe when he was charging against what he thought—often hastily—to be a spirit of evil sheltered under the vague authority of unknown and irresponsible organs. He writes to Mr. Ludlow that in his opinion the Bible is the history of God's conflict with evil, and that it assumes that evil is not to be crushed out by omnipotence, but to be vanquished in what may be called a fair fight. "The question is whether the unintelligibility of evil and the omnipotence of God is a reason for not regarding Him as carrying on a war against evil, and for not expecting that in that war evil will be vanquished. I know that there are some who think so. For God to make war instead of crushing evil, if it can be crushed at all, by a simple fiat, is for them a sinful absurdity. What I say is, that, if it be, the Bible is from beginning to end an absurdity, for it is the book of the wars of the Lord. It does not define evil, but it assumes evil; it assumes evil to be in a will; it assumes evil not to be vanquishable by an omnipotent fiat; it sets forth a process by which it has been overcome in a number of wills; it teaches us to pray, 'Thy will be done on earth as it is in heaven,' where it is done perfectly; it says that if we pray according to God's will He hears us, and we shall have the petition which we ask of Him." And it is as a knight-errant fighting in the wars of the Lord that Maurice must often be regarded. At the same time a knight-errant is not always in a judicial frame of mind, and I cannot help thinking that when Maurice was attacking "the religious world," or "the religious press," or any other anonymous organ of "religious" notions which seemed to him profoundly irreligious, he almost forgot that these people, however they might be hoodwinked by ignoring their individual responsibility, had still the consciences and spirits of men. "I have heard," he writes in one very able letter to Sir T. Acland, "of a poor creature in St. Luke's in a lucid moment snatching a lady by the arm who was visiting the asylum, with the exclamation, 'Have you thanked God for your reason to-day?' and then relapsing into fury. Surely one of these men [political journalists] might say to either of us, 'Have you thanked God to-day for having passed through a debating society with any portion of your souls undestroyed?' and at least to one of us, 'Have you meddled with periodicals, and have you thanked God that you still think, love, go to church, and find any one to love you?'" There is all the pent-up wrath here of a man who felt how full the press of his day was of unreal pretension and dishonest judgment, and doubtless both in that day and in this there was enough justification for wrath. But it is poured out as the soldier pours out his wrath on the foe whom he is fighting, not as the judge passes sentence on the offender whose case he has heard. And while the soldier-like element in Maurice was one of the noblest aspects of his nature, it often led him into extravagant expressions, which he would, on calmer consideration, have himself described as overstrained and perhaps uncharitable. For it is possible surely to be uncharitable to associations or sects, as well as to individuals. Indeed, he says in one letter to Archbishop Trench, that "the spirit dwells in the body, and in each of its members *as such*, and not as individuals. The spirit in an individual is a fearful contradiction." If that be so, the spirit which unites men together in any association, however temporary, is the true bond of that association, and if that be on the whole good, which no man will decide off-hand that it is not, even though its doings be anonymous and insufficiently weighted with responsibility, there must be uncharitableness in bitterly condemning it. Maurice, however, had seen so much of the evil in religious and political coteries and sects, that he was apt to charge at them whenever he came upon them, almost as if they must be spiritual freebooters and foes of truth and peace. Again, Maurice had none of that patience and toleration for what he found deficient in himself, which Fénélon presses on us as a duty wherever it does not cover a really false self-excuse. But this again is due to the militant spirit which was so strong in Maurice. He could not have tilted so chivalrously against all the moral and spiritual tyrants of the day, if he had not tilted with still more passionate fervour against the weaknesses and sins which he discovered in his own heart. In his indignation against himself he called himself cold-blooded. In reality Maurice had the hot blood of the genuine reformer — the reformer who begins by assailing himself.

But knight-errant as he was, there was no caprice or tolerance of caprice in Maurice. His aggressiveness was the aggressiveness of spiritual chivalry against the dogmatists who in his belief had repelled men from Christ, and nothing shocked him more than the prospect of obtaining followers for himself at the cost of the Church and the Church's Master. His whole teaching was a protest against the delusion of redemption through opinion, whether right or wrong, and an assertion of redemption through the life of God incarnate in the nature of man. "The light of the sun is not in you, but out of you; and yet you can see everything by it if you will open your eyes," was the analogy by which he loved to illustrate the difference between the power of opinion and the power of that truth of which even the correctest opinion is but a faint reflection. He held this so strongly that he made light even of the duty of bringing feeling into harmony with faith. "Faith first and feeling afterwards is, I believe, the rule which we are always trying to reverse," he writes; and that is one of the keys of his teaching. "In quietness and confidence is our strength," he says again, "but not in thinking of quietness and confidence, or grieving that we have so little of either." In a word, Maurice was one of the greatest of those teachers who have impressed upon us that it is not by virtue of any conscious state of ours that we can be redeemed, but by a power which can dispense, and dispense even for an indefinite time, with our own recognition of its beneficence; just as the body is restored to health by influences of the life-giving character of which we are often quite unaware. Once, when a lady asked him his belief as to our recognition of each other hereafter, he replied that that question always made him say to himself, "Ah, how little we have recognised each other here! may not that be the first great step in recognition?" and he would have applied the same remark in an even stronger sense to our recognition of the source of truth. Our recognition of the truth may be necessary to our own happiness, but it is the heat and light which proceeds from it, not our recognition of that heat and light, which heals us. And one may surely say the same of Maurice himself. How little did we recognise him here; and how much, in spite of that want of recognition, did he effect for us! May it not be the first step in our recognition of him hereafter, that we should understand how little in reality we ever recognised him truly here?

THE END

www.ingramcontent.com/pod-product-compliance
Lightning Source LLC
Chambersburg PA
CBHW030258240426
43673CB00040B/992